UNITY ALL IN ONE

A Handbook to Build 3D Games from Start to Finish and Learn C# in the Process

Patrick Felicia

UNITY ALL-IN-ONE: A HANDBOOK TO BUILD 3D GAMES FROM START TO FINISH

First published: November 2024

Published by Patrick Felicia

CREDITS

Author: Patrick Felicia

ABOUT THE AUTHOR

Patrick Felicia is an author and developer with deep expertise in game engines like Unity, Godot, and Unreal Engine. Holding a PhD in Computer Science, he has dedicated his career to making game development accessible, with a focus on practical guides that empower learners to build real-world skills in 2D and 3D game creation. Through his books, Patrick shares his hands-on experience, offering clear and comprehensive insights into programming, procedural generation, and game mechanics, making him a trusted resource for both beginners and seasoned developers.

SUPPORT AND RESOURCES FOR THIS BOOK

You can download the resource pack for this book; it includes solutions scripts for some of the sections in this book, as well as some of the files needed to complete some of the activities presented in this book.

To download these resources, please do the following.

If you are already a member of my list, you can just go to the member area (**http://learntocreategames.com/member/**) using the usual password and you will gain access to all the resources for this book.

If you are not yet on my list, you can do the following:

- Open the following link: **http://learntocreategames.com/books/**
- Select this book ("**Unity All-In-One**").
- On the new page, click on the link labelled "**Book Files**", or scroll down to the bottom of the page.
- In the section called "**Download your Free Resource Pack**", enter your email address and your first name, and click on the button labeled "**Yes, I want to receive my bonus pack**".
- After a few seconds, you should receive a link to your free start-up pack.
- When you receive the link, you can download all the resources to your computer.

This book is dedicated to Mathis

TABLE OF CONTENTS

Contents

PREFACE

After teaching Unity and Game Programming for over 10 years, I've often envisioned a comprehensive resource that not only introduces students to essential programming concepts but also demonstrates how to apply these concepts in practical and exciting ways within the context of game development.

Many resources I encountered either skimmed over critical details, leaving learners to wonder why certain techniques were used, or leaned too heavily on theory without providing the practical application that makes game development so engaging. Moreover, while those with programming backgrounds often find game development appealing, individuals with artistic or design expertise often struggle with the additional challenge of learning to code.

This book, *Unity All-In-One*, was written to bridge these gaps and offer a complete guide to building 3D games from the ground up. It is designed to empower readers to create dynamic, immersive, and interactive experiences, regardless of their prior coding or Unity experience.

Covering everything from the basics of Unity's interface and C# fundamentals to advanced game mechanics like AI navigation, adaptive gameplay, and dynamic UI, this book equips you with the skills to bring your creative visions to life.

This book is designed to:
- Be approachable for complete beginners while offering depth for intermediate learners.
- Keep you engaged with hands-on projects and real-world applications of game development concepts.
- Provide clear and thorough explanations of Unity's tools, scripting in C#, and key game design mechanics.
- Inspire you to build not just functional games but immersive worlds that captivate players.

By working through this book, you'll gain the confidence to tackle challenges such as creating NPC behaviors, designing adaptive difficulty systems, implementing dynamic animations, and optimizing game performance.

Whether you're new to Unity or looking to refine your skills, *Unity All-In-One* serves as a comprehensive and practical resource to guide you every step of the way.

My hope is that this book becomes your trusted companion as you embark on your journey to create engaging, professional-quality games
.

WHAT YOU NEED TO USE THIS BOOK

To complete the project in this book, you'll need the latest version of Unity and a computer that meets Unity's current system requirements. Unity is available for download from the official website (https://unity.com/download). Before installing, be sure to check the latest system requirements here: https://unity.com/unity/system-requirements.

- As of the most recent update, Unity supports the following operating systems for development:
- **Windows**: Windows 10 (64-bit) or higher
- **macOS**: macOS 10.15 (Catalina) or higher (64-bit)
- **Linux**: Ubuntu 20.04, Ubuntu 18.04, and CentOS 7

Unity now recommends a **DirectX 11** or **OpenGL 4.1** compatible graphics card. Most graphics cards manufactured after 2012 should meet this requirement, but for optimal performance with complex scenes, a newer or higher-performance GPU is recommended.

In terms of computer skills, this book assumes no prior experience with programming or Unity. All essential concepts will be introduced with step-by-step guidance. You only need to be able to perform basic tasks, such as downloading files, opening and saving projects, using drag-and-drop functionality, and typing. A general comfort with navigating Unity's interface will also be helpful, and the book provides support on this where needed.

WHO THIS BOOK IS FOR

If you can answer "yes" to any of these questions, then *Unity All-In-One* is the book for you:

1. Would you like to learn how to code in C# to create engaging 3D games from scratch?
2. Are you interested in mastering Unity's tools to design immersive environments, interactive NPCs, and adaptive gameplay mechanics?
3. Do you want to explore core game development techniques such as creating animations, implementing AI navigation, and building user interfaces?
4. Whether you're new to coding or have some experience, are you ready to dive deeper into C# and Unity to create polished, professional-quality games?
5. If so, this book will guide you step-by-step through the fundamentals and advanced features of Unity, helping you bring your game ideas to life!

WHO THIS BOOK IS NOT FOR

If you can answer "yes" to any of these questions, then *Unity All-In-One* may not be the best fit for you:

1. Can you already create fully interactive 3D games in Unity using advanced C# techniques?
2. Are you looking for a comprehensive reference book on Unity or C# rather than a practical, hands-on guide to game development?
3. Are you a professional developer seeking highly advanced, specialized techniques beyond the foundational concepts of Unity and C# covered in this book?

If these statements resonate, you may want to explore other advanced resources or books in this series, available on the official website (http://www.learntocreategames.com).

HOW YOU WILL LEARN FROM THIS BOOK

Because all students learn differently and have different expectations of a course, this book is designed to ensure that all readers find a learning mode that suits them. Therefore, it includes the following:

- A list of the learning objectives at the start of each chapter so that readers have a snapshot of the skills that will be covered.
- Each section includes an overview of the activities covered.
- Many of the activities are step-by-step, and learners are also given the opportunity to engage in deeper learning and problem-solving skills through the challenges offered at the end of each chapter.
- Each chapter ends-up with a quiz and challenges through which you can put your skills (and knowledge acquired) to the test. Challenges consist in coding, debugging, or creating new features based on the knowledge that you have acquired in the chapter.
- The book focuses on the core skills that you need. While some sections go into more detail, once concepts have been explained, links are provided to additional resources, where necessary.
- The code is introduced progressively and it is also explained in detail.
- You also gain access to several videos that help you along the way, especially for the most challenging topics.

FORMAT OF EACH CHAPTER AND WRITING CONVENTIONS

Throughout this book, and to make reading and learning easier, text formatting and icons will be used to highlight parts of the information provided and to make the book easy to read.

SPECIAL NOTES

Each chapter includes resource sections, so that you can further your understanding and mastery of Unity; these include:

- A quiz for each chapter: these quizzes usually include 10 questions that test your knowledge of the topics covered throughout the chapter. The solutions are provided on the companion website.
- Challenges: each chapter includes a challenge section where you are asked to combine your skills to solve a particular problem.

Author's notes appear as described below:

Author's suggestions appear in this box.

Code appears as described below:

```
public int score;
public string playersName = "Sam";
```

HOW CAN YOU LEARN BEST FROM THIS BOOK?

- **Talk to your friends about what you are doing.**
  We often think that we understand a topic until we have to explain it to friends and answer their questions. By explaining your different projects, what you just learned will become clearer to you.
- **Do the exercises.**
  All chapters include exercises that will help you to learn by doing. In other words, by completing these exercises, you will be able to better understand the topics and gain practical skills (i.e., rather than just reading).
- **Don't be afraid of making mistakes.**
  I usually tell my students that making mistakes is part of the learning process; the more mistakes you make and the more opportunities you have for learning. At the start, you may find the errors disconcerting, or you may find that Unity does not work as expected until you understand what went wrong.
- **Challenge yourself.**
  All chapters include a challenge section where you can decide to take on a particular challenge to improve your game or skills. These challenges are there for you to think creatively and to apply the knowledge that you have acquired in each chapter using a problem-based approach.
- **Learn in chunks.**
  It may be disconcerting to go through five or six chapters straight, as it may lower your motivation. Instead, give yourself enough time to learn, go at your own pace, and learn in small units (e.g., between 15 and 20 minutes per day). This will do at least two things for you: it will give your brain the time to "digest" the information that you have just learned, so that you can start fresh the following day. It will also make sure that you don't "burn-out" and that you keep your motivation levels high.

FEEDBACK

While I have done everything possible to produce a book of high quality and value, I always appreciate feedback from readers so that the book can be improved accordingly. If you would like to give feedback on this book, you can email me at **learntocreategames@gmail.com.**

IMPROVING THE BOOK

Although great care was taken in checking the content of this book, I am human, and some errors could remain in the book. As a result, it would be great if you could let me know of any issue or error you may have come across in this book, so that it can be solved and so that the book can be updated accordingly. To report an error, you can email me (learntocreategames@gmail.com) with the following information:

- Name of the book.
- The page or section where the error was detected.
- Describe the error and what you think the correction should be.

Once your email is received, the error will be checked, and, in the case of a valid error, it will be corrected, and the book will be updated to reflect the changes accordingly.

SUPPORTING THE AUTHOR

A lot of work has gone into this book, and it is the fruit of long hours of preparation, brainstorming, and finally writing. As a result, I would ask that you do not distribute any illegal copies of this book.

This means that if a friend wants a copy of this book, s/he will have to buy it through the official channels (i.e., through Amazon or the book's official website: http://www.learntocreategames.com/books).

If some of your friends are interested in the book, you can refer them to the book's official website **(http://www.learntocreategames.com/books)** where they can either buy the book, or join the mailing list to be notified of future promotional offers or enter a monthly draw and be in for a chance to receive a free copy of the book.

As an independent author, I pour my heart and soul into creating content that is both informative and engaging. Your feedback is not only a testament to the work I've done but also an essential component in helping others discover the book.

Reviews play a crucial role in the success of self-published authors. They offer potential readers a glimpse into the experiences of others and help them make informed decisions. A few words about what you enjoyed, what you learned, or how the book has helped you can go a long way. Positive reviews can boost the book's visibility on platforms like Amazon, making it more accessible to other aspiring game developers who can benefit from this resource.

So, if you find this book helpful, I kindly ask you to take a moment to leave a review on Amazon or your preferred online bookstore.

Writing a review doesn't have to be lengthy or complex. A few sentences about your favorite parts, the most valuable lessons you learned, or the projects you enjoyed the most can make a significant difference. Your review can inspire and encourage others to embark on their own game development journey with the confidence that this book will be a worthwhile companion.

Thank you for your support.

1

INSTALLING UNITY AND BECOMING FAMILIAR WITH THE INTERFACE

This chapter helps you to progressively become familiar with Unity and it will explain and illustrate how to install this software, and how the different views and core features can be employed.

After completing this section, you should be able to:

- Be more comfortable with Unity's interface.
- Understand the role and location of the different views in Unity.
- Know and use shortcuts to manipulate objects (e.g., move, scale, resize, duplicate, or delete) and move the view accordingly (e.g., pan or rotate).
- Use the **Inspector** view.
- Create and apply colors and textures to objects.
- Create and combine simple built-in shapes.
- Know how to search for and organize assets in your game efficiently.
- Navigate through your scene and see it from both first- and third-person views.

> If you need more help or information on the topics covered in this section, you can gain access to a FREE video training based on this book (i.e., 2-hour training) by using the following link: http://learntocreategames.com/. This training will show you exactly all of the steps covered in this book and may appeal to those who are more visual learners.

WHAT IS A GAME ENGINE AND SHOULD YOU USE ONE?

Unity makes it possible to create video games without knowing some of the underlying technologies of game development, so that potential game developers only need to focus on the game mechanics and employ a high-level approach to creating games using programming and scripting languages such as C# or JavaScript. The term high-level here refers to the fact that when you create a game with a game engine, you don't need to worry about how the software will render the game or how it will communicate with the graphics card to optimize the speed of your game. So, using a game engine would generally offer the following features and benefits:

- Accelerated development: game engines make it possible to focus on the game mechanics. Because built-in libraries are available for common mechanics and features, these do not need to be rebuilt from scratch, and programmers can use them immediately and save time (e.g., for the user interface or the artificial intelligence).

- Integrated Development Environment (IDE): an IDE helps to create, compile, and manage your code, and includes some useful tools that make development and debugging more efficient.
- Graphical User Interface (GUI): while some game engines are based on libraries, most common game engines make it possible for users to create objects seamlessly and to perform common tasks such as transforming, texturing, and animating assets, through drag and drop features. Another advantage of such software is that you can understand and preview how the game will look without having to compile the code beforehand (e.g., through scenes).
- Multi-platform deployment: with common game engines, it is possible to easily export the game that you have created to several platforms (e.g., for the web, iOS, or Android) without having to recode the entire game.

ADVANTAGES OF USING UNITY

There are several game engines available out there. However, Unity has proven to be one of the best game engines. It has been used by game developers for several years and has been employed to produce successful 3D and 2D games. Several of these titles can be seen on Unity's **website (https://unity.com/madewith).**
With Unity, you can create 2D or 3D games and produce several types of game genres including First-Person Shooters (FPS), Massive Multiplayer Online Role-Playing Games (MMORPG), casual games, adventure games, and much more.

In addition to being able to create high-quality games with an easy-to-use interface, Unity makes it possible to export games to a wide range of platforms, including mobile platforms (e.g., Android, iOS, or Windows), Virtual Reality platforms (e.g., Oculus Rift, Google Cardboard, or PlayStation VR) or desktop platforms (e.g., Windows, Mac or Linux).

Unity includes all the necessary tools that you need to create great games and it also simplifies the application of useful techniques to improve the quality of your game. For example, it includes Visual Studio, an IDE that will help you to code faster, built-in Artificial Intelligence (AI) modules (e.g., NavMesh navigation) that you can use with no prior knowledge of AI, lights, built-in objects, or a finite state machine that you can apply to your characters for customized behaviors and animations.

Finally, to control the game, you can use high-level programming and scripting languages such as C#. This is useful for those who have already been exposed to this language to transfer their skills to game programming in Unity.

DOWNLOADING UNITY HUB

Now that you have had an overview of Unity and game engines, it is time for us to start using Unity. However, before you can install and use Unity, you will need to download and install *Unity Hub* using the following steps:

1. Open the following link: **https://www.unity3d.com/download**. This will help you to check that your computer complies with Unity's requirements.
2. Once you have checked the requirements, we can download *Unity Hub* from the same.

3. Please follow the installation instructions.

INSTALLING UNITY

As mentioned in the previous section, you will need to install *Unity Hub* before you can install a version of Unity.

1. Once *Unity Hub* is installed, you can install a new version of Unity by going to the section called *Installs* and then selecting the option to **Install Editor**.

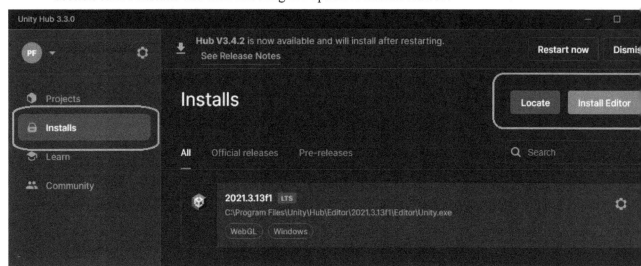

2. You can then select the version of Unity that you need (for example, Unity 2021.3) as per the next figure.

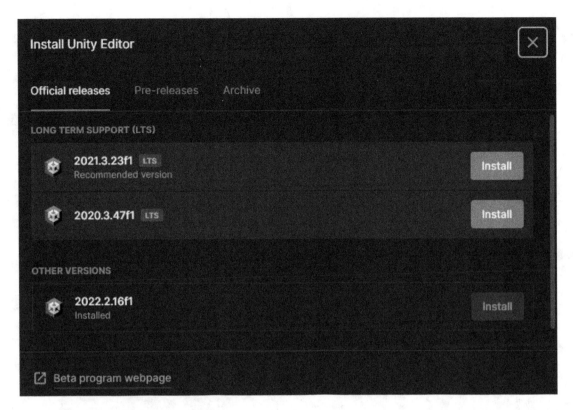

3. You can press the "**Next**" button.
4. You will be asked whether you want to install additional modules. For the time being you can leave all the options as default (i.e., no additional modules).

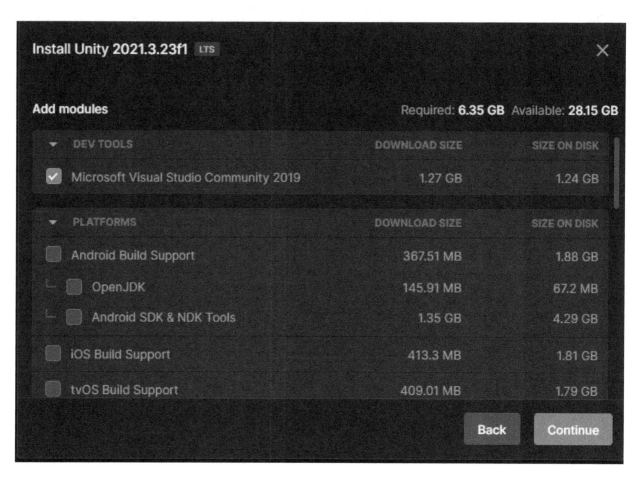

5. Click on the button labelled "**Continue**" and follow the instructions.

6. Once the new version of Unity is installed, it will be listed in ***Unity Hub*** in the section called **Installs**.

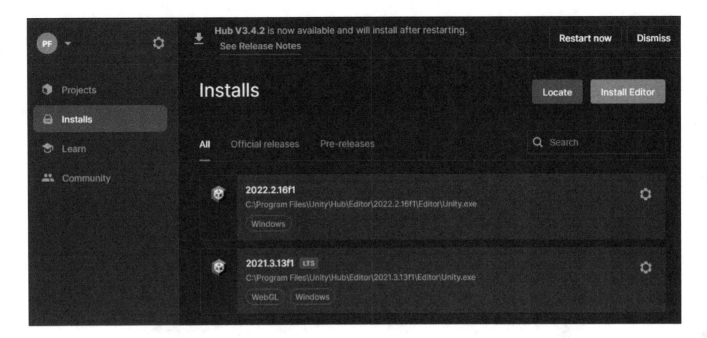

LAUNCHING UNITY

Once you have successfully installed Unity and its components, we can now launch it through **Unity Hub**. Upon the first time you open Unity, you may need to provide your email address, so that you can receive regular updates from the Unity team. This should be really useful to keep up to date with major announcements for this software. You may also be asked whether you would like to activate the Pro version. However, for the purpose of this tutorial, you only need to use the free version (i.e., personal edition).

After having provided your email details as well as choosing the free version of the software, we can start to enjoy Unity.

- You can now open a new project through **Unity Hub**.
- In **Unity Hub**, please select the section called *Projects* from the left menu.

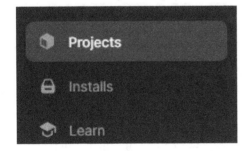

- Click on the button labelled "**New Project**".

- In the new window, give a name to your project, for example **Project1**.

When Unity starts-up, a window labeled **Unity Editor Update Check** appears. This window, illustrated below, is there to check whether you have the latest version of Unity and to let you know of any recent updates available. If an update is necessary, you can install it. If you would prefer not to see this message displayed every time you start Unity, you can uncheck the corresponding box labeled **Check for Updates** accordingly.

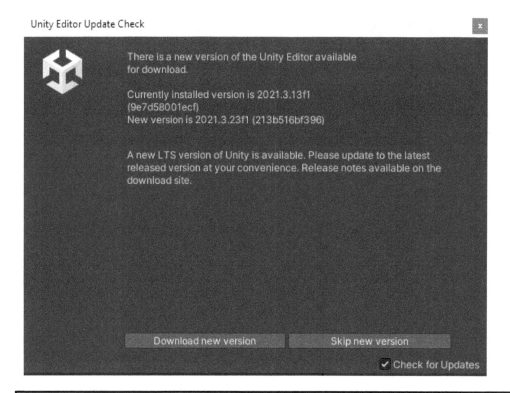

Unity provides links to official forums and documentation from the main (i.e., top) menu: **Help | Unity Forums** or **Help | Unity Manual**.

UNDERSTANDING AND BECOMING FAMILIAR WITH THE INTERFACE

After launching Unity, you will notice that it includes several windows organized in a (default) layout. Each of these windows includes a label in their top-left corner. These windows can be moved around and rearranged, if necessary, by either changing the layout (using the menu **Window | Layouts | ...**) or by dragging and dropping the corresponding tab for a window to a different location. This will move the view (or window) to where you would like it to appear within the window. In the default layout, the following views appear onscreen (as described in the next screenshot, clockwise from the top left corner):

1. The **Hierarchy** window (the corresponding shortcut is *CTRL+4*): this window or view lists all the objects currently present in your scene. These could include, for example,

basic shapes, 3D characters, or terrains. This view also makes it possible to identify a hierarchy between objects, and to identify, for example, whether an object has children or parents (we will explore this concept later).

> If you are using Mac OS, then CTRL can be replaced by CMD.

2. The **Scene** view (*CTRL+1*): this window displays the content of a scene (or the item listed in the **Hierarchy** view) so that you can visualize and modify them accordingly (e.g., move, scale, etc.) using the mouse.

3. The **Game** view (*CTRL+2*): this window makes it possible to visualize the scene as it will appear in the game (that is, through the lens of the active camera).

4. The **Inspector** view (*CTRL+3*): this window displays information (i.e., the properties) on the object currently selected.

5. The **Console** window (*SHIFT+CTRL+C*): this window displays messages that are printed from the code by the user, or warnings and error messages related to your project or code displayed by Unity.

6. The **Project** window (*CTRL+5*): this window includes all the assets available and used for your project, such as 3D models, sounds, or textures.

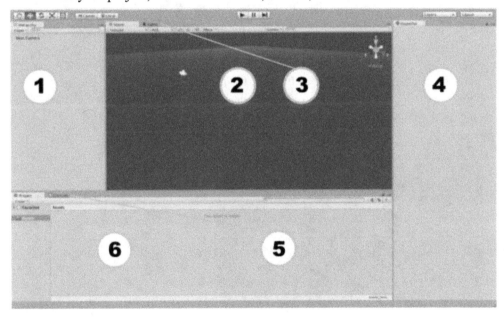

THE SCENE VIEW

We will use this view to create and visualize the scene for our game. When you create a project, you can include several scenes within. A scene is comparable to a level, and scenes that are included in the same project can share similar resources, so that assets are imported once and shared across (or used in) all scenes. The **Scene** and **Game** views are displayed in the same window, and both are represented by a corresponding tab. By default, the **Scene** view is active. However, it is possible to switch to the **Game** view by clicking on the tab labeled **Game**. For example, if we click successively on the **Game** and **Scene** tabs, we can see the view from both the perspectives of your eyes (i.e., the **Scene** view) and the active camera present in the scene (i.e., the **Game** view) as illustrated in the next figures.

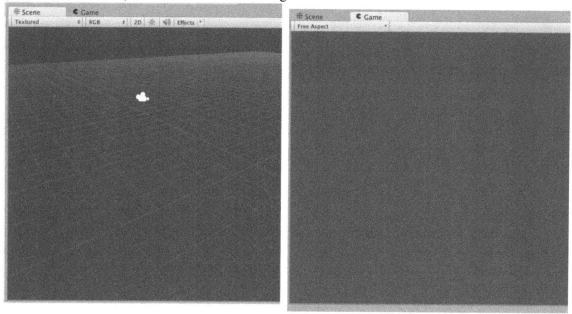

The Scene view   **The Game view**

Note that you can also rearrange the layout to be able to, for example, see both the **Scene** and **Game** views simultaneously. We could, for example, drag and drop the **Game** tab beside the **Console** tab to obtain the layout described on the next figure.

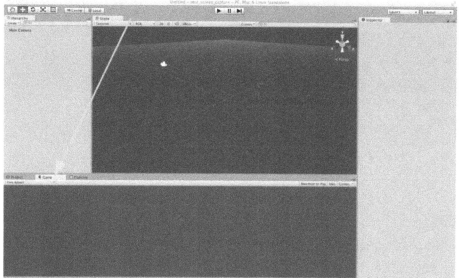

Changing the layout to display both Game and Scene views

In the previous figure, the **Game** tab that is usually to the right of the tab called **Scene** has been dragged to the right of the tab called **Project**. This way, you can see both the **Scene** view and the **Game** view simultaneously.

DISCOVERING AND NAVIGATING THROUGH THE SCENE

So that you can navigate easily in the current scene, several shortcuts and navigation modes are available. These make it possible to navigate through your scene just as you would in a First-Person Shooter or to literally "fly" through your scene. You can also zoom-in and zoom-out to focus on specific areas or objects, look around (i.e., using mouse look) or pan the view to focus on a specific part of the scene. The main modes of navigation are provided in the next table. However, we will look into these in more detail in the next section as we will be experimenting with them to explore (and modify) an existing scene.

Table 1: Navigation shortcuts

Navigation	Key or Mouse Combination
Activate Fly Mode	Keep MRB (Mouse Right Button) pressed.
Accelerate	Press Shift (in walk mode).
Move in four directions (left, right, forward and back)	Press W, A, S, or D (in fly mode).
Float Up and Down	Press Q or E (in fly mode).
Look around	Press *ALT* and drag the mouse left, right, forward or back.
Zoom in/out	Move the mouse wheel.
Pan the view	Press Q (to activate the hand tool) then drag and drop the mouse.

For example:

- In the default navigation mode, you can "walk" through the scene using the arrow keys (i.e., up, down, left and right).
- In the "flight" mode, which can be activated by pressing and holding the **Mouse Right Button** (MRB), we can navigate using the *W*, *A*, *S* and *D* keys.
- In the "flight mode", we can also look around us by dragging the mouse or float up and down using the keys *Q* and *E*.

As you can see, both modes are very useful to navigate through your scene and to visualize all its elements. In addition, you can also choose to display the scene along a particular axis (i.e., x, y, or z) using the **gizmo** that is displayed in the top-right corner of the **Scene** view as described on the next figure.

Gizmo

The gizmo available in the **Scene** view includes three axes that are color-coded: x (in red), y (in green) and z (in blue). By clicking on any of these axes (or corresponding letters), the scene will be seen accordingly (i.e., through the x-, y-, or z-axis).

If you are not familiar with 3D axes: **x**, and **z** usually refer to the width and depth, while **y** refers to the height. By default, in Unity, the z-axis is pointing towards the screen if the x-axis is pointing to the right and the y-axis is pointing upwards. This is often referred as a left-handed coordinate system.

Also note that by clicking on the middle of the gizmo (white box), we can switch between isometric and perspective views.

In addition to the navigation tools, Unity also offers ways to focus on a particular object by rotating around a specific point (i.e., by pressing the *ALT* key and dragging the mouse to the left, right, up or down), or double-clicking on an object (i.e., in the **Scene** or **Hierarchy** view), so that the camera in the **Scene** view is focused on this object (this can also be achieved by selecting the object in either the **Scene** or **Hierarchy** view and by then pressing *SHIFT+ F*), or by zooming-in and out (i.e., scrolling the mouse wheel forward or back).

While the shortcuts and keys described in this section should get you started with Unity and make it possible for you to navigate through your scene easily, there are, obviously, many more shortcuts that you could use, but that will not be presented in this book. Instead, you may look for and find these in the official documentation that is available both offline (using the top menu: **Help | Unity Manual** then select the sections **Working in Unity | The Main Windows | The Scene View | Scene View navigation**) and online (http://docs.unity3d.com/Documentation/Manual/SceneViewNavigation.html). When using the documentation, you can also search for particular words as illustrated on the next figure.

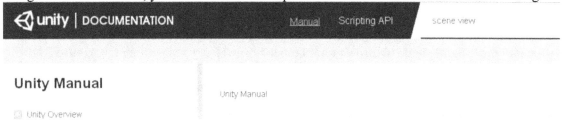

Using Unity's manual

THE HIERARCHY VIEW

As indicated by its name, this view lists and displays the name of all objects included in the scene (in alphabetical order, by default) along with the type of relationship or hierarchy between them. You may notice that before you add any object to the scene, a camera is already present in the scene so that it can be viewed in the **Game** view through its lenses.

This view offers several advantages when we need to manage all the objects present in the scene quickly and to perform organizational changes. For example, we could use this view to find objects based on their name, to duplicate objects, to amend the name of objects, to amend the properties of several objects simultaneously, or to change the hierarchy between objects.

For example, on the following figure, we can see that the scene includes seven objects including a camera, a directional light, four cubes, and an object called **group_of_cubes**.

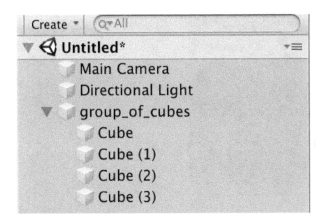

Creating a hierarchy between objects

We can also notice that all cubes are grouped under a "folder" (in Unity, this can be created as an empty object in the scene), which means that:

1. All four cubes are children of the object called **group_of_cubes**.
2. The object **group_of_cubes** is the parent of the four cubes.
3. If a transformation (i.e., scale or rotate) is applied to the parent (e.g., group of cubes) it will also be applied to the children (i.e., **Cube**, **Cube(1)**, **Cube(2)**, **Cube(3)** and **Cube(4)**).

> To change the hierarchy of the scene and make some objects children of a particular object, we only need to drag these objects atop the parent object.

THE PROJECT VIEW

This view includes and displays all the assets employed in your project (and across scenes), including: audio files, textures, scripts (e.g., scripts written in C#), materials, 3D models, scenes, or packages (i.e., zipped resources for Unity). All these assets, once present in the **Project** view, can be shared across scenes.

> In other words, if we create a project and then a scene, and import assets for our game, these assets will be available from any other scene within the same project.

As for the **Hierarchy** view, built-in folders and search capabilities are included to ease the management of all your assets.

By default, the **Project** view includes two windows divided vertically (left and right columns). As illustrated on the next figure, the left window includes a folder called assets and a series of "smart" folders (i.e., the content of these folders varies dynamically) called **Favorites**. The right window displays the content of the folder selected on the left-hand side.

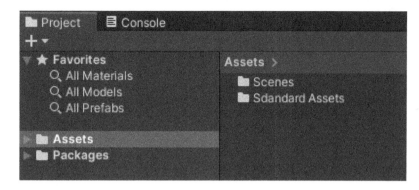

The project view

By clicking on any of the smart folders (e.g., **All Materials**, **All Models**, or **All Prefabs**) Unity will filter the assets to display only the relevant ones accordingly (e.g., materials, models, or prefabs). This can speed up the process of accessing specific assets and can be done, as for many of the functionalities present in Unity, in different ways. For example, you may notice a search window to the left of the **Project** view as illustrated in the next figure.

Searching for assets in the project

The **search** window in the **Project** folder can be used to search assets by their name or by their type, as illustrated in the next figure, by clicking on this icon 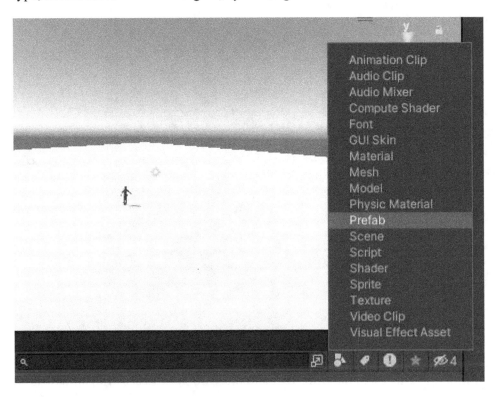.

Filtering through the assets in the project view

As we can see on the previous figure, we have the option to select the type of assets that we are looking for (e.g., **Texture**, **Prefab**, or **Script**). Note that this option can also be specified by typing **t:** followed by the type that we are looking for in the search window. For example, by typing **t:material** in the search window, Unity will only display assets of type **Material**.

THE INSPECTOR

This window displays the properties of the object currently selected (i.e., the object selected in the **Scene** or the **Hierarchy** view) and it makes it possible to modify the attributes of an object accordingly. All properties are categorized in **Components**.

By default, all objects present in the scene have a name, a default layer (we will look at this aspect later) and a component called **Transform**. However, it is possible to add components to an object using the button **Add Component** (see next figure) or the menu called **Component**.

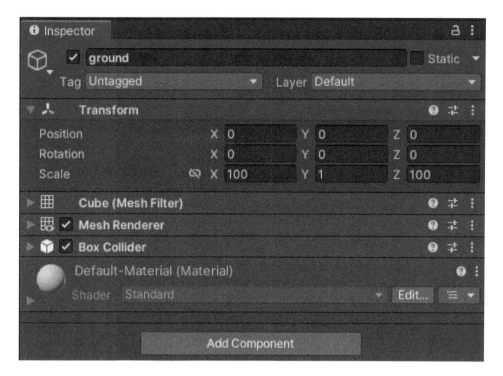

The Inspector window

You may also notice a tick box, in the **Inspector** window, to the left of the name of the object, that can be used to temporarily deactivate (and consequently reactivate) the object. This can be useful when you would like to temporarily remove an object from the scene without having to recreate it.

As we will see later, there are many types of components that can be added to an object to enhance it, including physics properties (to enhance how an object will behave realistically following the laws of physics), rendering (to enhance its appearance), or collision (to refine how it will detect collisions with other objects). For example, the default component **Transform** includes the position, rotation, and scale attributes of the object selected.

The attributes **tag**, **layer**, and **static**, while important, will be covered in later sections.

As we will see later, a scene can be edited and played. However, if we try to modify the attributes of an object while the game is playing, these will not be saved. In other words, for modifications to be saved in the scene, they have to be made while the game is stopped (i.e., not played).

THE CONSOLE VIEW

As seen previously, the console window will display messages from Unity, related to possible errors and warnings in your code that may prevent the game from playing, or messages that you can print through your own code (e.g., for debugging purposes).

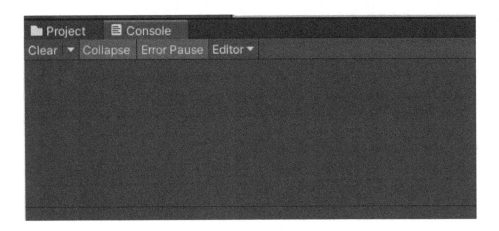

THE ASSET STORE WINDOW

This window, which is not displayed by default, connects you to the **Asset Store**, an online repository and marketplace where you can search for and find free or premium assets for your game. This window can be accessed through the main menu (i.e., **Window | Asset Store**) or by using the corresponding shortcut (*CTRL+9*) and will be displayed in your default browser.

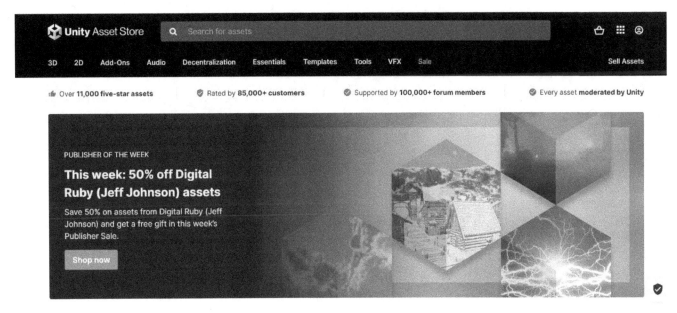

Quiz

It is now time to test your knowledge. Please specify whether the following statements are TRUE or FALSE. The answers are available at the end of the book.

1. The shortcut to open the **Console** window is CTRL + 1.
2. The shortcut to open the **Project** window is CTRL + 2.
3. The shortcut to open the **Hierarchy** window is CTRL + 4.
4. The **Console** window can display all the objects included in your scene.

5. The **Project** window can display messages or errors from your code.
6. Once an asset has been downloaded in the scene, it is not available in other scenes within the same project.
7. Once an object has been deactivated (i.e., using the tick box in the **Inspector**) it will be deleted from your project forever.
8. To make some objects children of other objects, you can select the option: **GameObject | Create Child**.
9. Unity is using a right-hand coordinate system.
10. Help on Unity is only available online (i.e., you need to be connected to the Internet to access it).

2
INTRODUCTION TO C#
PROGRAMMING

In this section, we will go through an introduction to C# programming and look at key aspects that you will need for your games, including:

- C# Syntax.
- Variable types and scope.
- Useful coding structures (e.g., loops or conditional statements).

So, after completing this chapter, you will be able to:

- Understand key concepts related to C# programming.
- Understand the concepts of variables and methods.
- Create a Flappy Bird game based on the concepts covered in this chapter.

The code solutions for this chapter are included in the **resource pack** that you can download by following the instructions included in the section entitled "**Support and Resources for this Book**".

INTRODUCTION

When you are using scripting in Unity, you are communicating with the Game Engine and asking it to perform actions. To communicate with the system, you are using a language or a set of words bound by a syntax that the computer and you know. This language consists of keywords, key phrases, and a syntax that ensures that the instructions are written and (more importantly) understood properly.

In computer science, this language needs to be exact, precise, unambiguous, and with a correct syntax. In other words, it needs to be **exact**.

When writing C# code, you will be following a syntax; this syntax will consist in a set of rules that will make it possible for you to communicate with Unity clearly and unambiguously. In addition to its syntax, C# also uses classes, and your C# scripts will, by default, be saved as classes.

In the next section, we will learn how to use this syntax. If you have already coded in JavaScript, some of the information provided in the rest of this chapter may look familiar and this prior exposure to JavaScript will definitely help you. This being said, UnityScript and C#, despite some relative similarities, are quite different in many aspects; for example, in C#, variables and functions are declared differently.

When scripting in C#, you will be using a specific syntax to communicate with Unity; this syntax will be made of sentences that will be used to convey information on what you would like the computer to do; these sentences or statements will include a combination of keywords, variables, methods, or events; and the next section will explain how you can confidently build these sentences together and consequently program in C#.

STATEMENTS

When you code in C#, you need to tell the system to execute your instructions (e.g., print information) using statements. A statement is literally an order or something that you ask the system to do. For example, in the next line of code, the statement will tell Unity to print a message in the **Console** window:

```
print ("Hello Word");
```

When writing statements, you will need to follow several rules, including the following:

- **The order of statements**: each statement is executed in the same order as it appears in the script. For example, in the next example, the code will print **hello**, then **world;** this is because the associated statements are in that particular sequence.

```
print ("hello");
print ("world");
```

- **Statements are separated by semi-colons** (i.e., semi-colon at the end of each statement).

Note that several statements can be added on the same line, as long as they are separated by a semi-colon.

- For example, the next line of code has a correct syntax, as all of its statements are separated by a semi-colon.

```
print("hello");print ("world");
```

- **Multiple spaces are ignored for statements**; however, it is good practice to add spaces around the operators **+**, **-**, **/**, or **%** for clarity. For example, in the next code snippet, we say that **a** is equal to **b**. You may notice that spaces have been included both before and after the operator **=**.

```
a = b;
```

- **Statements to be executed together (e.g., based on the same condition) can be grouped using code blocks**. In C#, code blocks are symbolized by curly brackets (e.g., **{** or **}**). So, in other words, if you needed to group several statements, you would include all of them within the same set of curly brackets, as follows:

```
{
        print ("hello stranger!");
        print ("today, we will learn about scripting");
}
```

As we have seen earlier, a statement usually employs or starts with a **keyword** (i.e., a word that the computer knows). Each of these keywords has a specific purpose, and common keywords, at this stage, could be used for the following actions:

- Printing a message in the **Console** window: the keyword is **print**.
- Declaring a variable: the keyword, in this case, depends on the type of the variable that is declared (e.g., **int** for integers, **string** for text, or **bool** for Boolean variables), and we will see more about these in the next sections.
- Declaring a method: the keyword to be used depends on the type of the data returned by the method. For example, in C#, the name of a method is preceded by the keyword **int** when the method returns an **integer**; it is preceded by the keyword **string** when the method returns a **string**, or by the keyword **void** when the method does not return any information.

What is called a **method** in C# is what used to be called a function in UnityScript; these terms (i.e., function and method) differ in at least two ways: in C# you need to specify the type of the data returned by this method, and the keyword **function** is not used anymore in C# for this purpose. We will see more about methods in the next sections.

- Marking a block of instructions to be executed based on a condition: the keywords are **if** and **else**.
- Exiting a function: the keyword is **return**.

COMMENTS

In C# (similarly to JavaScript), you can use comments to explain your code and to make it more readable by others. This becomes important as the size of your code increases; and it is also important if you work in a team, so that other team members can understand your code and make amendments in the right places, if and when it is needed.

Code that is commented is usually not executed. There are two ways to comment your code in C# using either **single-** or **multi-line** comments.

In single-line comments, a **double forward slash** is added at the start of a line or after a statement, so that this line (or part thereof) is commented, as illustrated in the next code snippet.

```
//the next line prints Hello in the console window
print ("Hello");
//the next line declares the variable name
string name;
name = "Hello";//sets the value of the variable name
```

In multi-line comments, any code between the characters forward slash and star " /*" and the characters star and forward slash "*/" will be commented, and this code will not be executed. This is also referred to as **comment blocks**.

```
/* the next lines after the comments will print the message "hello" in the console window
we then declare the variable name and assign a value
*/
print("Hello");
string name;
name = "Hello";//sets the value of the variable name
//print ("Hello World")
/*
        string name;
        name = "My Name";
*/
```

VARIABLES

A variable can be compared to a container that includes a value that may change over time. When using variables, we usually need to: (1) declare the variable by specifying its type, (2) assign a value to this variable, and (3) possibly combine this variable with other variables using operators, as illustrated in the next code snippet.

```
int myAge;//we declare the variable myAge
myAge = 20;// we set the variable myAge to 20
myAge = myAge + 1; //we add 1 to the variable myAge
```

In the previous example, we have declared a variable called **myAge** and its type is **int** (as in **integer**). We save the value **20** in this variable, and we then add **1** to it.

Note that, contrary to UnityScript, where the keyword **var** is used to declare a variable, in C# the variable is declared using its type followed by its name. As we will see later, we will also need to use what is called an **access modifier** in order to specify how and from where this variable can be accessed.

Also note that in the previous code, we have assigned the value **myAge + 1** to the variable **myAge**; the = operator is an assignment operator; in other words, it is there to assign a value to a variable and is not to be understood in a strict algebraic sense (i.e., that the values or variables on both sides of the = sign are equal).

To make C# coding easier and leaner, you can declare several variables of the same type in one statement. For example, in the next code snippet, we declare three variables **v1**, **v2**, and **v3** in one statement. This is because they are of the same type (i.e., they are **integers**).

```
int v1,v2,v3;
int v4=4, v5=5, v6=6;
```

In the code above, the first line declares the variables **v1**, **v2**, and **v3**. All three variables are **integers**. In the second line of code, not only do we declare three variables simultaneously, but we also initialize them by setting a value for each of these variables.

When using variables, there are a few things that we need to determine including their name, their type and their scope:

- **Name of a variable:** a variable is usually given a unique name so that it can be identified easily and uniquely. The name of a variable is usually referred to as an **identifier**. When defining an identifier, it can contain letters, digits, a minus, an underscore or a dollar sign, and it usually begins with a letter. Identifiers cannot be keywords, such as the keyword **if**, for example.
- **Type of variable:** variables can hold several types of data, including numbers (e.g., integers, doubles or floats), text (e.g., strings or characters), Boolean values (e.g., true or false), arrays, objects (we will see the concept of arrays later in this chapter) or **GameObjects** (i.e., any object included in your scene), as illustrated in the next code snippet.

```
string myName = "Patrick";//the text is declared using double quotes
int currentYear = 2017;//the year needs no decimals and is declared as an integer
float width = 100.45f;//the width is declared as a float (i.e., with decimals)
```

- **Variable declaration:** variables need to be declared so that the system knows what you are referring to if you use this variable in your code. The first step in using a variable is to declare or define this variable. At the declaration stage, the variable does not have to be assigned a value, as this can be done later. In the next example, we declare a variable called **myName** and then assign the value **"My Name"** to it.

```
string myName;
myName = "My Name"
```

- **Scope of a variable:** a variable can be accessed in specific contexts that depend on where in the script the variable was initially declared. We will look at this concept later.
- **Accessibility level:** as we will see later, a C# program consists of classes; for each of these classes, the methods and variables within can be accessed depending on their **accessibility** levels and we will look at this principle later.

Common variable types include:

- **String**: same as text.
- **Int**: integer (1, 2, 3, etc.).
- **Boolean**: true or false.
- **Float**: with a fractional value (e.g., 1.2f, 3.4f, etc.).
- **Arrays**: a group of variables of the same type. If this is unclear, not to worry, this concept will be explained further in this chapter.
- **GameObject**: a game object (any game object in your scene).

ARRAYS

You can optimize your code with arrays, as they make it easier to apply features and similar behaviors to a wide range of data. When you use arrays, you can manage to declare less variables (for variables storing the same type of information) and to also access them more easily. You can create either single-dimensional arrays or multi-dimensional arrays.

Let's look at the simplest form of arrays: **single-dimensional arrays**. For this concept, we can take the analogy of a group of 10 people who all have a name. If we wanted to store this information using a string variable, we would need to declare (and to set) ten different variables, as illustrated in the next code snippet.

```
string name1;string name2; ......
```

While this code is perfectly fine, it would be great to store this information in only one variable instead. For this purpose, we could use an array. An array is comparable to a list of items that we can access using an index. This index usually starts at 0 for the first element in the array.

So let's see how we store the names with an array.

- First we could declare the array as follows:

```
string [] names;
```

You will probably notice the syntax **dataType [] nameOfTheArray**. The opening and closing square brackets are used to specify that we declare an **array** that will include string values.

- Then we could initialize the array as follows:

```
names = new string [10];
```

In the previous code, we just specify that our new array, called **names**, will include 10 string variables.

- We can then store information in this array as described in the next code snippet.

```
names [0] = "Paul";
names [1] = "Mary";
...
names [9] = "Pat";
```

In the previous code, we store the name **Paul** as the first element in the array (remember the index starts at 0); we store the second element (with the index 1) as **Mary**, as well as the last element (with the index 9), **Pat**.

Note that for an array of size **n, the index of the first element is 0** and **the index of the last element is n-1**. So for an array of size 10, the index for the first element is 0, and the index of the last element is 9 (i.e., 10-1).

If you were to use arrays of integers or floats, or any other type of data, the process would be similar, as illustrated in the next code snippet.

```
int [] arrayOfInts; arrayOfInts [0] = 1;
float [] arrayOfFloats;arrayOfLoats[0]=2.4f;
```

Now, one of the cool things that you can do with arrays is that you can initialize your array in one line, saving you the headaches of writing 10 lines of code if you have 10 items in your array, as illustrated in the next example.

```
string [] names = new string [10] {"Paul","Mary","John","Mark", "Eva","Pat","Sinead","Elma","Flaithri",
"Eleanor"};
```

This is very handy, as you will see in the next chapters, and this should definitely save you a lot of time coding.

Now that we have looked into single-dimensional arrays, let's look at multidimensional arrays, which can also be very useful when storing information. This type of array (i.e., multidimensional arrays) can be compared to a building with several floors, each with several apartments. So let's say that we would like to store the number of tenants for each apartment. We would, in this case, create variables that would store this number for each of these apartments.
The first solution would be to create variables that store the number of tenants for each of these apartments with a variable that makes a reference to the floor, and the number of the apartment.

For example, the variable **ap0_1** could be defined to store the number of tenants in the first apartment on the ground floor, **ap0_2**, could be defined to store the number of tenants in the second apartment on the ground floor, **ap1_1** could be defined to store the number of tenants in the second apartment on the first floor, and **ap1_2**, could be defined to store the number of tenants in the third apartment on the first floor. So in term of coding, we could have the following:

```
int ap0_1 = 0;
int ap0_2 = 0;
...
```

However, we could also use arrays in this case, as illustrated in the next code snippet:

```
int [,] apArray = new int [10,10];
apArray [0,1] = 0;
apArray [0,2] = 0;
print (apArray[0]);
```

In the previous code:

- We declare our array. **int [,]** means a two-dimensional array with integers; in other words, we state that any element in this array will be defined and accessed based on two parameters: the floor level and the number of this apartment on that level.
- We also specify a size (or maximum) for each of these parameters. The maximum number of floors (or level) will be 10, and the maximum number of apartment per floor will be 10. So, for this example we can define levels, from level 0 to level 9 (i.e., 10 levels), and from apartment 0 to apartment 9 (i.e., 10 apartments).
- The last line of code prints the value of the first element of the array in the **Console** window.

One of the other interesting things with arrays is that, by using a loop, you can write a single line of code to access all the items in this array, and hence, write more efficient code.

CONSTANTS

So far, we have looked at variables and how you can store and access them seamlessly in your code. The assumption then was that a value may change over time, and that this value would be stored in a variable accordingly. However, there may be times when you know that a value will remain constant throughout your game. For example, you may want to define labels that refer to values that should not change over time, and in this case, you could use constants.

Let's see how this works: let's say that the player has three choices in the first menu of the game, that we will call 0, 1, and 2. Let's assume that you would like an easy way to remember these values so that you can process the corresponding choices. Let's look at the following code that illustrates this idea:

```
int userChoice = 2;
if (userChoice == 0) print ("you have decided to restart");
if (userChoice == 1) print ("you have decided to stop the game");
if (userChoice == 2) print ("you have decided to pause the game");
```

In the previous code:

- The variable **userChoice** is an integer and is set to **2**.
- We then check the value of the variable **userChoice** and print a message accordingly in the console window.

Now, as you add more code to your game, you may or may not remember that the value **0** corresponds to restarting the game; the same applies to the other two values defined previously. So instead, we could use constants to make it easier to remember (and to use) these values. Let's see how the previous example can be modified to employ constants instead.

```
const int CHOICE_RESTART = 0;
const int CHOICE_STOP = 1;
const int CHOICE_PAUSE = 2;
int userChoice = 2;
if (userChoice == CHOICE_RESTART) print ("you have decided to restart");
if (userChoice == CHOICE_STOP) print ("you have decided to stop the game");
if (userChoice == CHOICE_PAUSE) print ("you have decided to pause the game");
```

In the previous code:

- We declare three **constant** variables.
- These variables are then used to check the choice made by the user.

In the next example, we use a constant to calculate a tax rate; this is a good practice as the same value will be used across the program with no or little room for errors when it comes to using the exact same tax rate across your program.

```
const float VAT_RATE = 0.21f;
float priceBeforeVat = 23.0f
float priceAfterVat = pricebeforeVat * VAT_RATE;
```

In the previous code:

- We declare a **constant** float variable for the vat rate.

- We declare a **float** variable for the item's price before tax.
- We calculate the item's price after adding the tax.

It is a very good coding practice to use constants for values that don't change across your program. Using constants makes your code more readable, it saves work when you need to change a value in your code, and it also decreases possible occurrences of errors (e.g., for calculations).

OPERATORS

Once we have declared and assigned values to variables, we can then combine these variables using operators. There are different types of operators including: arithmetic operators, assignment operators, comparison operators and logical operators. So let's look at each of these operators:

- **Arithmetic operators** are used to perform arithmetic operations including additions, subtractions, multiplications, or divisions. Common arithmetic operators include +, -, *, /, or % (modulo).

```
int number1 = 1;// the variable number1 is declared
int number2 = 1;// the variable number2 is declared
int sum = number1 + number2;// We add two numbers and store them in the variable sum
int sub = number1 - number2;// We subtract two numbers and store them in the variable sub
```

- **Assignment operators** can be used to assign a value to a variable and include =, +=, -=, *=, /= or %=.

```
int number1 = 1;
int number2 = 1;
number1+=1; //same as number1 = number1 + 1;
number1-=1; //same as number1 = number1 - 1;
number1*=1; //same as number1 = number1 * 1;
number1/=1; //same as number1 = number1 / 1;
number1%=1; //same as number1 = number1 % 1;
```

Note that the = operator, when used with strings, will concatenate these strings (i.e., add them one after the other to create a new string). When used with a number and a string, the same will apply; for example **"Hello"+1** will result in **"Hello1"**.

- **Comparison operators** are often used in conditional statements to compare two values; comparison operators include ==, !=, >, <, <= and >=.

```
if (number1 == number2); //if number1 equals number2
if (number1 != number2); //if number1 and number2 have different values
if (number1 > number2); //if number1 is greater than number2
if (number1 >= number2); //if number1 is greater than or equal to number2
if (number1 < number2); //if number1 is less than number2
if (number1 <= number2); //if number1 is less than or equal to number2
```

CONDITIONAL STATEMENTS

Statements can be performed based on a condition, and in this case, they are called **conditional statements**. The syntax is usually as follows:

```
if (condition) statement;
```

This means **if the condition is verified (or true) then (and only then) the statement is executed**. When we assess a condition, we test whether a declaration is true. For example, by typing **if (a == b)**, we mean **"if it is true that a is equal to b"**. Similarly, if we type **if (a>=b)** we mean **"if it is true that a is greater than or equal to b"**

As we will see later, we can also combine conditions and decide to perform a statement if two (or more) conditions are true. For example, by typing **if (a == b && c == 2)** we mean **"if a is equal to b and c is equal to 2"**. In this case, using the operator **&&** means **AND**, and that both conditions will need to be true. We could compare this to making a decision on whether we will go sailing tomorrow. For example, **"if the weather is sunny and if the wind speed is less than 5km/h then I will go sailing"**.

We could translate this statement as follows.

```
if (weatherIsSunny == true && windSpeed < 5) IGoSailing = true;
```

When creating conditions, as for most natural languages, we can use the operator **OR** noted **||**. Taking the previous example, we could translate the following sentence **"if the weather is too hot or if the wind is faster than 5km/h then I will not go sailing "**, as follows.

```
if (weatherIsTooHot == true || windSpeed >5) IGoSailing = false;
```

Another example could be as follows.

```
if (myName == "Patrick") print("Hello Patrick");
else print ("Hello Stranger");
```

In the previous code:

- We assess the value of the variable called **myName**.
- The statement **print("Hello Patrick")** will be printed if the value of the variable **myName** is **"Patrick"**.
- Otherwise, the message **"Hello Stranger"** will be displayed instead.

When we deal with combining true or false statements, we are effectively applying what is called **Boolean logic**. Boolean logic deals with Boolean variables that have two possible values 1 and 0 (or true and false). By evaluating conditions, we are effectively processing Boolean numbers and applying Boolean logic. While you don't need to know about Boolean logic in depth, some operators for Boolean logic are important, including the **!** operator. It means **NOT** (or "the opposite"). This means that if a variable is true, its opposite will be false, and vice versa. For example, if we consider the variable **weatherIsGood = true**, the value of **!weatherIsGood** will be **false** (its opposite). So the condition **if (weatherIdGood == false)** could be also written **if (!weatherIsGood)** which would literally translate as "if the weather is **NOT** good".

SWITCH STATEMENTS

If you have understood the concept of conditional statements, then this section should be pretty much straight forward. Switch statements are a variation on the if/else statements that we have seen earlier. The idea behind the switch statements is that, depending on the value of a particular variable, we will switch to a particular portion of the code and perform one or several actions accordingly. The variable considered for the switch structure is usually of type **integer**. Let's look at a simple example:

```
int choice = 1;
switch (choice)
{
        case 1:
                print ("you chose 1");
                break;
        case 2:
                print ("you chose 2");
                break;
        case 3:
                print ("you chose 3");
                break;
        default:
                print ("Default option");
                break;
}
print ("We have exited the switch structure");
```

In the previous code:

- We declare the variable called **choice**, as an **integer** and initialize it to **1**.
- We then create a **switch** structure whereby, depending on the value of the variable **choice**, the program will switch to the relevant section (i.e., the portion of code starting with **case 1:**, **case 2:**, etc.). Note that in our code, we look for the values **1**, **2** or **3**. However, if the variable **choice** is not equal to 1 or 2 or 3, the program will go to the section called **default**. This is because this section is executed if all of the other possible choices (i.e., 1, 2, or 3) have not been fulfilled (or selected).

Note that each choice or branch starts with the keyword **case** and ends with the keyword **break**. The **break** keyword is there to specify that after executing the commands included in the branch (or the current choice), the program should exit the switch structure. Without any break statement we will remain in the switch structure and the next line of code will be executed.

So let's consider the previous example and see how this would work in practice. In our case, the variable **choice** is set to **1**, so we will enter the **switch** structure, and then look for the section that deals with a value of **1** for the variable **choice**. This will be the section that starts with **case 1:**; then the command **print ("you chose 1");** will be executed, followed by the command **break**, indicating that we should exit the switch structure; finally the command **print ("We have exited the switch structure")** will be executed.

Switch structures are very useful to structure your code and when dealing with mutually exclusive choices (i.e., only one of the choices can be processed) based on an integer value, especially in the case of menus. In addition, switch structures make for cleaner and easily understandable code.

LOOPS

There are times when you have to perform repetitive tasks as a programmer; many times, these can be fast forwarded using loops which are structures that will perform the same actions repetitively based on a condition. So, the process is usually as follows when using loops:

- Start the loop.
- Perform actions.
- Check for a condition.
- Exit the loop if the condition is fulfilled or keep looping otherwise.

Sometimes the condition is performed at the start of the loop, some other times it is performed at the end of the loop. As we will see in the next paragraph this will be the case for the **while** and **do-while** loop structures, respectively.

Let's look at the following example that is using a **while** loop.

```
int counter =0;
while (counter <=10)
{
        counter++;
}
```

In the previous code:

- We declare the variable counter and set its value to 0.
- We then create a loop that starts with the keyword **while** and for which the content (which is what is to be executed while we are looping) is delimited by opening and closing curly brackets.
- We set the condition to remain in this loop (i.e., **counter <=10**). So we will remain in this loop as long as the variable counter is less than or equal to 10.
- Within the loop, we increase the value of the variable **counter** by 1 and print its value.

So effectively:

- The first time we go through the loop: the variable **counter** is increased to **1**; we reach the end of the loop; we go back to the start of the loop and check if **counter** is less or equal to **10**; this is true in this case because **counter** equals 1.
- The second time we go through the loop: **counter** is increased to **2**; we reach the end of the loop; we go back to the start of the loop and check if **counter** is less or equal to 10; this is true in this case because **counter** equals **2**.
- ...
- The 11th time we go through the loop: **counter** is increased to **11**; we reach the end of the loop; we go back to the start of the loop and check if **counter** is less or equal to 10; this is now false as **counter** now equals **11**. As a result, we exit the loop.

So, as you can see, using a loop, we have managed to increment the value of the variable **counter** iteratively, from 0 to 11, but using less code than would be needed otherwise.

Now, we could create a slightly modified version of this loop, using a **do-while** loop structure instead, as illustrated in the next example:

```
int counter =0;
do
{
        counter++;
} while (counter <=10);
```

In the previous example, you may spot two differences, compared to the previous code:

- The **while** keyword is now at the end of the loop. So the condition will be evaluated (or assessed) at the end of the loop.
- A **do** keyword is now featured at the start of the loop.
- So here, we perform statements first and then check for the condition at the end of the loop.

Another variations of the code could be as follows:

```
for (int counter = 0; counter <=10; counter ++)
{
        print ("Counter = " + counter);
}
```

In the previous code:

- We declare a loop in a slightly different way: we state that we will use an integer variable called **counter** that will go from 0 to 10.
- This variable **counter** will be incremented by 1 every time we go through the loop.
- We remain in the loop as long as the variable **counter** is less than or equal to 10.
- The test for the condition, in this case, is performed at the start of the loop.

Loops are very useful to be able to perform repetitive actions for a finite number of objects, or to perform what is usually referred as recursive actions. For example, you could use loops to create (or instantiate) 100 objects at different locations in your game, or to go through an array of 100 items. So using loops will definitely save you some code and time :-).

QUIZ

It is now time to test your knowledge. Please specify whether the following statements are TRUE or FALSE. The answers are available at the end of the book.

1. The value of a variable always remains constant.
2. A method always returns information.
3. A method may not return information.
4. If a method is void, it will return an integer value.
5. An array can store several variables at a time.
6. A class usually includes a constructor.
7. A for loop can be used to go through all the elements of an array.
8. A public method is accessible from anywhere.
9. A private variable is accessible only from members of the class.
10. A protected variable is accessible only from members of the class.

3

CORE MECHANICS AND SIMPLE WORLD BUILDING

In this chapter, we will explore the foundational mechanics of building an interactive 3D game in Unity. By starting with simple concepts and gradually increasing complexity, you'll learn to create an engaging and functional game environment. This chapter is designed to introduce you to essential game development concepts such as world-building, player navigation, object interaction, and user interface integration.

We will cover the following topics:

- **Creating a Simple World with Boxes:** Learn how to set up a basic world using primitive shapes like cubes and planes, which will serve as the foundation for your game environment.
- **Navigating with an FPS (Create Your Own):** Build a first-person navigation system that allows players to explore the world with movement, jumping, and running mechanics.
- **Collecting Items:** Discover how to create collectible objects and track them as the player interacts with the game.
- **Creating a Simple Scoring System:** Implement a scoring mechanism to track the player's progress and add an element of challenge to your game.
- **Displaying Collected Items on Screen (Text and Images):** Design a user interface (UI) to show collected items and scores in real time.
- **Loading a New Scene + Smooth Scene Transitions:** Master scene management and add smooth transitions to enhance the player experience when moving between levels.
- **Avoiding Projectiles (Rigid Body Physics):** Use physics-based mechanics to introduce projectiles into the game, teaching players to dodge obstacles dynamically.
- **Adding Animated Elements: Moving Doors, Escalators, and Platforms:** Create interactive game elements with animations to add complexity and realism to your world.
- **Implementing a Mini Map:** Learn how to create a mini-map UI, making navigation easier and more intuitive for players.

So, by the end of this chapter, you will be able to:
- Set up a 3D game environment using Unity's tools and primitive shapes.
- Develop a first-person controller for navigating the game world.

- Implement item collection and scoring systems.
- Display collected items and scores on-screen using Unity's UI tools.
- Transition smoothly between scenes while maintaining player engagement.
- Integrate physics-based mechanics to create interactive gameplay.
- Add animated elements such as doors and platforms to enhance immersion.
- Create a mini-map UI to improve game navigation.

Overall, this chapter lays the groundwork for building a fully functional 3D game. Let's get started by creating a simple world with boxes, the first step toward crafting your game environment!

CREATING A SIMPLE WORLD WITH BOXES

INTRODUCTION

In this section, we will focus on setting up the foundation of your game world using Unity's primitive shapes, such as cubes and planes. These basic building blocks will help you design a simple yet functional environment where gameplay mechanics can be tested and refined. While this world may not be visually complex, it serves as an excellent starting point to understand the core principles of level design and object manipulation in Unity.

What You'll Learn in This Section:
- How to create and place 3D objects using Unity's interface.
- Techniques to organize and structure your game environment.
- Applying basic materials to enhance the appearance of objects.

By the end of this section, you will have a basic game environment created with simple shapes that can serve as a sandbox for developing and testing gameplay mechanics. Let's get started by creating and customizing your first 3D objects!

CREATING THE GROUND

Let's go ahead and create a new box for the ground:

- Create a new scene.
- Go to the **Hierarchy** window in Unity.
- Right-click anywhere in the **Hierarchy** and select **3D Object | Cube** from the context menu.
- This will create a new cube object in your scene.

We can now rename this cube "**ground**":

- In the **Hierarchy**, locate the newly created cube (it will likely be named "**Cube**").
- Right-click on the cube's name and select **Rename**, or simply select the cube and press F2 on your keyboard.
- Type **ground** and press Enter to rename it.

We can now set the size of the ground:

- Select the **ground** object in the **Hierarchy** to view its properties in the **Inspector** window.
- In the **Inspector**, find the **Transform** component.
- Locate the **Scale** property under **Transform** and change the **Scale** values to: **X**: 100; **Y**: 0.1 (to make it very thin like a floor); **Z**: 100
- This resizes the cube to create a flat, wide ground.

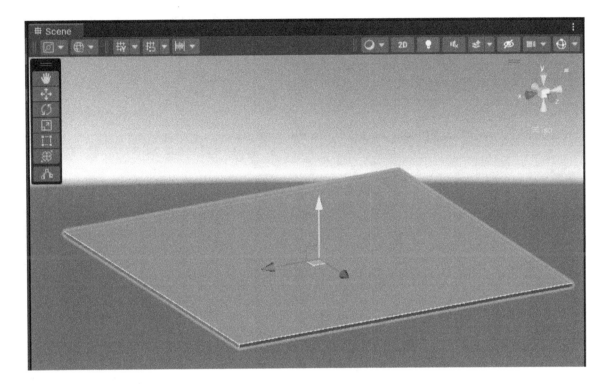

Next, we will position the ground:

- While the **ground** object is still selected, go to the **Position** property under the **Transform** component in the **Inspector**.
- Set the **Position** values to: **X**: 0; **Y**: 0; **Z**: 0
- This ensures the ground is centred at the origin of the scene.

Now that the ground has been created, let's verify the **Ground** setup:

- Look at the **Scene View** to confirm the changes.
- The ground should appear as a large, flat plane covering the area around the origin (0, 0, 0).

> **Tip**: If you don't see the changes in the scene, ensure the ground object is not hidden and that your camera is positioned correctly to view the object.

After completing these steps, you will have created a flat ground surface that can serve as the foundation for your game environment. This ground will act as the base for placing other objects and interacting with the game world.

CREATING THE WALLS

Now that we have created the ground, we can create simple walls made of cubes that will give a challenging, yet simple and easy to implement:

- Please create a new box and rename it **wall**.
- Change its size to **(20, 5, 20)**.
- Move it along so that it's slightly above the ground.

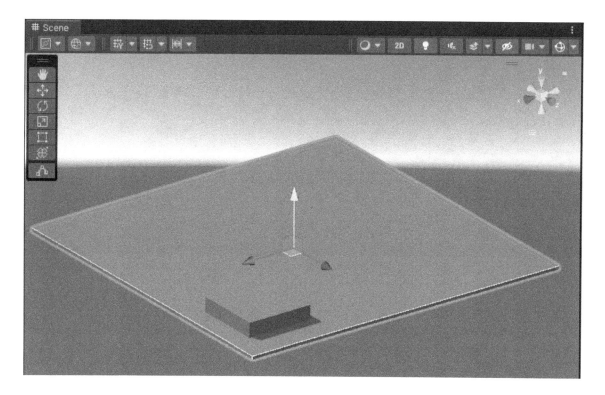

APPLYING COLOR TO THE WALLS

For more clarity, we can apply a red color to the box

- In the **Project** window, right-click and select **Create | New Material** from the contextual menu.
- This will create a new material.
- Rename this new material **red**.

We can now set its color to red:

- Select it, and, using the **Inspector** window, click on the white rectangle in the section called **Surface Inputs**.

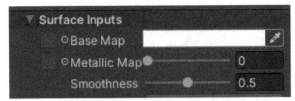

- In the new window, pick a red color.

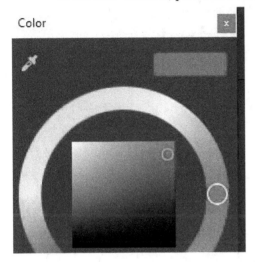

- Once this is done, you can drag and drop this material to the object **wall** and you should see that it turns red, as per the next figure.

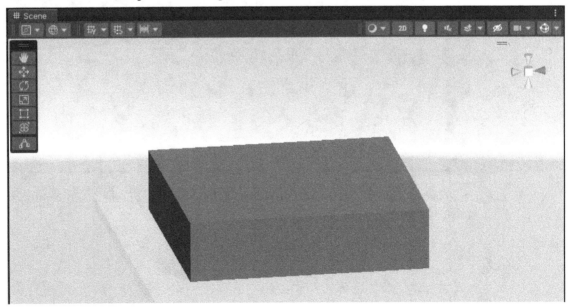

DUPLICATING THE WALL TO FORM THE LAYOUT

Now that the wall has been created and colored, we just need to duplicate it several times.

- Please duplicate the object **wall** (i.e., select it and press **CTRL + D**) twice to create two duplicates, and then move these duplicates so that they are aligned as per the next figure.

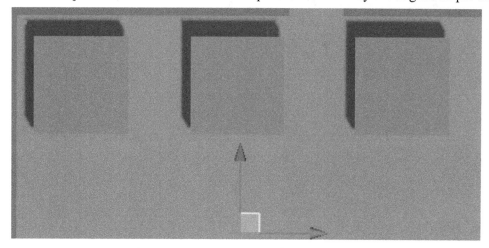

- Once this is done, you can select the three walls, press **CTRL + D** to create a new row, and move the new row so that it looks like the next figure.

- You can repeat the previous step to create a third row and obtain a layout similar to the next figure.

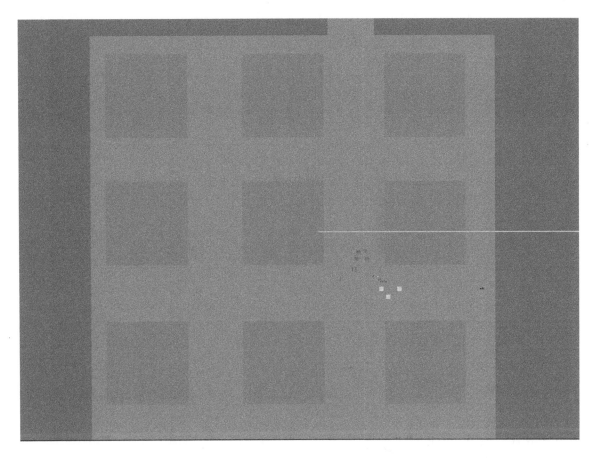

So, at this stage, you have managed to create a simple layout made of colored boxes; so, in the next section, we will get to navigate this layout by creating a First-Person Controller.

NAVIGATING WITH AN FPS (CREATE YOUR OWN)

INTRODUCTION

In the previous section, we laid the foundation for our game environment by creating a simple world using primitive shapes, with a flat ground that acts as the stage for player interaction. Now, we will shift our focus to giving the player the ability to navigate this world using a **First-Person Shooter (FPS) Controller**. This section introduces the mechanics of player movement, including walking, running, jumping, and camera control for a seamless exploration experience.

The goal of this section is to create a responsive and immersive FPS controller. Players will be able to:
- Move around the environment using keyboard controls.
- Look around the world with mouse inputs.
- Jump and run to interact dynamically with the surroundings.

This functionality is essential for most 3D games, particularly those requiring exploration, combat, or interaction with objects in a first-person perspective.

So, in this section we will do the following:

- Prepare the **Player** Object: We'll start by setting up a **Capsule** object to represent the player and adding essential components like a **CharacterController** and a **Camera**.
- Add Player Movement: We'll implement basic movement mechanics such as walking and running. Players will use keyboard inputs (W, A, S, D) to move in the game world.
- Jump and Gravity: We will introduce jumping mechanics to allow vertical movement and simulate real-world physics by adding gravity to the player's motion.
- Implement Camera Rotation: We will use mouse input to rotate the player's view horizontally and vertically, clamping the vertical rotation to create a realistic FPS experience.
- Fine-Tuning Movement: We will ensure smooth transitions between walking, running, and jumping while grounding the player properly on uneven surfaces.

Navigating the world is a core part of any 3D game. Without proper player movement and camera control, players cannot engage effectively with the environment or interact with game elements like objects, enemies, or puzzles. By the end of this section, you'll have a functional FPS controller that brings your game world to life.

Let's begin by preparing the player object and setting up the components required to implement FPS navigation!

SETTING UP THE PLAYER

To enable FPS navigation, the player object must be set up correctly in Unity, and then functionality will be added through the provided script. Follow these steps to configure the player in Unity, and then we will introduce the code in small, manageable snippets.

First, we are going to create a player object in the scene.
- In the **Hierarchy**, right-click and select **3D Object | Capsule**.
- Rename the capsule to **Player**.
- In the **Inspector**, set its y coordinate to 1 to place it slightly above the ground.

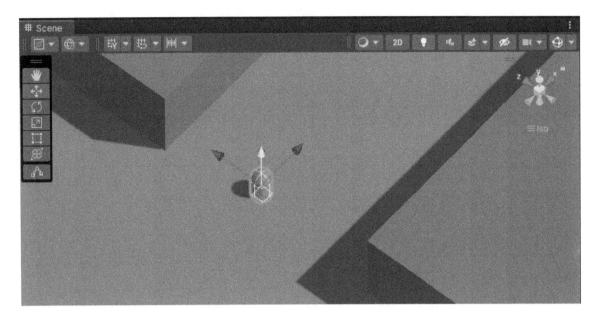

Next, we'll add a camera to the player object so the player can look around.

- Right-click the **Player** object in the **Hierarchy** and select **Camera**.
- Rename this camera **playerCamera**.
- Position the camera at the top of the capsule: In the **Inspector**, set the **Position** of the camera to **(0, 0.9, 0)**.

Now that the player and the camera are set, let's add the **CharacterController** to handle movement and collisions.
- Select the **Player** object in the **Hierarchy**.
- In the **Inspector**, click **Add Component** and search for **CharacterController**.
- Add the **CharacterController** component to the **Player**.

ADDING THE CODE

Now that the player object is set up, it's time to create the First-Person Controller script and attach it to the **Player**.
- In the **Project** window, right-click in your **Scripts** folder (or create one) and select **Create | C# Script**.

- Name the script **FPSController**.
- Double-click the script to open it in your code editor.
- Attach the script to the **Player** object: Drag the **FPSController** script from the **Project** window and drop it onto the **Player** object in the **Hierarchy**.

We will now build this script step by step by adding the following snippets. For each snippet, I'll explain what it does and where it should be placed in the script

- Please add the following code at the beginning of the class (before any functions):

```
// Movement speeds
public float walkSpeed = 5f;
public float runSpeed = 10f;
public float jumpHeight = 2f;

// Gravity
public float gravity = -9.81f;
private Vector3 velocity;
private bool isGrounded;

//Mouse Look
// Camera rotation
public Transform playerCamera;
public float mouseSensitivity = 100f;
private float xRotation = 0f;

// Components
private CharacterController controller;
```

In the previous code:

- **walkSpeed**: Defines the player's walking speed and is used to calculate movement speed when the player is not running.
- **runSpeed**: Determines the speed at which the player moves when running (sprinting) and is used to switch movement speed when the sprint key is held down.
- **jumpHeight**: Specifies how high the player can jump and is used to calculate the initial upward velocity during a jump.
- **gravity**: Simulates the downward pull on the player and is used to continuously decrease the vertical velocity, creating realistic falling behavior.
- **velocity**: Tracks the player's current movement in 3D space (particularly vertical motion) and is used for applying jumping and gravity effects.
- **isGrounded**: checks whether the player is touching the ground.
- **playerCamera:** stores the Transform of the player's camera, which holds data about its position, rotation, and scale. It allows the script to manipulate the camera for first-person perspective actions, such as rotation or positioning relative to the player.
- **mouseSensitivity**: sets the sensitivity of the camera's response to mouse input. The value is adjustable in the **Inspector**, enabling the user to tweak how fast the camera moves based on mouse movement.
- **xRotation**: tracks the camera's vertical rotation (up and down movement). It ensures the camera's rotation on the x-axis can be controlled and clamped to prevent unnatural movements (e.g., looking directly behind).

- **controller**: references the **CharacterController** component attached to the player. The CharacterController handles collision detection and player movement without the need for rigid body physics.

So overall, in this code we define variables for managing the player's camera and movement. These include sensitivity settings for camera rotation, tracking the camera's vertical movement, and enabling player movement through a **CharacterController** component. Together, these elements form the foundation for a smooth first-person control system

- Add this code to the Start function.

```
controller = GetComponent<CharacterController>();
playerCamera = GameObject.Find("playerCamera").transform;
```

Now that we have defined the variables necessary to move the player, we will define functions that will either move the player or rotate the camera.

Let's implement the function **RotateCamera** that will effectively rotate the camera when we move the mouse (i.e., **MouseLook**).

MouseLook refers to a control mechanism in a game environment that allows players to look around and control their view using the mouse. It is commonly used in first-person or third-person games to simulate the player's head movement, enabling intuitive camera rotation and interaction with the game world.

- Please add this function:

```
void RotateCamera()
{
    // Get mouse movement inputs
    float mouseX = Input.GetAxis("Mouse X") * mouseSensitivity * Time.deltaTime;
    float mouseY = Input.GetAxis("Mouse Y") * mouseSensitivity * Time.deltaTime;

    // Rotate player horizontally
    transform.Rotate(Vector3.up * mouseX);

    // Rotate camera vertically
    xRotation -= mouseY;
    xRotation = Mathf.Clamp(xRotation, -90f, 90f); // Limit vertical rotation
    playerCamera.localRotation = Quaternion.Euler(xRotation, 0f, 0f);
}
```

In the previous code, we do the following:

- **Define a reference for the player's camera**: This allows the script to manipulate the camera separately from the player's body, enabling vertical rotation for looking up and down.

- **Set the mouse sensitivity**: This variable controls how responsive the camera rotation is to mouse movement. Higher values result in faster and more sensitive camera rotation, while lower values provide slower movement.
- **Track the vertical rotation of the camera**: A variable is used to store the current vertical angle of the camera, ensuring smooth and controlled vertical rotation.
- **Capture mouse input for rotation**: Horizontal mouse movement is mapped to control the player's horizontal rotation. Vertical mouse movement is used to tilt the camera up and down, enhancing the first-person experience.
- **Rotate the player horizontally**: The player object is rotated left or right based on horizontal mouse input, creating a smooth turning effect.
- **Rotate the camera vertically**: The camera is tilted up or down based on vertical mouse input. The vertical rotation is clamped to prevent the player from looking too far up or down, ensuring a realistic range of motion.

So overall, with this code we capture mouse movement to enable camera control, we rotate the player horizontally to allow looking around in the environment, we tilt the camera vertically within a realistic range for looking up and down and we finally create a responsive and immersive first-person perspective.

Next, we will define a function called **MovePlayer** that will handle the player's movement:

- Please add this function:

```
private void MovePlayer()
{
        // Ground check
        isGrounded = controller.isGrounded;

        // Reset velocity when grounded
        if (isGrounded && velocity.y < 0)
        {
                velocity.y = -2f; // Keep a slight downward force to keep the player grounded
        }

        // Get movement inputs
        float horizontal = Input.GetAxis("Horizontal");
        float vertical = Input.GetAxis("Vertical");
}
```

In the previous code, we perform the following actions:

- **Ground Check:** We use the **isGrounded** property of the **Character Controller** to determine if the player is currently in contact with the ground. This avoids using external collision objects or methods, simplifying the ground detection logic.
- **Reset Velocity When Grounded:** If the player is grounded and their vertical velocity (**velocity.y**) is less than zero, it is reset to a small negative value. This ensures the player stays grounded and prevents issues like "floating" slightly above the ground.
- **Capture Movement Inputs:** We retrieve horizontal and vertical movement values from the player's input using **Input.GetAxis**. These inputs correspond to the player's desired direction of movement, typically mapped to the keyboard (e.g., WASD or arrow keys).

So overall, with this code, we check if the player is grounded, reset their velocity to maintain proper ground contact, and capture input for horizontal and vertical movement, laying the foundation for smooth and responsive player movement.

Next, we will define the characters speed and movement:

- Please add this code to the function **MovePlayer**:

```
// Determine speed (shift to run)
float speed = Input.GetKey(KeyCode.LeftShift) ? runSpeed : walkSpeed;

// Calculate movement direction
Vector3 move = transform.right * horizontal + transform.forward * vertical;

// Apply movement
controller.Move(move * speed * Time.deltaTime);
```

In the previous code, we do the following:

- **Determine Speed:** The speed variable is assigned based on whether the **LeftShift** key is pressed. If the key is pressed, the **runSpeed** value is used, allowing the player to sprint. If the key is not pressed, the **walkSpeed** value is used, enabling normal walking. This provides a simple mechanism to toggle between walking and running speeds.
- **Calculate Movement Direction:** A Vector3 called move is calculated to determine the player's movement direction. The horizontal movement is aligned with the player's right direction (**transform.right**), and vertical movement is aligned with the player's forward direction (**transform.forward**). Combining these two directions creates a vector that points in the desired movement direction based on player input.
- **Apply Movement:** The calculated movement vector (move) is multiplied by the determined speed and Time.deltaTime to ensure frame-independent movement. The CharacterController.Move method is then used to apply this movement to the player.

So overall, with this code, we dynamically determine the player's movement speed (walk or run), calculate the movement direction based on input and the player's orientation, and apply this movement to the player using the **CharacterController** for smooth and frame-rate-independent movement.

Now that the character can move in all directions, we will handle the jumping movement:

- Next, please add this code to the function **MovePlayer**:

```
// Jump
if (Input.GetButtonDown("Jump") && isGrounded)
{
        velocity.y = Mathf.Sqrt(jumpHeight * -2f * gravity); // Jump physics calculation
}

// Apply gravity
velocity.y += gravity * Time.deltaTime;
controller.Move(velocity * Time.deltaTime);
```

In the previous code, we perform the following actions:

- **Handle Jumping:** The if condition checks whether the player has pressed the "Jump" button (**Input.GetButtonDown("Jump")**) and is grounded (**isGrounded** is true). If both conditions are met, the player's vertical velocity (**velocity.y**) is calculated to make the player jump.
- **Apply Gravity:** Gravity is applied to the player's vertical velocity by adding a value calculated as **gravity * Time.deltaTime**. This ensures that gravity affects the player gradually over time.
- **Move the Player:** The **controller.Move** method applies the updated velocity (including the vertical component) to the player, making the jump and gravity effects visible in the game.

So overall, with this code, we allow the player to jump if they are grounded and have pressed the "**Jump**" button; we apply the effects of gravity to ensure a realistic fall, and we move the player vertically in response to these forces. This combination creates a smooth jumping and falling mechanic in the game

Finally, we just need to call these functions, that we have just defined, from the **Update** function to ensure that they run every frame; so please add this code to the **Update** function:

```
void Update()
    {
    // Handle player movement
    MovePlayer();

    // Handle camera rotation
    RotateCamera();
    }
```

In the previous code, we call the function **MovePlayer** and **RotateCamera** so that player and the camera movement are handled every frame.

So overall, with the code that we have just added in this section, we:
1. Initialized variables to control movement, gravity, and camera sensitivity.
2. Enabled walking and running with smooth keyboard input.
3. Added jumping mechanics and gravity for realistic vertical movement.
4. Implemented camera rotation to complete the FPS navigation system.

You can now save your code and play the scene to check that you can move on the ground and use the **MouseLook** to look around too, as per the next figure.

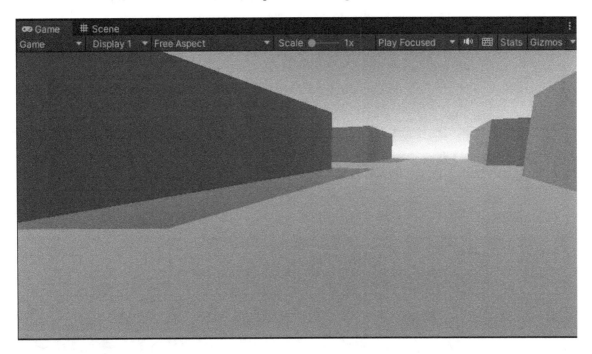

Now that the player can fully explore the 3D environment built in the previous section, we'll integrate collectible items into the scene to make it interactive.

COLLECTING ITEMS

INTRODUCTION

In this section, we will implement a system for collecting items in the game. By interacting with objects in the environment, players can progress toward completing tasks or advancing to the next level. We will set up a mechanism to detect when a player collects an item, track the number of items collected, and visually update the user interface (UI) to reflect the progress. Once all items are collected, the player will transition to the next scene.

This system introduces a common gameplay mechanic and demonstrates how to use Unity's collision detection and UI components effectively.

By the end of this section, you will:
- Add collectible items to your game world.
- Detect when the player interacts with these items.
- Update the UI to track the player's progress.
- Trigger a scene transition once all items are collected.

ADDING COLLECTIBLE ITEMS TO THE SCENE

Now, we'll add the collectible items to the world. Each item will be represented as a **Cube**. For this purpose, we will create a collectible cube, make it a prefab, and then duplicate this cube several times to create three more cubes to be collected.

A **prefab** in Unity is a reusable asset that acts as a blueprint for a game object, allowing developers to create and manage multiple instances of the same object efficiently. Prefabs are particularly useful for maintaining consistency, making updates across all instances simultaneously, and simplifying the creation of complex, repeatable objects like enemies, collectibles, or UI elements

Let's create our first cube:

- Right-click in the **Hierarchy** and select **3D Object | Cube**.
- This will create a new cube that you can rename **box**.
- Leave its size as default **(1, 1, 1)**.

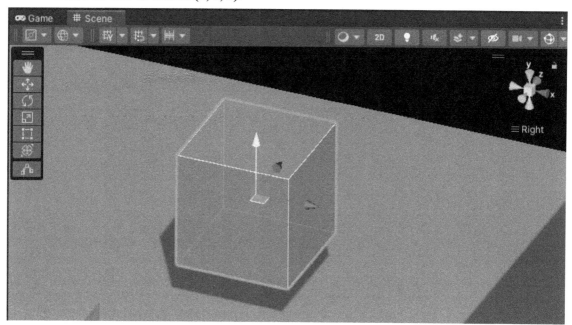

Next, we will assign a **Tag** to this cube:

- Select the object "**box**".
- Go to the **Inspector**, and set its **Tag** to "**box**."

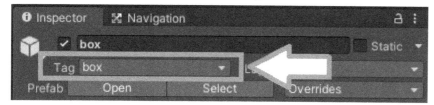

If this tag is not available yet, you can create/apply it by using the **Add Tag** option as follows:

- Click on the drop-down menu to the right of the tag **Label**.

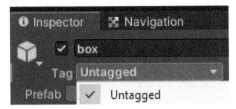

- Select the option "**Add Tag**".
- In the new window, press the + button to create a new tag.

- Add the name of your new tag in the new contextual menu and press **Save**.

- You should see that your tag has been created.

- You just need to select your object and select the tag from the tag list.

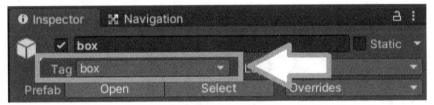

- Once you tag has been added to the box, you can drag and drop this box to the **Project** window, and this will create a prefab called **box**.

- You can then drag and drop this prefab to the scene to create three more collectible cubes.
- Rename them **box2**, **box3**, and **box4**.

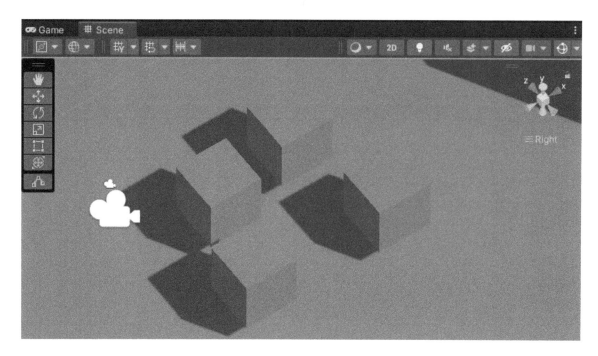

Last but not least, we will apply a texture to the **box** prefab so that this texture can be applied to all objects based on this prefab (i.e., **box2**, **box3**, and **box4**).

- Please select the object called **box** in the **Hierarchy**.
- In the **Inspector**, click on the button **Open**, as per the next figure:

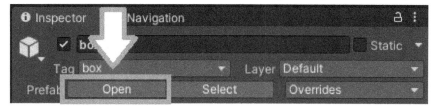

- This will open the prefab.

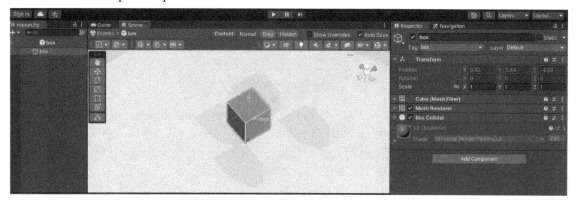

- Next, import the texture **box_texture** in your project: drag and drop the file **box_texture** from your file system (it is in the books resource pack) to the **Project** window.
- Then drag this texture from the **Project** window to the **box** in the **Scene** view.

- You should see that the box now has a texture on it, as per the next figure.

- You can now close the prefab by pressing the left arrow located in the **Hierarchy**, as per the next figure:

- You should now see that all boxes are now textured.

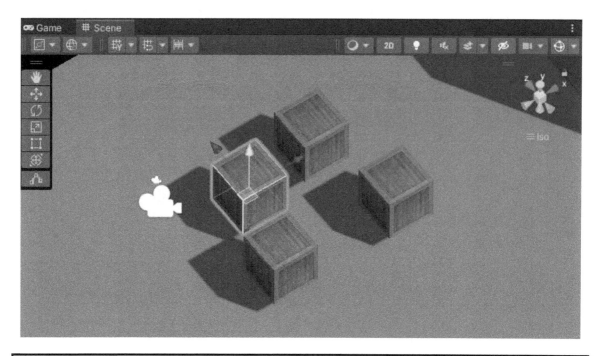

Prefabs allow developers to create reusable, scalable objects with preconfigured components, saving time and ensuring consistency. They enable quick updates across all instances, support modular design, and simplify scene management. Prefabs are ideal for creating repetitive game elements like enemies, collectibles, or UI components efficiently.

ADDING THE CODE TO COLLECT BOXES

Now that we have created the boxes to be collected, we will implement the code to collect them; the idea is to:

- Detect collision between the player and the boxes, using a function called **OnControlliderHit**.
- Check for the tag of the objects that the player collides with.
- Destroy (i.e., collect) the object if its tag is "**box**".

With this in mind, let's go ahead and create a new class that will handle the box collection:

- Please create a new script called **BoxCollecto**r, and attach it to the object **Player**.
- Open the script.
- Add this code to the script.

```
private void OnControllerColliderHit(ControllerColliderHit hit)
{
        // Check if the collided object has the tag "box"
        if (hit.gameObject.CompareTag("box"))
        {
                        // Destroy the box
                Destroy(hit.gameObject);
        }
}
```

In the previous code, we do the following:

- Detect collisions with the **OnControllerColliderHit** method: This method is automatically called when the player's **CharacterController** collides with another object in the scene. The hit parameter provides information about the object involved in the collision.
- Check the tag of the collided object:The code uses **hit.gameObject.CompareTag("box")** to verify if the collided object is tagged as **"box"**. This ensures the logic only applies to objects with this specific tag, ignoring other collisions.
- Destroy the collided object: When the collided object is confirmed to have the **"box"** tag, the **Destroy** method removes it from the scene. This prevents the object from remaining in the environment after it has been interacted with.

So overall, with this code we detect collisions between the player and objects using the **CharacterController**, we identify objects tagged as **"box"** to ensure the interaction is relevant and we remove the collided object from the game world by destroying it.

Please check that you script **BoxCollector** is error-free and attached to the object **Player**; once this is done, you can play the scene, navigate towards the boxes and check that they disappear as you collide with them.

IMPLEMENTING A SIMPLE SCORE AND A USER INTERFACE

In the previous section, we managed to introduce some code that made it possible to collect (i.e., destroy boxes), so now we will improve this by introducing two new features:

- Every time we collect a box, we will increase the score by 1.
- We will also display a brief message in the **Console** window acknowledging that we have collected a box.
- We will display the boxes collected onscreen using an image.

Let's go ahead and implement these three features.

INCREASING THE SCORE

To keep track of the score, we will simply create a variable that will increase every time we collect a box.

- Please add this code at the beginning of the class **BoxCollector**:

```
private int boxCount = 0;
```

- Then add this code in the function **OnControllerColliderHit**, within the conditional statement, as per the next code (new code in bold).

```
private void OnControllerColliderHit(ControllerColliderHit hit)
{
        // Check if the collided object has the tag "box"
        if (hit.gameObject.CompareTag("box"))
        {
                // Increase the box count
                boxCount++;
                Debug.Log("Box Collected! Total Boxes: " + boxCount);
```

In the previous code, we do the following:

- Check if the collided object has the tag "**box**": The condition **hit.gameObject.CompareTag("box")** verifies if the object involved in the collision is tagged as "**box**". This ensures the logic only applies to specific objects marked as collectible boxes.
- Increment the box count (**boxCount++**): When a collision with a box occurs, the **boxCount** variable is increased by one. This keeps track of the total number of boxes collected by the player.
- Log the updated box count: The message "**Box Collected! Total Boxes: "** + **boxCount** is printed to the **Console**. This provides immediate feedback during development or debugging, showing the total number of collected boxes.

So overall, with this code we verify if the collided object is a collectible box using its tag, we update the total number of boxes collected by incrementing a counter and we log the current box count to the **Console** for debugging and testing purposes.

You can now play the scene and check that a message is displayed in the **Console** window every time you collect a box.

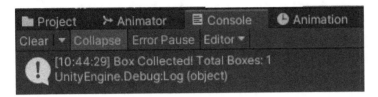

ADDING UI ELEMENTS

In the previous section, we have implemented a score system; however, it would be great to visually provide feedback to the player. To do so, we will implement a system whereby we display the number of boxes collected as part of the user interface (i.e., 1 square when one box has been collected, two squares for two boxes collected, etc.).

First, let's add four **Image** objects to your canvas:

- Switch to the **2D** mode by pressing the corresponding button, as per the next figure:

- Right-click in the **Hierarchy** and select **UI | Image.**
- This will create a new image object.
- Rename it **bx1**.

- You may need to zoom-out to be able to see this image in your **Scene** view.
- Position this image in a visible area on the canvas, for example, in the bottom-left corner.

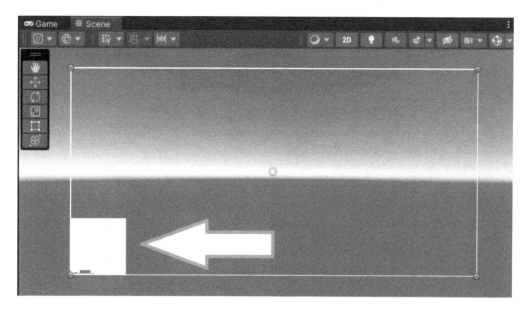

- Duplicate this image three times, rename the duplicates **bx2**, **bx3**, and **bx4**, and place them alongside the first image, aligned, and similarly to the next figure.

CODING THE DISPLAY OF THE UI BOXES

Now that each of the UI elements have been created, it's time to manage their display with our script.

- Please open the script **BoxCollector**.
- Add this code at the beginning of the script:

```
using UnityEngine.UI;
```

- Add this code at the beginning of the class.

```
public Image box1;
public Image box2;
public Image box3;
 public Image box4;
```

In the previous code, we do the following:

- **Define references to UI images**: Each Image variable corresponds to a specific UI element in the game. These images are linked to visual indicators that represent the progress of the player collecting boxes.
- **Enable flexible control over the UI**: These public variables allow us to assign specific UI elements (images) from the Unity editor, if needed. This makes it easy to modify or update the visuals without changing the code.
- **Provide clear identification for collected items**: Each variable, **box1**, **box2**, **box3**, and **box4**, is tied to a unique collectible. As items are collected in the game, the corresponding UI image can be activated to show the player's progress.

So overall, with this code, we enable the game to visually track and display the player's progress in collecting items. Each Image variable provides a direct connection to a specific UI element, allowing the game to dynamically update the visual indicators as the player collects boxes. This enhances user feedback and provides a clear and engaging way to monitor game progression.

After defining these variables, it's time to deactivate all the pictures, and then activate them one by one as we collect boxes:

- Please add this code to the **Start** function in the script **BoxCollector**:

```
box1.gameObject.SetActive(false);
box2.gameObject.SetActive(false);
box3.gameObject.SetActive(false);
box4.gameObject.SetActive(false);
```

In the previous code, we do the following:

- Deactivate the UI elements at the start of the game: Each **SetActive(false)** call ensures that the corresponding UI image (**box1**, **box2**, **box3**, **box4**) is hidden when the game begins. This prevents the visual indicators from appearing before the player collects any items.

- Maintain a clean user interface initially: By deactivating these elements, the game interface remains uncluttered until they are needed. This approach enhances the player's experience by showing only relevant information.

- Prepare for dynamic updates: These images are designed to be activated later during gameplay when the player collects corresponding items. Deactivating them initially allows the game to manage their visibility programmatically.

Overall, this code ensures that the UI elements representing collected boxes are hidden at the start of the game. This creates a clean interface while allowing the images to be activated dynamically as the player progresses, providing clear and responsive feedback for their actions

Next, we will create a function that hides/shows the UI pictures based on the number of boxes collected:

- Please add this method to the script:

```
private void UpdateUI()
{
        // Show the appropriate UI image based on the box count
        switch (boxCount)
        {
                case 1:
                        box1.gameObject.SetActive(true);
                        break;
                case 2:
                        box2.gameObject.SetActive(true);
                        break;
                case 3:
                        box3.gameObject.SetActive(true);
                        break;
                case 4:
                        box4.gameObject.SetActive(true);

                        break;
                default:
                        Debug.Log("All boxes collected or no boxes collected yet.");
                        break;
        }
}
```

In the previous code, we do the following:

- **Use a switch statement to manage UI updates**: The switch statement checks the value of the **boxCount** variable to determine how many boxes the player has collected. Based on this value, the code performs the appropriate actions.
- **Activate the corresponding UI element**: Each case in the switch statement corresponds to a specific number of collected boxes: If **boxCount** equals 1, the first image (box1) is activated to indicate one box has been collected. If boxCount equals 2, the second image (box2) is displayed, and so on until the fourth box.
- **Provide feedback for unexpected scenarios**: The default case logs a message if the **boxCount** does not match any predefined values (e.g., no boxes collected yet or all boxes collected). This is useful for debugging or testing.
- **Ensure dynamic updates**: The code dynamically updates the UI, showing progress to the player as they collect more items. This creates a responsive and engaging user experience.

Overall, this code dynamically updates the UI based on the number of collected boxes. By activating the appropriate image for each **boxCount**, it provides clear feedback to the player about their progress. The use of a switch statement ensures that only the relevant UI element is displayed at any given time, enhancing the game's interactivity and player engagement

Last, we just need to call this function every time we collect a box:

- Please add this code to the function **OnControllerColliderHit** (new code in bold):

```
if (hit.gameObject.CompareTag("box"))
{
        // Increase the box count
        boxCount++;
        Debug.Log("Box Collected! Total Boxes: " + boxCount);
        UpdateUI();
```

In the previous code, we just call the function **UpdateUI** so that the user interface is updated whenever we collect a box.

- You can now check that your code is error-free.
- Select the **Player** object in the **Hierarchy**, you should see empty placeholders for the script **BoxCollector** and we need to initialize these variables.

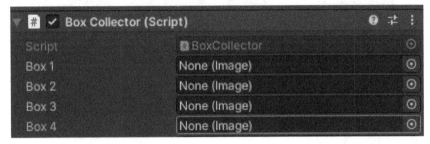

- Drag and drop the object **bx1** to the placeholder **Box1**, the object bx2 to the placeholder box2, and so on, as per the next figure.

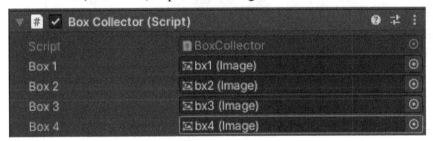

You can now play the scene. As you collect boxes, you should see that new boxes are appearing in the User Interface as per the next figure.

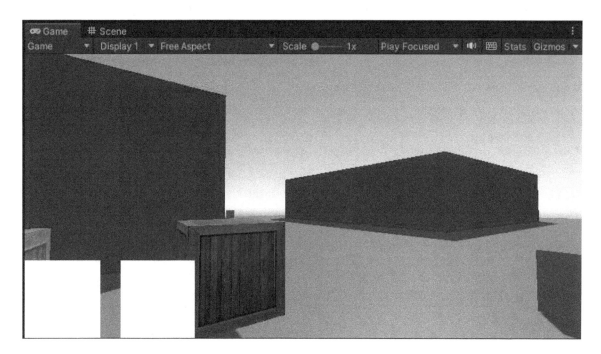

Last but not least, we could change the image displayed to something more appealing than a blank box and we will use one of the textures included in the resource pack for this purpose:

- Import the texture **box_texture_ui** from the resource pack to the **Project** window.
- Select this texture (i.e., click on it).
- Using the **Inspector**, set its type to **Sprite (2D and UI)**.

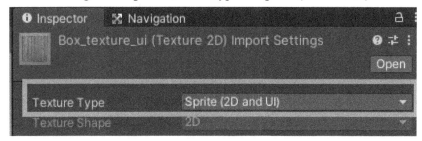

- Apply this change by scrolling down in the **Inspector**, and by pressing the button labelled "**Apply**".

- Next, select all three UI boxes (i.e., **bx1**, **bx2**, **bx3**, and **bx4**) using **CTRL + LMB** (**L**eft **M**ouse **B**utton).
- Drag and drop the texture **box_texture_ui** to the attribute **Image | Source Image** so that the texture is applied to all three images.

You now can play the scene and check that these textures are displayed every time a new box has been collected

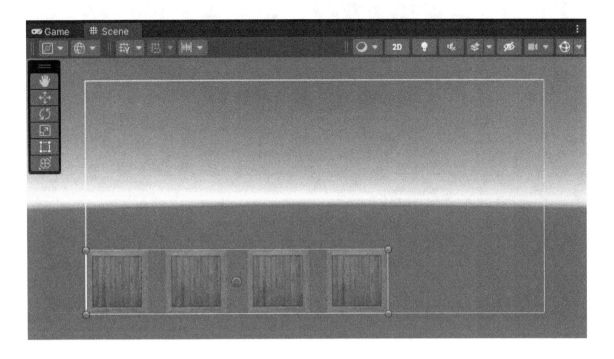

LOADING A NEW SCENE + SMOOTH SCENE TRANSITIONS

In the previous section, we have implemented features whereby the player was able to collect boxes; we also created a script that would update the UI accordingly. In this section, we will create a mechanism by which the player will transition to another level when s/he has collected four boxes or more. So, in this section we will:

- Create a new level based on the current one.
- Detect when the player has collected four boxes.
- Transfer the player to the new level when this happens.
- Apply a transition effect (fade in/out) for this transition to be even smoother.

CREATING A NEW LEVEL

So first, let's create the new level:

- Save your current scene: **File | Save As**.
- Give it a name, for example **level1**.
- Locate this scene in the **Project** folder.
- Duplicated it: select it and press **CTRL + D**.
- Rename the duplicate **level2**.
- Open the duplicate scene (i.e., **level2**).
- Change the color of the buildings, as per the next screenshots (I have chosen a green color for **level2**, and red color for **level1**).

- You can add any other objects to that level, if you wish.
- Save your scene (**File | Save**).
- Open the scene **level1**.

ADDING CODE FOR THE TRANSITION BETWEEN LEVELS

It's now time to add the code to ensure that the player transitions to the second level after collecting 4 boxes.

- Please add the following code at the beginning of the script **BoxCollector**:

```
using UnityEngine.SceneManagement;
```

In the previous code, we import the **SceneManagement** namespace. This line allows access to Unity's **SceneManager** class and its related functionality, which is used to manage scenes in the game. We therefore enable scene management features.

By including this namespace, the script can perform operations like loading new scenes, reloading the current scene, or transitioning between levels. This facilitates scene transitions and functions such as **SceneManager.LoadScene()** become available, enabling seamless scene changes based on player actions or game events.

- Add the following code to the function **OnControllerColliderHit,** inside the conditional statement, just after the code **boxCount++;**.

```
if (boxCount >= 4) LoadNewScene();
```

In the previous code, we check if the player has collected enough boxes; the condition **boxCount >= 4** ensures that the action is triggered only when the player has collected at least four boxes. This acts as a threshold to determine progress. We then call the **LoadNewScene** method:

When the condition is met, the **LoadNewScene** method is executed. This method handles the transition to the next scene, signaling the completion of the current task or level.

So overall this line checks whether the player has achieved the required objective (collecting four or more boxes). If so, it transitions the game to the next scene, advancing the gameplay and maintaining progression.

- Add this function to the script:

```
void LoadNewScene()
{
        Debug.Log("Load New Scene");
        SceneManager.LoadScene("level2");
}
```

In the previous code, we do the following:

- Define a method to load a new scene: The **LoadNewScene** method is created to handle scene transitions in the game. It can be called whenever the game needs to move to a different level or area.
- Log a message for debugging purposes: The **Debug.Log("Load New Scene");** line prints a message to the console. This is useful during development to confirm that the method was executed successfully.
- Use the **SceneManager.LoadScene** method: The **SceneManager.LoadScene("level2");** function transitions the game to the scene named "level2". This method replaces the current scene with the specified one, effectively advancing the gameplay.

So overall, this code defines a method that transitions the game to a new scene while providing a debug message for tracking. It ensures seamless movement between levels, supporting progression in the game's structure.

Now that the code for the transition to the next level has been created, you can check that your code is error-free, and make sure that the scene **level2** can be loaded:

- Select: **File | Build Settings**.
- In the new window, drag and drop the scene **level2** from the **Project** window to the **Build Settings** window, as per the next figure.

- Close the **Build Settings** window.
- Play the scene.
- Collect 4 boxes.
- Check that you are moved to **level2**.

CREATING A SMOOTHER TRANSITION

At present, we can transition from **level1** to **level2** after collecting four boxes; however, we could improve this transition and make it smoother. This could be achieved, for example, by introducing a fade in/out effect. So, in this section, we will create such an effect; this will consist of the following steps:

- Creating a black UI image that covers the screen.
- Deactivating this image at the start.
- Activating it just before we change scene.
- Progressively decreasing its opacity as we move to the **level2** scene.

First let's create the black image that will be used for the transition effect.

- Create a new image: Select **GameObject | UI | Image**.
- This will create a new image that you can rename **TransitionImage**.
- Select this image and inspect its properties in the **Inspector**.
- Set the color property to **Black**.

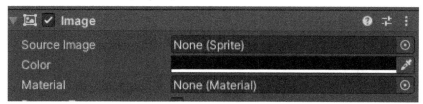

- Set the attribute **Anchor Preset** to **Stretch/Stretch**.

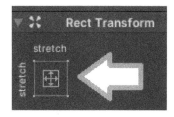

- Set the Attributes **Left**, **Right**, **Top**, **Bottom** and **PosZ** to **0**.

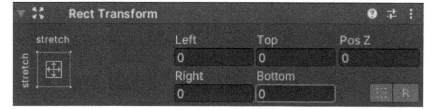

- Set the **Anchors** property to: **Min = (0,0)**; **Max = (1,1)**.

- If you switch to a 2D view, you should see that this image now occupies the full game view, as per the next figures.

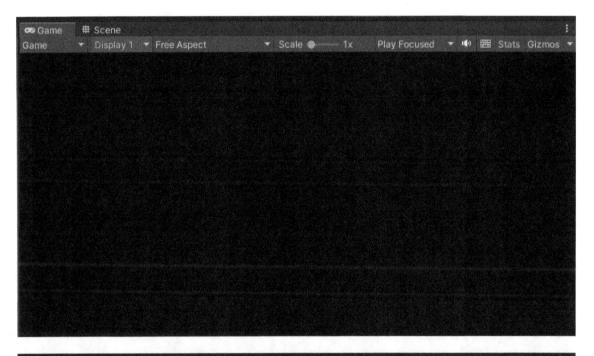

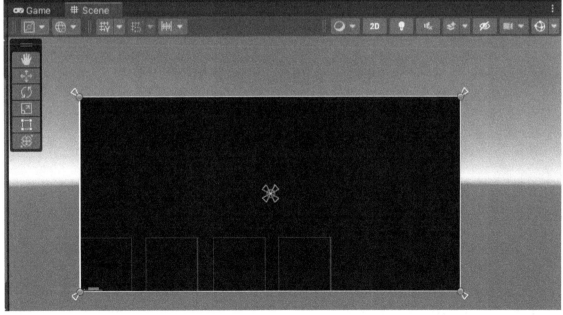

Now that the image has been created, let's write the code to handle the smooth transition between levels:

- Add this code at the beginning of the class **BoxCollector**:

```
public Image transitionImage; // UI Image for the fade effect
public float fadeDuration = 1f; // Duration of the fade effect
```

- Add this code to the **Start** function:

```
if (transitionImage != null)
{
        transitionImage.color = new Color(0f, 0f, 0f, 0f); // Fully transparent
        transitionImage.gameObject.SetActive(false);
}
```

In the previous code, we do the following:

- **Check if the transitionImage is not null**: The condition if (**transitionImage != null**) ensures that the transitionImage variable has been assigned a valid reference in the Unity Editor. This prevents runtime errors if the variable was left unassigned.
- **Set the initial color of the transitionImage to fully transparent**: The **transitionImage.color = new Color(0f, 0f, 0f, 0f);** line assigns a fully transparent black color to the image. This ensures that the image starts invisible and does not obstruct the player's view when the game begins.
- Deactivate the **transitionImage** GameObject: The **transitionImage.gameObject.SetActive(false);** line disables the transition image in the scene. This keeps it hidden and ready to be activated later when a scene transition is triggered.

Overall, this code ensures that the transition image starts fully transparent and deactivated, preparing it for use during a fade effect. It safeguards against errors by checking if the image is assigned and maintains a clean game interface until the transition effect is required.

It is now time to define the function that will effectively operate the cross-fading:

- Please add this function:

```
private IEnumerator LoadSceneWithTransition(string sceneName)
{
                Debug.Log("starting transition");
    // Fade out to black
    yield return StartCoroutine(FadeToBlack());

    // Load the new scene
    SceneManager.LoadScene(sceneName);

    // Fade in from black
    yield return StartCoroutine(FadeFromBlack());
}
```

In the previous code we do the following:

- Define a coroutine to handle scene transitions: The method **LoadSceneWithTransition** is a coroutine, allowing the game to manage timing for fade effects and scene loading without freezing the game.
- Log the start of the transition: The **Debug.Log** statement outputs a message to the **Console**, confirming the transition process has started. This is helpful for debugging.
- Perform a fade-out effect: The method **StartCoroutine(FadeToBlack())** initiates a smooth fade-to-black effect, visually signaling the transition to the player. The yield return ensures this effect completes before moving to the next step.
- Load the specified new scene: **The SceneManager.LoadScene(sceneName)** method replaces the current scene with the one specified in the **sceneName** parameter.
- Perform a fade-in effect: The method **StartCoroutine(FadeFromBlack())** initiates a fade-in effect from black, making the new scene appear smoothly. The yield return ensures the fade completes before the transition coroutine finishes.

So overall, with this code, we manage a visually smooth scene transition by implementing a fade-out, loading the new scene, and performing a fade-in effect while maintaining a responsive game experience.

A **coroutine** is a method that allows code to execute over multiple frames without freezing the game. It is ideal for tasks requiring gradual updates or delays, like animations or loading sequences. Unlike regular methods, coroutines can pause execution using yield and resume later. Coroutines are essential for smooth, time-based operations that need to run alongside other gameplay processes. In this context, the coroutine manages the fade-to-black effect, gradually increasing transparency over time while ensuring the game remains responsive. This approach creates visually seamless transitions between scenes without disrupting the player experience or halting other game logic.

- We can now add the functions **FadeFromBlack** and **FadeToBlack**:

```
private IEnumerator FadeToBlack()
  {
    // Ensure the transition image is active and starts transparent
    transitionImage.gameObject.SetActive(true);
    Color color = transitionImage.color;
    color.a = 0f;
    transitionImage.color = color;

    // Gradually increase the alpha value to create a fade-out effect
    float timer = 0f;
    while (timer < fadeDuration)
    {
      timer += Time.deltaTime;
      color.a = Mathf.Clamp01(timer / fadeDuration);
      transitionImage.color = color;
      yield return null;
    }
  }
```

In the previous code, we do the following:

- Activate the transition image: The **transitionImage.gameObject.SetActive(true)** line ensures that the transition image is visible and ready for the fade effect.
- Initialize the image color as fully transparent: The **transitionImage.color** is set to a transparent color by setting the alpha value (**color.a**) to 0f. This ensures the fade effect starts from an invisible state.
- Prepare for gradual fade-out: A while loop is used to gradually increase the alpha value of the image color over time, creating the fade-to-black effect.
- Increment the timer to track the fade duration: The **timer** variable starts at **0f** and is incremented each frame using **Time.deltaTime**, ensuring the fade effect is frame-rate independent.
- Adjust the transparency of the image: The alpha value (**color.a**) is calculated as the proportion of the elapsed time to the total **fadeDuration**. The **Mathf.Clamp01** ensures the value stays between 0 and 1 for smooth transitions.
- Update the transition image color: The new **alpha** value is applied to the **transitionImage.color** every frame, gradually making the image more opaque.
- Yield execution until the next frame: The yield return null statement pauses the coroutine until the next frame, allowing other game processes to continue while the fade effect runs.

So overall, with this code, we create a smooth fade-to-black effect by gradually increasing the transparency of the transition image, ensuring the process is visually seamless and frame-rate independent.

- Please add this function:

```
private IEnumerator FadeFromBlack()
{
   // Gradually decrease the alpha value to create a fade-in effect
   Color color = transitionImage.color;
   float timer = fadeDuration;
   while (timer > 0f)
   {
      timer -= Time.deltaTime;
      color.a = Mathf.Clamp01(timer / fadeDuration);
      transitionImage.color = color;
      yield return null;
   }

   // Ensure the transition image is hidden after the fade-in
   transitionImage.gameObject.SetActive(false);
}
```

In the previous code we do the following:

- Initialize the color and timer for the fade-in effect: The method begins by storing the current color of the **transitionImage**. The timer is set to the **fadeDuration**, ensuring the fade-in effect starts fully opaque and gradually becomes transparent.
- Decrease the **alpha** value over time: A while loop runs as long as the timer is greater than 0. In each frame, the timer is decreased using Time.deltaTime, ensuring the effect is smooth and frame-rate independent.
- Adjust the transparency of the image: The **alpha** value (**color.a**) is recalculated proportionally based on the remaining timer. The **Mathf.Clamp01** function ensures the alpha value stays between 0 and 1 for consistent results.
- Update the transition image color: The adjusted transparency is applied to the **transitionImage**, gradually fading it out to reveal the new scene.
- Pause execution until the next frame: The yield return null statement allows other game processes to continue while the fade-in effect updates each frame.
- Deactivate the transition image: Once the fade-in is complete, the **transitionImage** is deactivated to make it fully invisible and inactive, cleaning up the UI for the gameplay.

So overall, with this code, we create a smooth fade-in effect by gradually reducing the alpha value of the transition image, ensuring the new scene is revealed seamlessly and without interrupting other game processes.

- Finally, modify the **LoadNewScene** function to call the new function that we have just created:

```
void LoadNewScene()
{
        Debug.Log("Load New Scene");
        //SceneManager.LoadScene("level2");
        StartCoroutine(LoadSceneWithTransition("level2"));

}
```

- You can now save your code and check that it is error-free.
- In Unity, select the object **Player**, you should now see an empty placeholder for the script **BoxCollector** called **Transition Image**, as illustrated in the next figure.

- Drag and drop the object **TransitionIlmage** from the **Hierarchy** to this empty placeholder.

- You can now play the game and observe the transition with a fade in/out.
- You should see that, while accessing **level2**, the current scene becomes progressively darker, before transitioning to **level2**, as per the next figure.

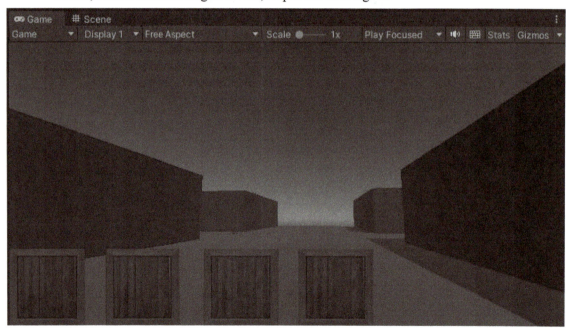

AVOIDING PROJECTILES (RIGID BODY PHYSICS)

While the previous section has helped you to create collect and account for collectible boxes, this section will be dedicated to creating a simple robot (symbolized by a box) that will throw projectiles towards the player, using rigid body physics and projectiles that are subject to gravity.

So, for this section, we will do the following:

- Create the robot.
- Create the projectile.
- Create a script that will throw the projectile towards the player.
- Ensure that the robot is always looking towards the player before throwing the projectile.

CREATING THE ROBOT AND THE PROJECTILE

Let's create our robot and the projectile:

- Create a new cube and rename it **Robot**.
- Create a new sphere and rename it **projectile**.
- Add a **Rigid Body** component to it.

- Create (or reuse) a red material and apply it to the projectile so that it can be easily seen.

> To create a new material, right-click in the Project Folder, select **Create | Material**, and set a color for that material, using the color attribute.

- Once this is done, drag and drop the object **projectile** to the **Project** window to create a prefab that will be named **projectile** by default.

CREATING THE SCRIPT TO THROW THE PROJECTILE

Now that the we have created the robot and the projectile, we need to create the code that will be used to throw the projectile:

- Create a new script called **RobotProjectileThrower**.
- Attach this script to the object **Robot**.
- Open the script.
- Add this code at the beginning of the class.

```
public GameObject projectilePrefab; // Prefab for the projectile (sphere)
public Transform throwPoint; // Point from where the projectile will be thrown
public Transform player; // Reference to the player's Transform
float throwForce = 70; // Force applied to the projectile
public float throwInterval = 2f; // Time interval between throws
float throwTimer;
```

In the previous code:

- The **projectile** prefab is a pre-designed object, such as a sphere, that serves as the base for creating projectiles dynamically during the game. It is used to spawn identical projectiles with predefined properties.
- The **throwPoint** variable determines where the projectile is instantiated in the game world. It is usually positioned in front of the throwing object, such as a character or enemy.
- The **player** variable provides the position and orientation of the player. This allows the throwing mechanism to aim projectiles accurately at the player's location.
- The **throwForce** variable sets the speed and distance of the projectile. Higher values make the projectile travel faster and farther, simulating realistic movement.
- The **throwInterval** variable defines the time delay between successive projectile launches. This ensures controlled timing, such as cooldowns, for throwing mechanics.

Overall, these variables enable a dynamic system for spawning and throwing projectiles with precision, speed, and timing, enhancing the interactivity of the gameplay.

Now that we have defined the variables necessary for throwing the projectile, we will create two functions: one to look in the direction of the player, and another one to throw the projectile towards the player.

- Please add this function to the script **RobotProjectileThrower**:

```
private void LookAtPlayer()
{
        Vector3 directionToPlayer = player.position - transform.position;
        directionToPlayer.y = 0f; // Ignore the vertical axis to prevent tilting
        Quaternion lookRotation = Quaternion.LookRotation(directionToPlayer);
        transform.rotation = Quaternion.Slerp(transform.rotation, lookRotation, Time.deltaTime * 5f);
}
```

In the previous code:

- The **LookAtPlayer** method ensures that the robot continuously faces the player, which is important for interactions like aiming or targeting.
- A **direction vector** is calculated by subtracting the robot's position from the player's position. This determines where the player is relative to the robot.
- The **y-axis value is set to zero**, so the robot only rotates horizontally. This prevents the robot from tilting up or down, maintaining a natural movement regardless of height differences.
- A **quaternion rotation** is created to align the robot with the calculated direction vector. This defines the target orientation for the robot to face the player.
- The robot's current rotation is smoothly interpolated toward the target rotation using spherical linear interpolation (Slerp). This creates a gradual and natural-looking rotation instead of an abrupt movement.

Overall, this method allows the robot to face the player dynamically, ensuring smooth and realistic adjustments to its orientation during gameplay.

- Next, please add this function:

```
private void ThrowProjectile()
{

        GameObject projectile = Instantiate(projectilePrefab, throwPoint.position, throwPoint.rotation);
        Rigidbody rb = projectile.GetComponent<Rigidbody>();
        if (rb == null)
        {
                rb = projectile.AddComponent<Rigidbody>();
        }
        Vector3 directionToPlayer = (player.position - throwPoint.position).normalized;
        rb.AddForce(directionToPlayer * throwForce, ForceMode.Impulse);
        Destroy(projectile, 4);

}
```

In the previous code:

- The **ThrowProjectile** method creates and launches a projectile toward the player, simulating a dynamic and interactive attack or gameplay mechanic.
- A new projectile is instantiated using the projectilePrefab. It is spawned at the specified throwPoint position and orientation, ensuring it appears and faces the correct direction.
- A **rigidbody** component is retrieved from the instantiated projectile. The rigidbody is necessary for applying physics-based movement to the projectile.
- If the projectile doesn't already have a rigidbody, a **new rigidbody is added** dynamically. This ensures the projectile can respond to physics forces even if the prefab was not preconfigured with one.
- A **direction** vector is calculated by subtracting the **throwPoint** position from the player's position. This normalized vector represents the direction from the throw point to the player, ensuring the projectile is aimed accurately.
- A **force** is applied to the **rigidbody** in the calculated direction, using the specified **throwForce** value. The **ForceMode.Impulse** ensures the force is applied instantly, propelling the projectile toward the player.
- We destroy the projectile after 4 seconds.

Overall, this method dynamically creates a projectile, calculates the correct direction, and launches it toward the player using physics, enhancing gameplay with interactive and realistic projectile mechanics.

Now that these two functions have been created, it's time to use them from the **Update** function; so please add the following code to the **Update** function:

```
LookAtPlayer();
throwTimer += Time.deltaTime;
if (throwTimer >= throwInterval)
{
        ThrowProjectile();
        throwTimer = 0f;
}
```

In the previous code:

- We ensure the robot continuously faces the player by calling the method that handles its rotation, maintaining accurate aiming and a realistic interaction.
- We track the time elapsed since the last projectile was thrown by incrementing a timer variable with the time passed in the current frame. This ensures a consistent countdown between throws.
- We check if the elapsed time exceeds the predefined interval, signalling that it is time to throw another projectile.
- We create and launch a new projectile toward the player when the timer reaches the required interval, ensuring the robot attacks at regular intervals.
- We reset the timer to zero after a projectile is thrown, restarting the countdown for the next attack and maintaining a steady rhythm.

Overall, with this code, we manage smooth and consistent projectile-throwing behavior where the robot dynamically tracks the player and launches projectiles at regular intervals to maintain engaging gameplay mechanics.

FINAL SETUP

Before we can use this script, we need to do a few things:

- Please check that the script is error-free.
- Check that this script is attached to the object **Robot**.
- Add an **Empty** object as a child of the object **Robot**, and rename this object **throwPoint**.

- For this object (**throwPoint**) set the position to **(0, 0, 0.37)**.
- Select the object **Robot** and look at the Component **RobotProjectileThrower** in the **Inspector**, and you should see several empty placeholders.

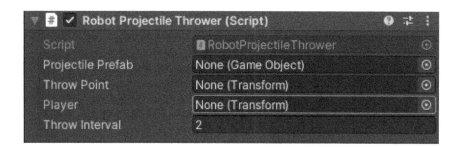

- You can now set these variables by dragging and dropping the projectile **prefab** from the **Project** window to the attribute **Projectile Prefab**, the object **throwPoint** (child of the object **Robot**) to the attribute **Throw Point**, and finally the object **Player** to the attribute **Player**, as per the next figure.

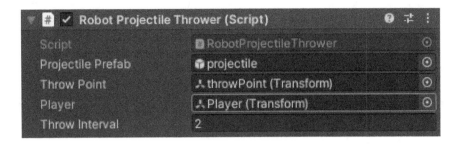

Now that the robot is set up you can test the scene:

- Place the robot away from the player.
- Remove the object called **projectile** from the scene.
- Play the scene and check that it throws red balls towards the player, as illustrated in the next screenshot.

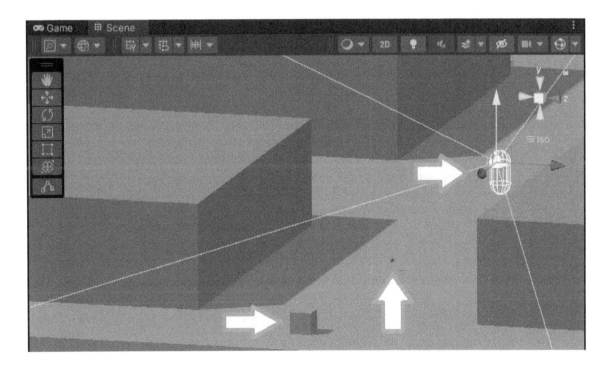

CREATING MULTIPLE ROBOTS

Now that you have checked that the robot works, we can do a few things to facilitate further changes and also improve the gameplay:

- Restart the current level every time the player is touched by a projectile.
- Create a prefab for the robot so that it can be duplicated easily, if need be.

First, let's look into restarting the current level upon collision with a projectile:

- Create a new script called **Projectile**.

- Attach this script to the prefab **Projectile**.
- Open the script and add this code at the beginning of the script.

```
using UnityEngine.SceneManagement;
```

- Add this function:

```
private void OnCollisionEnter(Collision collision)
{
    // Check if the collided object's name matches the player's name
    if (collision.gameObject.name == "Player")
    {
        Debug.Log("Projectile hit the player!");

        // Reload the current level
        SceneManager.LoadScene(SceneManager.GetActiveScene().name);
    }
}
```

In the previous code we do the following:

- **Detect collisions using OnCollisionEnter:** This method is automatically triggered whenever the projectile collides with another object in the game world. The collision parameter contains details about the object involved in the collision.
- **Check if the collided object's name matches "Player":** The condition compares the name of the collided object (**collision.gameObject.nam**e) with "Player". This ensures the logic only executes when the projectile hits the player, ignoring other objects.
- **Log a message when the player is hit:** The Debug.Log statement outputs a message to the console, confirming that the projectile successfully collided with the player. This is useful for debugging and verifying the functionality.
- **Reload the current level:** The **SceneManager.LoadScene** function reloads the active scene by retrieving its name using **SceneManager.GetActiveScene()**.name. This resets the game to its initial state, effectively simulating a "game over" or retry scenario.

Overall, with this code, we detect when a projectile collides with the player, log the event for debugging, and reload the current level to reset the game, maintaining engaging and reactive gameplay.

- You can now check that your code is error-free and then play the scene; once the player is hit by a projectile, the level should restart.

Last but not least, we will create a prefab with the robot and add duplicates in parts of the environment to increase the challenge.

- Drag and drop the object **Robot** to the **Project** folder.
- This will create a new prefab called **Robot**.
- Drag and drop this prefab several times in the scene to create additional robots.
- For clarity, you can also apply a blue color to the **Robot** prefab.

You can then test the scene and check that all robots shoot projectiles at the player.

IMPLEMENTING A MINI MAP

In this section, we will create a simple mini-map that will be used by the player to have an overall view of the level, and to highlight objects of interest and their position in relation to the player.

ADDING THE CAMERA AND RENDING ITS CONTENT

- Please add a new **Camera** as a child of the object **Player** and rename it **topView** (Select **GameObject | Camera** from the top menu).

Adding a new camera allows us to create a second perspective in the game. By making it a child of the Player object, the camera moves and rotates along with the player, ensuring the view stays aligned with the player's position. Renaming it to **topView** makes its purpose clear: to provide an overhead perspective, often used for maps or strategic views

- Set its position to **(0, 50, 0)** and its rotation to **(90, 0, 0)**. Positioning the camera 50 units above the player gives it a bird's-eye view of the scene. Rotating it to face directly downward **(90, 0, 0)** ensures the camera captures the top-down perspective accurately. This setup is ideal for displaying environments or tracking movement in gameplay scenarios like navigation or exploration.
- Set the attribute **Rendering | Priority** to **1**.

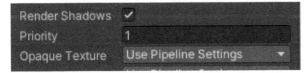

- The rendering priority determines which camera has precedence when multiple cameras are active. By setting the priority to 1, we ensure that the **topView** camera overlays its view on top of other active cameras, such as the main player camera.
- Set the attribute **Output | ViewPort** to X=.75, Y = .75, W=.25 and H = .75, as per the next figure.

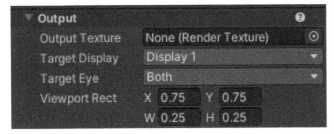

Adjusting the viewport defines where the **topView** camera's output will appear on the screen. These values create a smaller, inset window (often referred to as a "mini-map") in the top-right corner of the game view. X and Y set the position of the viewport (relative to the screen). W (width) and H (height) define the size of the viewport.

You can now play the scene and check that you can see a bird view of the level in the top right corner of the screen, as per the next figure.

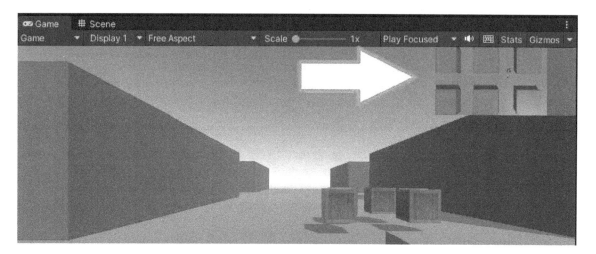

SUMMARY

In this chapter, we explored foundational techniques for building a simple and interactive 3D game environment using Unity. Starting with basic concepts, we created a world made of boxes, implemented player navigation through a First-Person Controller, and introduced collectible items with interactive UI feedback.

We learned how to create a structured game environment using Unity's tools, adding a flat ground and walls to form the level layout. A First-Person Controller allowed the player to explore this environment with realistic movement, including jumping and running. By integrating a system for collecting items, we added an engaging gameplay mechanic, visually represented through UI elements.

Additionally, we implemented smooth scene transitions with fade-in and fade-out effects to enhance player immersion. We also introduced physics-based projectile mechanics, enabling a robot to throw projectiles at the player dynamically. Finally, we created a mini-map to provide an overhead view of the level, enhancing navigation.

By completing this chapter, you have gained practical skills in world-building, player interaction, and UI design. These elements form the foundation for crafting a fully interactive and engaging game experience.

.

QUIZ: TEST YOUR KNOWLEDGE

Please specify whether the following statements are True or False (the solutions are at the end of the book).

1. The ground object in the game environment was created using a cube resized to form a flat surface.
2. The walls of the game environment were initially created as spheres to add variety to the level.
3. The First-Person Controller enables players to navigate the environment using keyboard inputs for movement and mouse inputs for camera control.
4. Jumping mechanics in the FPS controller are implemented using Unity's built-in CharacterController component.
5. The collectible items were created as spheres and tagged as "collectible" for collision detection.
6. The player's progress in collecting items is visually represented using UI images that activate dynamically.
7. The transition effect between scenes includes a fade-to-black animation followed by a fade-from-black animation.
8. The robot throwing projectiles uses physics-based rigid body mechanics to launch objects toward the player.
9. The mini-map is displayed in the bottom-left corner of the game view, providing a bird's-eye view of the level.
10. Prefabs allow developers to create reusable and scalable game objects, like collectible boxes and robot enemies.

CHALLENGE

Now that you've mastered the core mechanics and features covered in this chapter, it's time to put your skills to the test by enhancing your game level. This challenge is designed to help you apply what you've learned and expand on the functionality of your game. Follow the steps below to create a more dynamic and engaging level:

- Add two new types of collectibles to the game: A "special" box that awards double points when collected and a "hidden" box that is placed in a hard-to-reach area, requiring strategic exploration to find.
- Update the UI to reflect the collection of these new items.

.

4

ADDING WEAPONS AND AMMUNITIONS

In the previous chapter, we laid the foundation for creating a functional and interactive game environment. Now, it's time to take the gameplay experience to the next level by introducing core mechanics that enhance player engagement and add depth to your game. This chapter focuses on implementing weapon systems, inventories, and damage mechanics, which are essential features in many action, survival, and adventure games.

We will begin by creating and testing a basic weapon system, allowing the player to interact dynamically with the environment. Then, we will dive into inventory management using arrays for simplicity, equipping you with the skills to handle item storage and usage efficiently. To make the experience more immersive, we'll introduce ammunition collection and management, tying it to the weapon system. Finally, we'll implement damage calculation and effects, enabling the player to interact with the targets.

By the end of this chapter, you'll be able to:

- Add a weapon system to your game and test it on static targets.
- Build both basic and advanced inventory systems for managing items and ammunition.
- Enable the player to collect ammunition and use it strategically.
- Create dynamic interactions by calculating and applying damage to targets.

Let's get started with the first step: adding a weapon to your game!

DETECTING OBJECTS AHEAD USING RAY-CASTING

At this stage, we would like to detect what is in front of the player so that when we use our weapon (e.g., gun), we know whether an object is in the line of fire before shooting. To do so, we will use ray casting. So, we will create some code to be able to detect what is in front of the player using a ray.

A ray is a bit like a laser beam; it is cast over a distance and usually employed to detect if an object is in the line of fire. In our case, we will cast a ray from the player (forward) and detect if it "collides" with another object. Before we do this, we can also use a ray in debug mode (i.e., only visible in the scene view), just to check its direction and length.

Rays can be used for many applications, from weapons to controlling objects (e.g., opening a door only if you are facing it rather than using collision).

The first ray that we create will be used for testing purposes; it will only be visible in the scene view for the time being and will help us to gauge whether the ray casting technique used for collision detection will be successful.

- Please create a new script called **ManageWeapons**.
- Open this script and modify it as illustrated below.

```
public class ManageWeapons : MonoBehaviour
{
        Camera playersCamera;
        Ray rayFromPlayer;
        // Use this for initialization
        void Start ()
        {
                playersCamera = GameObject.Find ("playerCamera").GetComponent<Camera>();
        }

        // Update is called once per frame
        void Update ()
        {

        }
}
```

In the previous code:

- We declare a new **GameObject** called **playersCamera**. This camera will be used for ray casting.
- We also declare a new ray called **rayFromPlayer** that will also be used for our ray casting.
- In the method **Start**, this camera is then initialized with the camera that is linked to the First-Person Controller.

Since the game, in this scene, will be using a First-Person view, the scene will be viewed through the eyes of the player; so we will cast a ray as if it was originating from the eyes of the player; since the scene is rendered through the camera attached to the First-Person controller, we will cast a ray from the middle of this lens (or the screen) and forward.

- Let's further modify this script.

```
void Update ()
{
        rayFromPlayer = playersCamera.ScreenPointToRay (new Vector3 (Screen.width/2,
Screen.height/2, 0));
        Debug.DrawRay(rayFromPlayer.origin, rayFromPlayer.direction * 100, Color.red);

}
```

In the previous code, we do the following:

- We initialize our ray defined earlier; this ray will originate from the camera used for the **First-Person Controller**, from the center of the screen, which is defined by the x and y coordinates **Screen.width/2** (i.e., half the screen's width) and **Screen.height/2** (i.e., half the screen's height); the z coordinate is ignored. So, at this stage, we know where the ray will start. By default, the ray will point outward.
- On the next line, we use the static method **DrawRay** and specify three parameters: the origin of the ray, its direction, and its color. By using **ray.origin** we will start the ray from the middle of the screen. By using **rayFromPlayer.direction*100**, we specify that the ray's length is 100 meters.

We are now ready to use this script:

- Please save your code and check that there are no errors left.
- Drag and drop the script **ManageWeapons** from the **Project** window to the object **Player**.
- Change the layout of your scene so that you can see both the **Scene** and the **Game** view simultaneously (e.g., drag the **Scene** view to the right of the **Console** tab).
- Deactivate the robots present in the scene: select all Robots, and then, in the **Inspector** untick the box in the top-left corner of the **Inspector**.

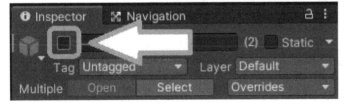

- Play the scene.

- Check that you can see a ray cast from the camera of the Player Controller, as described on the next figure.

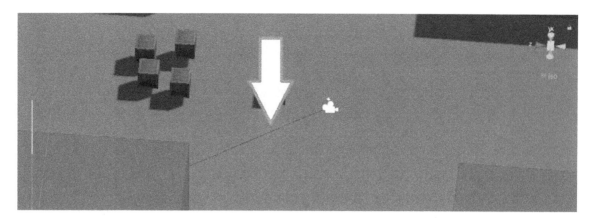

Once this done, we can now apply a real ray casting method, by using a ray that will point in the exact same direction, but that will, in addition, detect any objects ahead of the player. The new ray will detect any collider attached to an object in front of the player.

- Please open the script **ManageWeapons**, and modify it as follows (new code highlighted in bold).

```
public class ManageWeapons : MonoBehaviour
{
        Camera playersCamera;
        Ray rayFromPlayer;
        RaycastHit hit;
```

In the previous code, we declare an object of type **RaycastHit**; this object will be used to store information about the collision between the ray cast from the player (i.e., from its camera), and the object in front of the player.

- We will then modify the **Update** method to cast the ray and detect any object in sight (the new code is highlighted in bold):

```
void Update ()
{
        rayFromPlayer = playersCamera.ScreenPointToRay (new Vector3 (Screen.width/2,
Screen.height/2, 1000));
        Debug.DrawRay(rayFromPlayer.origin, rayFromPlayer.direction * 100 , Color.red);
        if (Physics.Raycast(rayFromPlayer, out hit, 100))
        {
                print (" The object " + hit.collider.gameObject.name +" is in front of the player");
        }
}
```

In the previous code:

- We cast a ray using the keyword **Physics.RayCast**; the method **RayCast** takes three parameters: the ray (**rayFromPlayer**), an object where the information linked to the collision between the ray and another collider is stored (**hit**), and the length of the ray (**100**). The keyword **out** is used so that the information returned about the collision is easily accessible (as a reference rather than a structure; this is comparable to a type conversion or casting).

- If this ray hits an object (i.e., its collider), we print a message that displays the name of this object. To obtain this name, we access the collider involved in the collision, then the corresponding **GameObject** using **hit.collider.gameObject.name**.
- Please play the scene, and as you walk towards some of the walls, for example **Bulding(1)**, the message **"Building (1) is in front of the player "** should be displayed in the **Console** window.

> The method **Debug.DrawRay** will create a ray that we can see in the scene view and that can be used for debugging purposes to check that a ray effectively points in the right direction; however, **Debug.DrawRay** does not detect collisions with objects. So, while it is useful to check the direction of a particular ray in the **Scene** view, this ray needs to be combined to a different method to be able to detect collisions; one of these methods is called **Physics.Raycast**.

- Finally, we will then make sure that the ray is cast only when a specific key has been pressed, by adding the following code to the **Update** method (new code highlighted in bold).
- Please modify the code in the **Update** function, as follows:

```
if (Input.GetKeyDown(KeyCode.F))
{
        if (Physics.Raycast(rayFromPlayer, out hit, 100))
        {
                print (" The object " + hit.collider.gameObject.name +" is in front of the player");
        }
}
```

- In the previous code, the ray is cast only when the key **F** is pressed.

Last but not least, and to improve accuracy when fire the gun, we will include a crosshair.
- Import the **crosshair** image from the resource pack to your **Project** window.
- Create a new **RawImage** Object (**Game Object | UI | RawImage**).
- Rename it **crosshair**.
- Using the **Inspector** window, change its position to **(0, 0, 0)** so that it is displayed in the center of the screen.

And finally, set its texture in the section **RawImage**, by dragging and dropping the **crosshair** texture from your **Project** window (i.e., where you have imported this texture) to the variable **Texture**, as per the next figure.

- Once this is done, the **Game** view should look as follows:

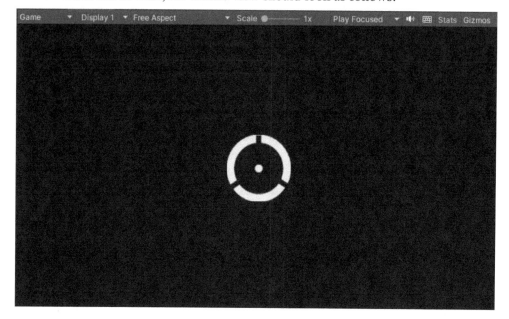

- To see the other UI elements, you can temporarily deactivate the object **transitionImage**, and the Scene view will look as follows then.

- Now, we can play the scene and use the crosshair to aim at the boxes or walls and check that a corresponding message is displayed in the **Console** window.

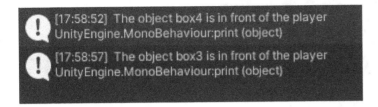

CREATING A WEAPON

While we are now able to detect the objects we are aiming at, we will try to manage ammunitions for this particular gun. At present, the player can shoot indefinitely; so we could just give the player an initial amount of bullets, and make it possible to fire the gun only if there are bullets left. Son for this purpose, we will create a variable that tracks the number of bullets left, and check its value every time the player want to fire the gun.

- Please open the script **ManageWeapons** (if it's not already open).

- Add this code at the beginning of the class.

```
private int gunAmmo = 3;
```

In the previous code, we declare a new variable that will be used to store the number of ammunitions left.

- Then, we can modify the code to manage these ammunitions, as follows (new code in bold):

```
if (Input.GetKeyDown(KeyCode.F)&& gunAmmo > 0)
{
        if (Physics.Raycast(rayFromPlayer, out hit, 100))
        {
                print (" The object " + hit.collider.gameObject.name +" is in front of the player");
        }
        gunAmmo --;
        print ("You have "+gunAmmo + " bullets left");
}
```

In the previous code:

- We check that we have enough ammunition before firing the gun.
- If this is the case, we decrease the number of bullets left.
- We then display the number of bullets left in the **Console** window.

Please play the scene, and check that the ammunition decreases as you fire the gun (i.e., press **F**) along based on the message in the **Console** window.

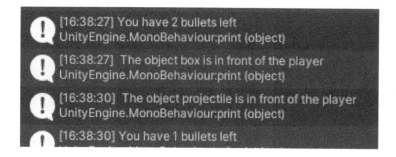

MANAGING DAMAGE

So, at this stage, we have managed to create a weapon and fire bullets accurately using ray casting and a crosshair. Ultimately, this weapon will be used to eliminate targets (for example robots), and it would be great to be able to manage the targets by knowing how many times they have been hit and when they should be destroyed (e.g., after being hit three times). So, for this purpose, we will create three static targets to be used for testing purposes, along with a script that will store a target's health, count how many times it was hit, decrease its health whenever it has been hit, and destroy it after its health has reached 0.

First, let's create four targets:

- Create a new **Cube**.
- Rename this cube **target1**.
- Create and apply a tag called **target** to this target.
- Using the **Rect** tool and/or the **Move** tool, rescale the target on the y-axis so that its **scale** property is **(1, 6.5, 1)**. At this stage, what really matters is that this target can be seen (and targeted) easily.
- You can also paint this target in red by either applying an existing material that you have created in the previous scene, or by creating a new color material for this scene (i.e., select **Create | Material** from the **Project** window, change the color of the material and drag and drop it onto the target).

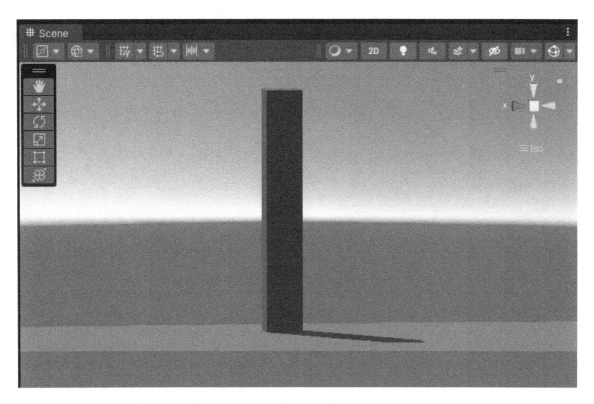

- Make a prefab from this target and call the prefab **target**.
- Use this prefab to create three identical targets. You can rename these targets **target2**, **target3**, and **target4**.
- Move these targets apart, so that they are aligned and about three meters apart; for example, they could be at the positions.

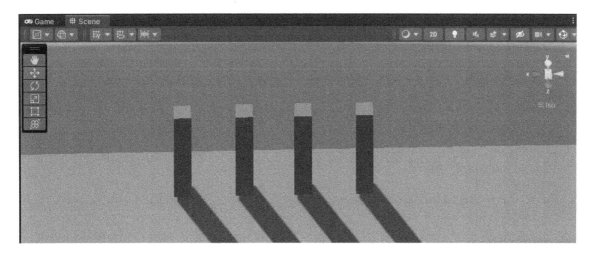

Next, we will create a script that will manage the targets' health:

- Please create a new C# script and rename it **ManageNPC**.
- Add this code at the beginning of the class.

```
private int health;
```

- Add the following code (new code in bold).

```
void Start ()
{
        health = 100;
}
public void GotHit()
{
        health -=50;
}
```

In the previous code:

- We declare two variables: **health** and **smoke**; the former is used to track the NPCs' health, and the latter is used so that we can instantiate particles (e.g., explosions) when and where the NPC has been destroyed.
- We then initialize the health to 100 in the **Start** function.
- We also create a method **GotHit** that is declared as **public**. This means that it will be accessible from outside this script. This method will be called whenever the object has been hit; when this happens, the health is decreased by **50**.

Next, we will add the code that will handle the destruction of each box

- Please add the next code to the script (i.e., within the class **ManageNPC**; new code is in bold).

```
public void Destroy()
{

        Destroy(gameObject);

}
void Update ()
{
        if (health <=0) Destroy();
}
```

In the previous code:

- In the method **Update**, we check the status of the health. If the health is **0** or less, then we call the method **Destroy**.
- In the method **Destroy**, we instantiate a **GameObject** (e.g., smoke) at the position of the NPC.

Once these changes have been made, we can:

- Save the script.

- Drag and drop this script on the prefab **target**.

Once this is done, we just need to modify the script **ManageWeapons** so that we can modify the health of each target when it has been hit:

- Please open the script **ManageWeapons**.
- Add this code at the beginning of the class.

```
GameObject objectTargeted;
```

- Modify the code as follows (new code in bold).

```
if (Physics.Raycast(rayFromPlayer, out hit, 100))
{
        print (" The object " + hit.collider.gameObject.name +" is in front of the player");
        if (hit.collider.gameObject.tag == "target")
        {
                objectTargeted = hit.collider.gameObject;
                objectTargeted.GetComponent<ManageNPC>().GotHit();
        }

}
```

In the previous code:

- We create a new **GameObject** called **objectTargeted**.
- We then set this object with the object that is in the line of sight.

- If the tag of this object is **target** we will access its script called **ManageNPC** and call (or evoke) the method **GotHit**.

The last thing we need to do is to set the initial number of bullets, **gunAmmo**, to **10** (instead of three, in the script **ManageWeapons**) so that we can test the game properly.

- Please make these changes (i.e., set the initial number of ammos to **10**).
- Make sure that the script **ManageNPC** is attached to the prefab **target**.
- Please play the scene.
- Shoot at each target twice and check that they disappear.

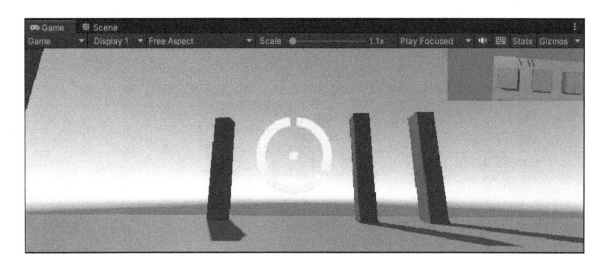

COLLECTING AND MANAGING AMMUNITIONS

At this stage, the game level is working well, however our player may run out of ammunitions. So, it would be good to create ammunitions that can be collected by the player. To do so, we will create (and add a texture to) boxes that will be used as ammunition; we will also give them a label and detect whenever the player collides with them. We will also get to create prefabs with these so that they can be reused later (i.e., in different levels).

So, let's create these ammunition boxes:

- Please create a new cube.
- Rename it **ammo_gun**.
- Move it slightly away from the targets and above the ground.
- Use a texture of your choice or import a texture from the resource pack and apply it to the box (for example the texture **ammunition_texture**).

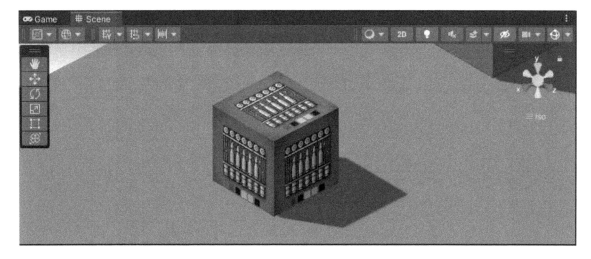

- Create a new tag called **ammo_gun** and apply it to this cube.

Once this is done, we just need to detect collisions between this cube and the player, and increase the player's ammunitions accordingly.

- Open the script **ManageWeapons**.
- Add this code:

```
public void IncreaseGunAmmo(int increasedGunAmmo)
{
        print ("Increasing Gun Ammo by "+increasedGunAmmo);
        gunAmmo += increasedGunAmmo;
        if (gunAmmo > 10) gunAmmo = 10;
}
```

In the previous code, we manage the player's gun ammunition through a dynamic method that increases ammo, provides feedback, and enforces a maximum limit:

- A message is printed to the console to display the amount of ammunition being added. This helps with debugging and ensures the feature is functioning correctly.
- The **gunAmmo** variable is incremented by the specified value, allowing flexibility in how much ammunition is added in different scenarios.
- A conditional check ensures that the ammunition does not exceed a maximum limit of 10. If the ammo count surpasses this limit, it is reset to the cap, maintaining balanced gameplay.

Overall, this code provides a way to dynamically increase and cap gun ammunition while offering feedback for debugging. Since this method is public, it will be accessible from outside its class.

Next, we will manage the ammunition collection:

- Please open the class **BoxCollector**, and add the following code to the function **OnControllerColliderHit**:

```
if (hit.gameObject.CompareTag("ammo_gun"))
{
        GetComponent<ManageWeapons>().IncreaseGunAmmo(5);
        Destroy (hit.collider.gameObject);
}
```

In the previous code, when we collide with an ammunition box, we call the function **IncreaseGunAmmo**, passing **5** as a parameter, so that the players **gunAmmo** variable is increased by **5**; we then destroy the box.

You can now play the scene. As you play the scene, please check that you can shoot at the targets several times, that you can collect ammunition, and also that your ammunition levels have been updated accordingly, as per the next figure.

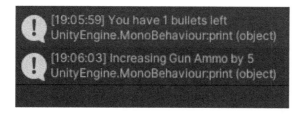

BUILDING A WEAPON MANAGEMENT SYSTEM WITH ARRAYS

At present, we have a relatively simple weapon management system that works with one weapon. We can collect ammunition and also shoot at targets. However, in the next sections, we will be adding more types of weapons (i.e., automatic gun and grenade), so we need to find a way to manage these simply, using structures that make it easy to track the ammunitions for each of them or the time it takes to reload a weapon. So, before even creating new weapons, we will make sure that we have a structure in place that will make it possible to track the following information, for each of them:

- Whether the player has this weapon.
- The reload time for this weapon.
- The name of the weapon.
- The ammunitions that the player is carrying (or currently has) for this weapon.
- The maximum number of ammunitions that the player can carry for this weapon.

To do so, we will be using a combination of arrays and constant variables. The process will be as follows.

- We will create an array for each of the variables that are common across the weapons: an array for the weapons' name, an array for their reload time, an array to check whether the player has this weapon, an array for the corresponding ammunitions, and an array for the maximum number of ammunitions that can be carried for this weapon.
- We will then create an index for each of these weapons; for example, a gun could be referred to as index 0, the automatic gun could be referred as index 1, and the grenade launcher could be referred to as index 2. These indexes will be used to access information in the arrays for a particular weapon.
- Whenever the player presses the tab key, we will switch between the active weapons (i.e., the one that the player is carrying).
- When the player presses the **F** key, we check that there is enough ammunition for the current weapons, and then, if this is the case, we fire this weapon.
- As the player tries to shoot another time, we check the reload time for this weapon (e.g., 2 for a normal gun, .5 for an automatic gun, etc.).
- When we collect an ammo pack, we check its type and update the ammunition levels for the weapon that we currently carry.

So, this is the general principle for our weapon inventory; now that it is clearer, let's implement the corresponding code.

- Please open the script **ManageWeapons** and add the following code at the beginning of the class (new code in bold).

```
private const int WEAPON_GUN = 0;
private const int WEAPON_AUTO_GUN = 1;
private const int WEAPON_GRENADE = 2;

private int activeWeapon = WEAPON_GUN;
private float timer;
private bool timerStarted;
private bool canShoot = true;
private int currentWeapon;

private bool [] hasWeapon;
private int [] ammos;
private int [] maxAmmos;
private float [] reloadTime;
private string [] weaponName;
```

In the previous code:

- We first declare a set of three constant variables, **WEAPON_GUN**, **WEAPON_AUTO_GUN**, and **WEAPON_GRENADE**. These variables are constant, so their value will always be the same.
- We then declare four other variables: **activeWeapon**, **timer** (this will be used to simulate the reload time), **timerStarted** (this will be used to check whether the reload has started), **canShoot** (this will be used to check if the player can shoot or whether the reload time has elapsed).
- Finally, we also declare five arrays that will share common properties across weapons including: whether the player has this weapon (**hasWeapon**), the number of ammos for a particular weapon (**ammos**), the maximum number of ammos for this weapon (**maxAmmos**), the reload time (**reloadTime**), and the name of this weapon (**weaponName**).

Now, we just need to initialize these variables; so, let's add the following code to the **Start** function:

```
ammos = new int [3];
hasWeapon = new bool [3];
maxAmmos = new int [3];
reloadTime = new float [3];
weaponName = new string[3];
```

In the previous code, we initialize all the arrays that we have declared previously; they are initialized using the syntax **new dataType [size]**. Because we only plan on having three different weapons for now, we set a size of 3 for all these arrays.

Note that each element of the arrays will be accessible using the syntax **arrayName [index]**; for example the first element of the array **ammos** will be accessible using **ammos [0]**; for each array, the first element starts at **0**, so the last element will be, in our case, at the index **2** (i.e., the size of the array minus 1). Although you can also initialize an array without specifying its size, it is good practice to set its size at the beginning if we know that it will not change overtime.

Also note that many of the errors related to the use of arrays are often linked to their size. For example, you may try to access an array element at the index 7, whereas the size of the array is 5; in this case Unity may display a message telling your that you are **"out of bounds"** which means that you are trying to access an element that is outside the bounds of this array. We will look into these types of errors later but this is something to keep in mind.

After initializing the arrays we can initialize some of the values in these arrays; please add the following code to the **Start** method (after the previous code):

```
hasWeapon [WEAPON_GUN] = true;
hasWeapon [WEAPON_AUTO_GUN] = false;
hasWeapon [WEAPON_GRENADE] = false;

weaponName[WEAPON_GUN] = "GUN";
weaponName[WEAPON_AUTO_GUN] = "AUTOMATIC GUN";
weaponName[WEAPON_GRENADE] = "GRENADE";

ammos [WEAPON_GUN] = 10;
ammos [WEAPON_AUTO_GUN] = 0;
ammos [WEAPON_GRENADE] = 0;

maxAmmos [WEAPON_GUN] = 20;
maxAmmos [WEAPON_AUTO_GUN] = 20;
maxAmmos [WEAPON_GRENADE] = 5;

currentWeapon = WEAPON_GUN;
```

In the previous code:

- We first set the content of the array **hasWeapon**. For each element of the array, we use the constant variables defined earlier. So the first element of the array (index 0), is referred to using the constant variable **WEAPON_GUN**, the second element (1) is referred to using the constant variable **WEAPON_GUN_AUTO_GUN**, and so on. Using these notations, we set the elements of the array **hasweapon** to specify that we initially only have a gun.
- Then, using the same principle, we initialize the values for the array **ammos** (i.e., 10 ammos for the gun, and no ammos for the other weapons), **maxAmmos** (i.e., 20 ammos for the gun and the automatic gun, and 5 grenades).
- Finally we specify that the current weapon is the gun.

Once this is done, we need to find a system that switches between the weapons that we have whenever we press the *Tab* key on the keyboard; so, the following method will be used:

- Pressing the tab key will change the index of the current weapon (0 for gun, 1 for the automatic gun, or 2 for grenades).
- If we have only one weapon, then pressing the Tab key will not cause any change.
- If we have the three weapons, pressing the tab key will select the gun, the automatic gun, or the grenades.
- If we have two weapons, pressing the tab key will toggle between these two weapons.

Let's implement this system:

- Please add the following code to the **Update** method (just before the end of this method) in the script **ManageWeapons**:

```
if (Input.GetKeyDown(KeyCode.Tab))
{
        if (hasWeapon[WEAPON_GUN] && hasWeapon[WEAPON_AUTO_GUN] &&
hasWeapon[WEAPON_GRENADE])
        {
                currentWeapon++;
                if (currentWeapon>2) currentWeapon = 0;
        }
        else if (hasWeapon[WEAPON_GUN] && hasWeapon[WEAPON_AUTO_GUN])
        {
                if (currentWeapon == WEAPON_GUN) currentWeapon = WEAPON_AUTO_GUN;
                else currentWeapon = WEAPON_GUN;
        }
        else if (hasWeapon[WEAPON_GUN] && hasWeapon[WEAPON_GRENADE])
        {
                if (currentWeapon == WEAPON_GUN) currentWeapon = WEAPON_GRENADE;
                else currentWeapon = WEAPON_GUN;
                }
        else if (hasWeapon[WEAPON_AUTO_GUN] && hasWeapon[WEAPON_GRENADE])
        {
                if (currentWeapon == WEAPON_AUTO_GUN) currentWeapon = WEAPON_GRENADE;
                else currentWeapon = WEAPON_AUTO_GUN;
        }
        else
        {
        }
        print ("Current Weapon: "+ weaponName[currentWeapon] + "("+ammos[currentWeapon]+")");
}
```

In the previous code:

- We first check whether the **Tab** key has been pressed.
- If this is the case, we check how many and what types of weapons the player currently has.

- In the case of three weapons, we increase the index of the current weapon; if this count is more that **2** (remember that the index starts at 0 so the third item would be at the index 2) then it is set to 1; this way we can loop through the three weapons (i.e., index goes from 0, to 1, 2, and back to 0).
- In the case where the player has two weapons (i.e., gun and automatic gun, gun and grenade, or grenade and automatic gun), we switch between the current and the second weapon.
- Finally, if the player has only one weapon, nothing happens.
- We also print a message, in the **Console** window, that indicates the current weapon and the corresponding ammunitions.

Last but not least, you can modify the code in the **Start** method as follows.

```
hasWeapon [WEAPON_AUTO_GUN] = true;
```

Please save your code and test the scene. As you press the *Tab* key, you should see the message **"Current Weapon: AUTOMATIC GUN (10)"** and **"Current Weapon: GUN (10)"** in the **Console** window, as illustrated in the next figure.

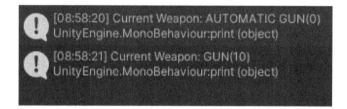

Well, our system is working properly; now we just need to link it to the firing system, so that we can shoot depending on the current weapon and ammunitions available for this weapon.

- Please modify the **Update** method as follows (new code in bold).

```
if (Input.GetKeyDown(KeyCode.F))
{
        if (currentWeapon == WEAPON_GUN && ammos [WEAPON_GUN] >=1 && canShoot)
        {
                ammos [currentWeapon]--;
                if (Physics.Raycast(rayFromPlayer, out hit, 100))
                {
                                print (" The object " + hit.collider.gameObject.name +" is in front of
the player");
                                GameObject objectTargeted;
                                if (hit.collider.gameObject.tag == "target")
                                {
                                        print ("hit a target");
                                        objectTargeted = hit.collider.gameObject;
                                        objectTargeted.GetComponent<ManageNPC>().GotHit();
                                }
                }
                canShoot = false;
                timer = 0.0f;
                timerStarted = true;
                //gunAmmo --;
        }
}
```

In the previous code:

- We check that the key **F** has been pressed.
- We then check whether the current weapon is a gun and that we have enough ammunition left.
- If this is the case, we decrease the number of ammunitions and proceed as we did before.
- After we have managed to fire the gun, we set the variable **canShoot** to false; this is so that the gun can't be fired while it is reloading.
- We then set up the timer that calculates how much time it will take for the gun to reload; when this timer is up, the player will be able to use the weapon again, provided that there is enough ammunition. So here, the time (for the timer) is set to 0 and it will then start. These variables **timer** and **timerStarted** will be used in the code that we yet need to add in the script.

Before we can add this timer, we need to set the reload time for each weapon.

- Please add the following code at the end of the **Start** method, for the script **ManageWeapons**.

```
reloadTime [WEAPON_GUN] = 2.0f;
reloadTime [WEAPON_AUTO_GUN] = 0.5f;
reloadTime [WEAPON_GRENADE] = 3.0f;
```

In the previous code, we indicate that it will take 2 seconds for the gun to reload, .5 seconds for the automatic gun to reload, and 3 seconds to be able to throw another grenade.

- Add the following code at the beginning of the **Update** method:

```
if (timerStarted)
{
        timer += Time.deltaTime;
        if (timer >= reloadTime [currentWeapon])
        {
                timerStarted = false;
                canShoot = true;
        }
}
```

- In this code, if the timer is started (this will happen just after a weapon has been used), we increase the time.
- Once the time reaches the reload time for the current weapon, we can then stop the timer and make it possible for the player to shoot again.

So, let's test this system; before we do so, let's modify the code slightly so that we have enough ammunition for the automatic gun.

- Please modify the following code in the **Update** method:

```
if (Input.GetKeyDown(KeyCode.F))
{
        if ((currentWeapon == WEAPON_GUN  || currentWeapon == WEAPON_AUTO_GUN) &&
ammos [currentWeapon] >=1 && canShoot)
        {
```

In the previous code, we check whether the gun or the automatic gun are selected; we also check that we have enough ammunitions and that the current weapon can be used (i.e., when the reload time has elapsed).

We can also modify the number of initial ammunitions for the automatic gun, by modifying the code in the **Start** method as follows (new code in bold):

```
ammos [WEAPON_GUN] = 10;
ammos [WEAPON_AUTO_GUN] = 10;
ammos [WEAPON_GRENADE] = 0;
```

To make sure that we hear when the gun is shot, and to tell the difference between the two guns, we will also add a sound when one of these is fired.

- Please import the **gun_shot** sound for the resource pack into your project.
- Select the object **Player**.
- Then add an **Audio Source** component to it by selecting: **Component | Audio | AudioSource** from the top menu.
- Once this is done, a new **Audio Source** component should be added to this object.
- You can look at its properties in the **Inspector** window.
- In the section called **Audio Source**, uncheck the option **Play on Awake** and drag and drop the **gun_shot** sound from the **Project** window to the variable called **Audio Clip**, as illustrated on the next figure.

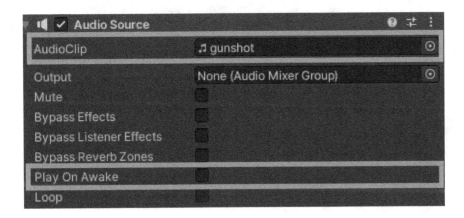

Once this is done, we can trigger this sound through our script.

- Please open the script **ManageWeapons**.
- Modify the code in the **Update** method as follows (new code highlighted in bold).

```
if ((currentWeapon == WEAPON_GUN || currentWeapon == WEAPON_AUTO_GUN) && ammos
[currentWeapon] >=1 && canShoot)
{
        ammos [currentWeapon]--;
        GetComponent<AudioSource>().Play();
```

In the previous code, we access the **AudioSource** component on the object **FirstPersonCharacter** and play the default **AudioClip** associated with this **Audio Source**.

The last change that we will apply will be to display the current weapon onscreen.

- Please create a new **Text** object (**Game Object | UI | Text - TextMeshPro**).
- Rename this object **userInfo**.
- Please move this object to the bottom-left corner of the window (if it is not already there). You may switch to the 2D mode temporarily for this.

[113]

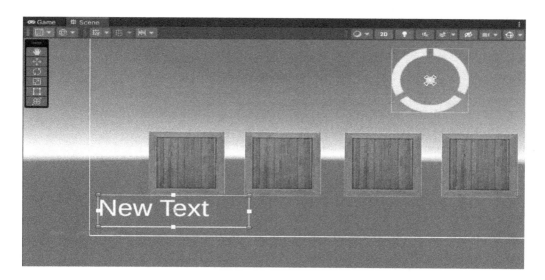

To move the **Text UI** component you can temporarily switch to the 2D mode, this will display the screen boundaries (i.e., white rectangle) and make it easier to position the **Text UI** component. To activate or deactivate the 2D mode, you can click on the 2D icon located below the tab labeled scene, as described on the next figure.

- You may change the color of the font and the alignment for this text if you wish by amending the corresponding attributes in the **Inspector** for the section **TextMesh Pro,** as per the next figure.

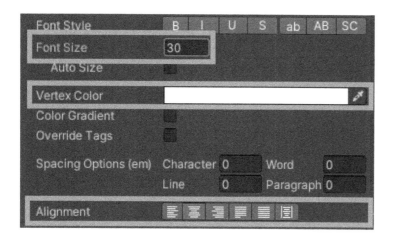

Next, we will modify the text for this object from the script to display the name of the current weapon:

- Please add the following code at the start of the script **ManageWeapons**:

```
using TMPro;
```

In the previous code:

- We include the **TextMeshPro namespace**, enabling the script to use TextMeshPro's features for advanced text rendering and manipulation in Unity.
- **TextMeshPro** is a text-rendering solution in Unity, offering better performance and a wider range of customization options compared to the default UI Text and TextMesh components.
- By adding the namespace **TMPro**, the script can directly access TextMeshPro's classes, methods, and properties, such as TextMeshProUGUI, for creating and managing text elements in the Unity UI.

Overall, this line integrates the powerful features of TextMeshPro into the script, enabling the use of highly customizable text elements in the game.

- Then add the following code at the end of the method **Update**.

```
GameObject.Find("userInfo").GetComponent<TextMeshProUGUI>().text =
weaponName[currentWeapon]+ "("+ammos[currentWeapon]+")";
```

In the previous code, we access the **Text UI** object named **userInfo**, then its **Text** component; we then change the value of the text to the name of the current weapon.
We are now ready to go, so please:

- Save your code, and check for any error in the **Console** window.
- Play the scene.
- As you play the scene, try to switch between the two guns and see how the reload delay varies as you try to press the **F** key several times consecutively.

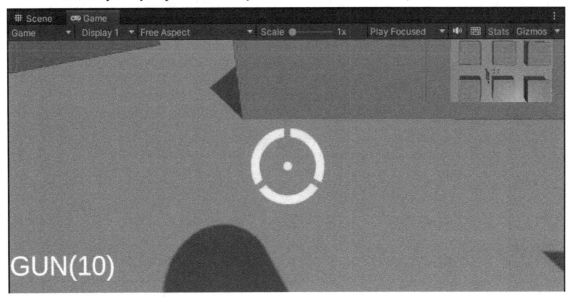

Now, at this stage, all works well; this being said we could just make a small change; that is, making it possible for the player to shoot repeatedly but without having to press the F key again; in other words, the weapon should fire, as long as the F key is kept pressed (or is down) and that we have sufficient ammos. For this, we just need to change the type of event detected. Instead of using the event **GetKeyDown**, we will use the event **GetKey**.

While the first event (**GetKeyDown**) is triggered only when the key has been pressed, the second one (**GetKey**) is triggered as long as the key is being pressed.

- Please modify the **Update** method in your code, for the conditional statement that checks whether the player has pressed the **F** key as follows:

```
if (Input.GetKey(KeyCode.F))
```

Play the scene and check that you can now fire consecutive shots by just keeping the F key pressed.

MANAGING THE COLLECTION OF AMMUNITIONS

Well, so far, we have managed to define two different weapons and to fire them based on the corresponding ammunitions. What we need to do now is to make it possible, as we have done before, for the player to collect ammunitions, and to then update the game information accordingly. For this, we will need to do the following:

- Detect collision with ammo packs.
- Increase the number of ammunitions for a particular weapon.
- Destroy the ammo pack.

So, let's modify the script **ManageWeapons** to create the code that will handle the collection of ammunition.

- Please add the following function:

```
public void ManageAmmoCollection (string tagOfAmmo)
{
        int indexOfAmmoBeingUpdated = 0;
        if (tagOfAmmo =="ammo_gun") indexOfAmmoBeingUpdated = WEAPON_GUN;
        if (tagOfAmmo =="ammo_automatic_gun") indexOfAmmoBeingUpdated =
WEAPON_AUTO_GUN;
        if (tagOfAmmo =="ammo_grenade") indexOfAmmoBeingUpdated = WEAPON_GRENADE;
        ammos [indexOfAmmoBeingUpdated] +=5;
        if (ammos [indexOfAmmoBeingUpdated] > maxAmmos[indexOfAmmoBeingUpdated])
ammos[indexOfAmmoBeingUpdated] = maxAmmos[indexOfAmmoBeingUpdated];

}
```

In the previous code:

- We create a new public function that takes the tag of the ammo collected as a parameter.
- We then check whether this object is an ammo pack (e.g., for a gun, an automatic gun or grenades).

- If this is the case, we check what type of ammunition we have collided with and we keep track of its type using the variable **indexOfAmmoBeingUpdated**.
- Once this is done, we increase the number of ammos for the corresponding weapon (i.e., using the variable **indexOfAmmoBeingUpdated**).
- We then check that we have not reached the maximum number of ammos that we can carry for this particular weapon.

Now that this function has been defined, we just need to call it from the script **BoxCollector**, after a collision has been detected with an ammo pack.

- Please open the script **BoxCollector**.
- Add this code at the beginning of the class:

```
HashSet<string> ammoTags = new HashSet<string> { "ammo_gun", "ammo_automatic_gun",
"ammo_grenade" };
```

In the previous code, we define a **HashSet<string>** to store a collection of unique tags for ammunition types.

A HashSet is a collection type in C# that stores unique values. It does not allow duplicate entries, ensuring each tag appears only once. It provides fast lookups for checking whether an item exists in the collection, which is particularly useful for operations like checking tags.

- The HashSet is initialized with three strings: **"ammo_gun"**, **"ammo_automatic_gun"**, and **"ammo_grenade"**. These represent tags used to identify different types of ammunition in the game (i.e., gun, auto_gun and grenade).
- This HashSet can be used to efficiently check whether a given string (e.g., the tag of a game object) belongs to the predefined set of ammo tags.
- Using a HashSet for this purpose is optimal because lookups are faster compared to lists or arrays, especially when the collection grows larger.

So overall, this code creates a collection of unique ammunition tags that can be checked quickly during gameplay. It is a robust and efficient way to manage and validate tags for different types of ammo in the game.

- Next please comment the following code in the function **OnControllerColliderHit**.

```
/* if (hit.gameObject.CompareTag("ammo_gun"))
{
        GetComponent<ManageWeapons>().IncreaseGunAmmo(5);

        Destroy (hit.collider.gameObject);
} */
```

- And add this code below:

```
if (ammoTags.Contains(hit.gameObject.tag))
{
        GetComponent<ManageWeapons>().ManageAmmoCollection(hit.gameObject.tag);
        Destroy (hit.gameObject);
}
```

In the previous code:

- We check if the tag of a collided object is part of a predefined set of valid tags and then take appropriate actions.
- We validate the tag of the collided object against a collection of valid tags. This ensures the logic applies only to specific objects of interest, such as ammunition.
- If the tag is valid, we retrieve a component responsible for managing weapons and call a method to handle the collection of ammunition.
- We destroy the ammo pack.

Overall, with this code, we efficiently validate and process interactions with specific game objects, we handle ammo collection, and we remove items from the game world.

Before we start to collect ammunitions, we will create ammunitions for the automatic gun and the grenades. At this stage, you should have an ammo pack called **ammo_gun**.

- Add a text label to that object (i.e., **ammo_gun**): Right-click on that object in the hierarchy, and **select 3D Object | Text – TextMeshPro**, and rename the new object **label**.

- Select this object in the **Hierarchy window** and then switch to the **Inspector**.
- Change its position to **(0, 1, 0)**.

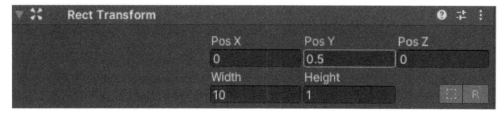

- Set the text to **GUN**.

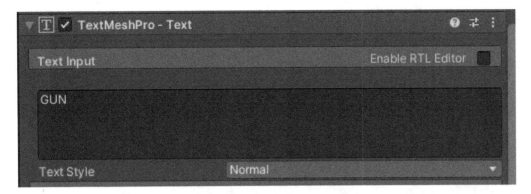

- Set the font size to **5** and the alignment to **Center**, as per the next figure.

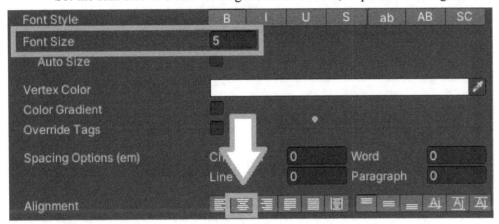

- Once this is done, you ammo pack should look like the next figure.

So, with this in mind, please play the scene, collect this ammo pack and check that the number of ammos for your gun has increased, as per the next figure.

We could now create a prefab from this ammo pack, duplicate the object used for the ammunition object, and change the duplicate's tag to **ammo_automatic_gun**.

- Drag and drop the object **ammo_gun** to the **Project** window; this will create a new prefab called **ammo_gun**.
- Duplicate this prefab and rename it **ammo_auto**.
- Create a new tag called **ammo_automatic_gun**.
- Apply this tag **ammo_automatic_gun** to the prefab **ammo_auto**.
- Change the text of label for this prefab to **AUTO**.

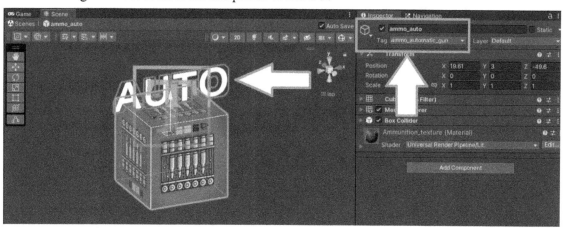

- You can close the prefab **ammo_auto** and repeat the same steps to create a prefab called **ammo_grenade**, with a tag called **ammo_grenade**, and a label entitled **GRENADE** as per the next figure

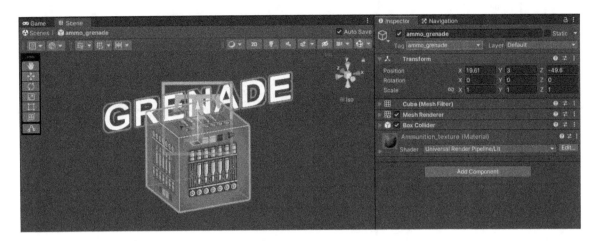

You should have now three types of ammunition, and we will add some more of them to the level:

- Drag and drop the prefab **ammo_auto** to the **Scene** view slightly apart from the other ammo pack, as illustrated in the next figure.

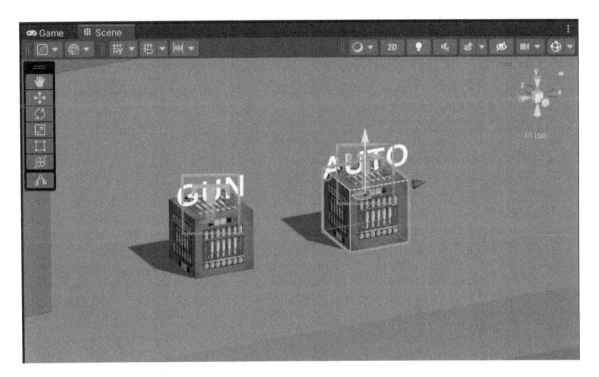

- Play the scene and check that after collecting this pack (**ammo_auto**), your ammos for the automatic gun increase accordingly.

By creating prefabs for these ammo packs, we have created templates that can be reused (or instantiated) either from the scene view (i.e., by dragging and dropping these prefabs to the scene), or from the code, by instantiating these prefabs while the game is playing. This is interesting, for example when you would like to balance the game difficulty and spawn some ammos when the player is in trouble and needs them.

CREATING A GRENADE LAUNCHER

At this stage our weapon management system works well; however, we just need to add the ability to throw grenades (and to also pick-up corresponding ammos). For this purpose, we will use rigid body physics, as we have in the last chapter, to propel the grenade and to also apply damage, where applicable. For this purpose, we will do the following:

- Create a launcher attached to the player.
- When the **F** key is pressed and the grenade launcher is selected, we will propel a grenade in the direction where the player is looking, provided that we have enough ammunition.
- The grenade will explode after a few seconds.
- Upon explosion, all objects within a specific radius of the grenade will be destroyed.

So, let's get started.

- Create a new empty object (**Game Object | Empty Object**) and rename it **launcher**.
- Drag and drop this object on top of the object **Player**, so that the launcher becomes a child of the object **Player**.
- Modify its position to **(0, 0, 0.5)**.
- Create a new **Sphere** object (**Game Object | 3D Object | Sphere**).
- Rename this object **grenade**.
- Modify its scale properties to **(0.2, 0.3, 0.2)**.
- You can also add a color to it if you wish (e.g., red).

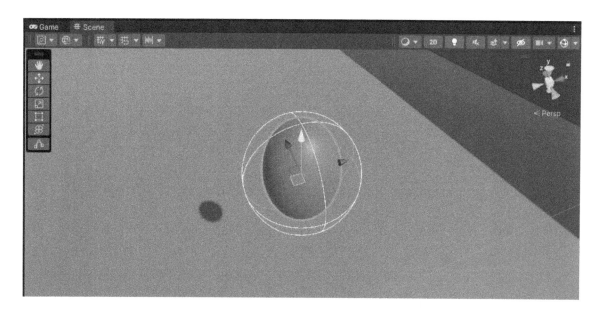

- Add a **Rigidbody** component to this object (i.e., to the grenade) by selecting: **Component | Physics | Rigidbody**.

Once this is done, we can start to modify our script **ManageWeapons** so that we can propel this grenade:

- Open the script **ManageWeapons**.
- Add the following code at the beginning of the class, to declare a placeholder that will be accessed from the **Inspector** to set the grenade that will be launched:

```
public GameObject grenade;
```

- Also modify the code in the **Start** method, to specify that we will start the game with a grenade launcher, as follows:

```
hasWeapon [WEAPON_GRENADE] = true;
```

- You can also add the following line within the **Start** method, so that we start with 10 grenades.

```
ammos [WEAPON_GRENADE] = 10;
```

Then we just need to add code to manage the grenades. The code that we are about to add will simply check whether we have a grenade, and the corresponding ammunitions for it. It will also instantiate and propel a grenade in the air.

- Please add the following code in the **Update** function, just after the code that deals with the guns (but within the conditional statements that deals with the key **F;** if ensure, you can always check the solution code included in the resource pack).

```
if (currentWeapon == WEAPON_GRENADE && ammos [WEAPON_GRENADE] >=1 && canShoot)
{
        ammos [currentWeapon]--;
        GameObject launcher = GameObject.Find("launcher");
        GameObject grenadeF = (GameObject) (Instantiate (grenade, launcher.transform.position,
Quaternion.identity));
        grenadeF.GetComponent<Rigidbody>().AddForce(launcher.transform.forward*500);
        canShoot = false;
        timer = 0.0f;
        timerStarted = true;
}
```

In the previous code:

- We check if the grenade launcher is selected and that we have enough ammunition.
- We then decrease the corresponding level of ammunition.
- We identify the **launcher** object.
- We create a new instance of the object **grenade** (i.e., a public variable that will be set later by dragging and dropping the **grenade** object on it in the **Inspector**).
- The new projectile is then propelled using the method **AddForce**.

Once this is done, we can save our code and add grenades to the scene:

- Save your code.
- Create a new grenade prefab by dragging the **grenade** object to the **Project** window.

If you are prompted to choose the type of prefab that you want to create, please choose the option **"Original Prefab"**.

- Once this is done, we can deactivate the **grenade** object already present in the scene.
- We can also select the object **Player** and drag and drop the prefab **grenade** (from the **Project** window) to the field called **grenade** for the script **ManageWeapons** attached to the object **Player**

- Once this is done, you can now test the scene, switch between weapons, and check that you can throw a grenade.

After this, we just need to create an explosion and also check if other objects are close to the grenade as it explodes. For this purpose, we will create a new script that will be attached to the grenade that has been instantiated.

- Please create a new C# script called **GrenadeTrigger**.
- Open the script and add the following code to it (new code in bold).

```
public class GrenadeTrigger : MonoBehaviour {
public float grenadeTimer;
public bool grenadeTimerStatrted;
public float grenadeTimerLimit;
public bool grenadeExplode;
public GameObject explosion;
private float radius = 5.0f;
private float power = 500.0f;
private float timer;
private  float explosionTime;
private bool hasExploded;
```

In the previous script, we declare several variables that will be necessary to control and launch the grenade: variables that will determine when the grenade should explode (e.g., **grenadeTimer**, **grenadeTimerStarted**, and **grenadeTimerLimit**), a variable that checks whether the grenade has exploded (**grenadeExplode**), the radius within which objects will be affected by the explosion, and the power of the explosion.

- Then we can modify the method **Start** as follows:

```
private void Start ()
{
        timer = 0.0f; explosionTime = 2.0f;
        hasExploded = false;
}
```

In the previous code:

- We set the explosion time to 2 seconds, so that the grenade explodes two seconds after it has been propelled.
- We also specify that it has not exploded yet when launched.

Finally, we will modify the method **Update** as follows:

```
void Update()
{
        timer+=Time.deltaTime;
        if (timer >= explosionTime)
        {
                if (hasExploded == false)
                {
                        Vector3 explosionPos = gameObject.transform.position;
                        Collider [] colliders = Physics.OverlapSphere (explosionPos, radius);
                        for (int i = 0; i < colliders.Length; i++)
                        {

                        }

                        hasExploded = true;
                        Destroy (gameObject);
                }
        }
}
```

In the previous code:

- We update the time.
- We also check whether the grenade should detonate (based on **explosionTime**).
- In this case, we look for all objects around the grenade with a collider. For this purpose, we use the method **Physics.OverlapSphere**.

The method **Physics.OverlapSphere** checks for the presence of rigid bodies within a specific radius; in our case, once they have been found, the colliders of these objects are saved in the variable called **colliders**.

- Lastly, please add this code within the loop in the **Update** function:

```
if (colliders [i].gameObject.tag  == "target")
{
        GameObject objectTargeted = colliders [i].gameObject;
        objectTargeted.GetComponent<ManageNPC>().GotHitByGrenade();
}
```

In the previous code, if there are any targets within the radius; if that's the case, we call the function **GotHitByGrenade** that is in the script attached to the target; this function, as we have seen previously, will destroy the target. However, this method does not exist yet, and you may have an error in the **Console** window for this reason.

So, let's modify the script **ManageNPC** accordingly:

- Please open the script **ManageNPC**.
- Add the following code to it:

```
public void GotHitByGrenade()
{
        print ("Hit by grenade");
        health = 0;
}
```

In the previous code, we set the health of the NPC to **0** if it has been hit by a grenade.

Now that the code is compiled correctly, we can update the prefab **grenade** and drag and drop the script **GrenadeTrigger** on the prefab **grenade**.

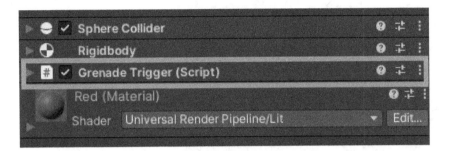

You can now test the scene by throwing a grenade and checking that it eliminates any NPC nearby.

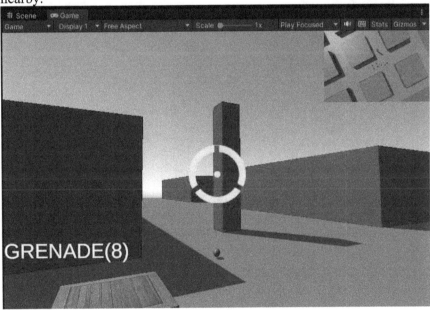

After completing that test, it would be great to add a more visual effects, for example, using an explosion at the point of impact. For this purpose, we will employ Unity's native Particle System.

- In the Unity menu bar, select **GameObject > Effects > Particle System**.
- This will create a new Particle System in your scene.
- Rename it **explosion**.

We can now configure the Particle System:

- Select the object **explosion** in the **Hierarchy** and open the **Inspector**.
- Adjust the following settings under the **Main** module:
  - o **Duration**: Set this to 1 (a short explosion effect).
  - o **Looping**: Uncheck this (the explosion should happen once).
  - o **Start Lifetime**: Set this to 0.5 to 1 seconds (how long particles last).
  - o **Start Speed**: Set this to 10 or higher for fast particle movement.
  - o **Start Size**: Set this to 1 or 2 for larger particles.

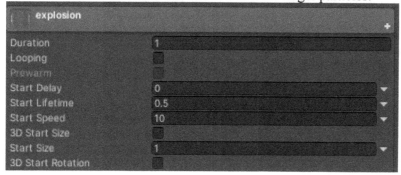

- Expand the **Emission** module.
- Set the **Rate Over Time** to 0.
- Click the + icon under **Bursts** and set the **Count** attribute a high value (e.g., 100 or 200) for an impactful burst.

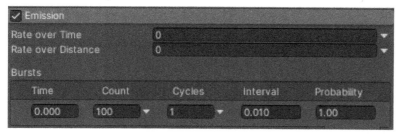

- Expand the **Shape** module.
- Choose **Sphere** as the shape.
- Adjust the **Radius** to control the spread of the particles (e.g., 1 to 2).

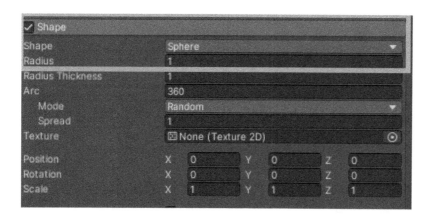

- Expand the **Color over Lifetime** module and check the box to enable it.
- Tick the box to the left of the label "**Color Over Time**".
- Click the **Color Gradient** bar.
- It will open the Gradient Color window

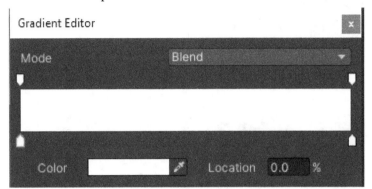

- This window can be used to set different colors at the start, middle, and/or end of the animation.
  Each keyframe is represented by a white tab. For example, in the figure above, you can see two pairs of tabs: two for the start (on the left) and two for the end (on the right).
- You can specify the color at each of these keyframes (e.g., start and end) by clicking on the corresponding tabs.

- By default, the color is already set to white for the start and end. To specify a yellow color in the middle, you just need to add a tab in the center. To do this, click below the white rectangle around the middle, as shown in the next figure.

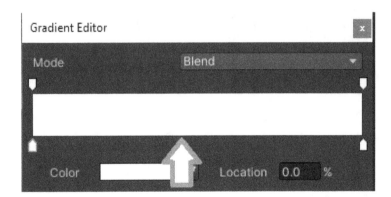

- This will create a new tab in the middle.

- Click on that tab, and select a brown color.

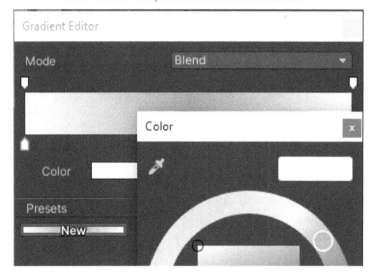

- You should see that the middle color is brown.

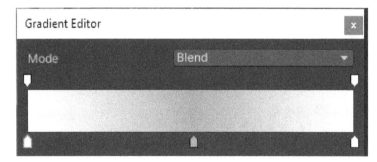

- Expand the **Size over Lifetime** module and check the box to enable it.
- Click on the downward facing arrow to the right of the label **Size**.

- Select the option "**Random Between Two Constants**".

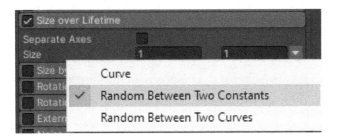

- Set the values to 100 and 0 so that the curve gradually shrinks to zero.

Now that we have set-up the explosion, please do the following:

- Create a prefab from the object **explosion**.
- Open the prefab **Grenade**.
- In the Inspector, locate the script **GrenadeTrigger** and the empty placeholder called **explosion**.

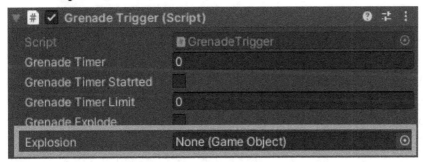

- Drag and drop the prefab explosion (that you have just created) to the placeholder.

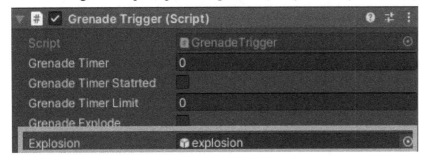

- Close the **Grenade** prefab.
- Open the script **GrenadeTrigger** and add the following code in the **Update** method (new code in bold).

```
GameObject.Instantiate (explosion, transform.position, Quaternion.identity);
hasExploded = true;
Destroy (gameObject);
```

- In the previous code we instantiate a new explosion at the point where the grenade has detonated.
- Please save your code and test the scene.

As you try to launch a grenade, it will explode and remove any target around it.

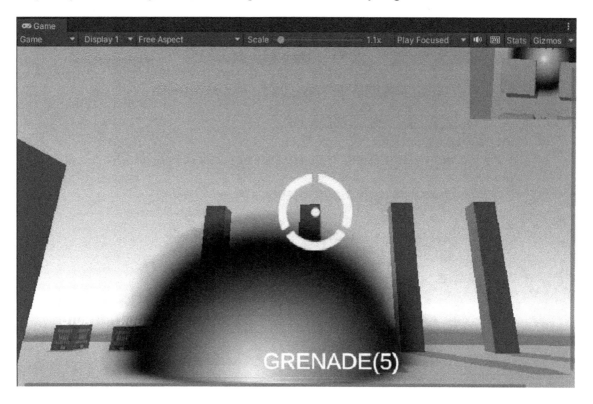

Last but not least, we just need to add a grenade ammo to the scene; so please drag and drop one or several **ammo_grenade** prefabs to the **Scene**.

Once this is done, you can test the scene, launch grenades, and collect more grenades then.

As you play the scene, you may notice that the initial number of grenades is 10 and that it then drops to 5 after collecting the grenade ammos; this is because we have initialized the number of grenades to 10 in our code and set the maximum to 5; so we could change our code in the **Start** method for the script **ManageWeapons** as follows:

```
maxAmmos [WEAPON_GRENADE] = 10;
```

SUMMARY

Well done on completing this chapter! You have successfully created a complete weapon system using new concepts and tools such as arrays and particle systems. Throughout this chapter, you have implemented ways for the player to detect targets, eliminate them with a wide range of weapons, and collect ammunition. Along the way, you explored particle systems, ray-casting, tags, and rigid bodies to develop a functional grenade launcher.

QUIZ: TEST YOUR KNOWLEDGE

Please specify whether the following statements are True or False (the solutions are at the end of the book).

1. The script ManageWeapons uses raycasting to detect objects in the player's line of sight.
2. A Debug.DrawRay is used to detect collisions between the ray and objects in the scene.
3. The crosshair helps players aim by aligning with the center of the screen.
4. The Physics.Raycast method requires a ray and outputs collision data when the ray intersects with an object.
5. Ammo collection is managed by increasing the player's gunAmmo variable directly without any checks for maximum ammo.
6. The weapon management system uses arrays to store properties such as ammo count, reload times, and weapon availability.

[133]

7. The grenade launcher propels grenades using Unity's AddForce method applied to a Rigidbody component.
8. The Physics.OverlapSphere function identifies all objects within a defined radius and applies damage to them.
9. The particle system for explosions is configured to loop continuously for repeated effects.
10. The ManageNPC script destroys targets instantly after a single hit, regardless of health.

CHALLENGE

Now that you know how to implement a weapon system, modify it as follows:

- Modify the damage to the target depending on the type of weapon (gun or automatic gun)
- Modify the reload time of each weapon.
- Create a particle effect that is applied at the point of impact of the bullets.

5
SIMPLE AI AND NAVIGATION

In the previous chapter, we laid the groundwork for creating interactive gameplay mechanics by implementing weapon systems, inventory management, and damage mechanics. These foundational systems added depth to the player's experience, providing tools for dynamic interaction with the game environment. Now, we will take a significant step forward by introducing artificial intelligence (AI) and navigation systems, allowing non-player characters (NPCs) to move, behave, and interact within the game world intelligently and dynamically.

In this chapter, we focus on integrating simple AI systems and pathfinding to bring NPCs to life, combining technical concepts with creative execution. These activities will help you expand your skills in NPC navigation, behavior management, and interactive environments. By the end of this chapter, you will have built a robust foundation for more advanced AI systems, with NPCs capable of navigating, responding to the player, and interacting with the environment.

So, in this chapter you will learn about:

- Simple NavMesh Navigation with a Box Robot: Configure Unity's NavMesh system for NPCs to navigate to a target, creating the basis for dynamic movement in your game.
- Adding Costs and Areas to Navigation: Fine-tune NPC pathfinding by assigning movement costs and defining navigation areas, allowing for more strategic and controlled NPC behavior.
- Using a Simple Finite State Machine (FSM): Implement a basic FSM to control NPC behaviors dynamically, enabling transitions between states like idle, patrol, and chase.
- Waypoints: Random and Fixed Points: Set up waypoints to guide NPCs along fixed or random paths, enhancing the realism of their movement patterns.
- Adding Health and Damage to NPCs: Create health and damage systems for NPCs, allowing them to take damage from the player and enhancing the challenge of gameplay.
- Using 3D Animated Characters for NPCs: Import and animate 3D character models, replacing placeholder objects with fully realized NPCs to elevate the visual appeal of your game.

By completing this chapter, you will:

- Master the basics of AI-driven NPC navigation using Unity's NavMesh system.
- Understand how to implement and manage navigation costs and areas for strategic movement.

- Develop a solid understanding of finite state machines (FSMs) for dynamic behavior control.
- Gain experience in setting up waypoint systems to add variety to NPC movement.
- Enhance gameplay with NPC health and damage mechanics.
- Improve player immersion through advanced camera mechanics and perspective switching.

This chapter is a stepping stone to advanced AI systems and game mechanics, empowering you to create more dynamic, engaging, and polished gameplay experiences. Let's get started with creating our first simple navigation system!

SIMPLE AI NAVIGATION

In this section we will add simple navigation to the robots already present in the level, by making it possible for them to either follow a path, or to follow the player.

- Select the **Robot** prefab and open it.
- If you don't have a **Robot** prefab yet, you just need to drag and drop one of the robots present in the scene to the **Project** window.
- Add a **NavMeshAgent** component to that object.

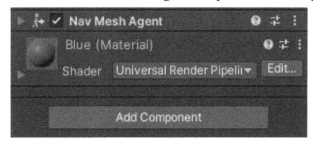

- Deactivate the component **RobotProjectileThrower** for now, as we just want the **Robot** to follow the player for now.

- Create a new script called **MoveRobot** and attach it to the **Robot** prefab.
- Close the prefab.
- Open the script **MoveRobot**.
- Add this code at the beginning of the script.

```
using UnityEngine.AI;
```

- Add this code at the beginning of the class:

```
GameObject target;
NavMeshAgent navmeshAgent;
```

- Add this code to the **Start** function.

```
navmeshAgent = GetComponent<NavMeshAgent>();
target = GameObject.Find("Player");
```

- Add this code to the **Update** function:

```
navmeshAgent.SetDestination(target.transform.position);
navmeshAgent.isStopped = false;
```

- Save your code.
- Reactivate the two robots already present in the scene (or create two based on this prefab).

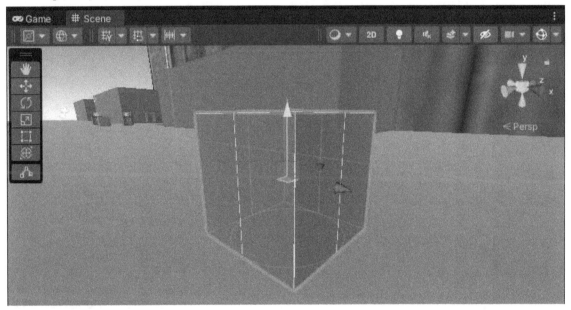

So, at this stage, we are almost ready to enable the robots to follow the player, we just need to make the ground navigable.

- Open the Package Manager: In the **Unity Editor**, go to the top menu and select **Window > Package Manager**.
- Search for the Navigation Package: In the **Package Manager** window, search for **AI Navigation** or **Navigation** in the search bar.
- Install the Package: Select the **AI Navigation** package from the list and click **Install**.
- Select the **ground** object
- In the **Hierarchy** window, click on the object that represents your ground or floor (e.g., "**Ground**").
- With the **ground** object selected, go to the **Inspector** window.
- Click the **Add Component** button.
- Search for **NavMeshSurface**, select it from the list and add it to your **ground** object.

- Under the **NavMeshSurface** component in the **Inspector**, adjust the following settings.
- For the attribute **Agent Type**: Select the appropriate agent type (e.g., "Humanoid") based on your NPCs.
- For the attribute **Include Layers**: Ensure that the layer of your ground object is included (e.g., "Default").
- For the attribute **Collect Objects**: Choose **All** to include all objects in the scene for navigation, or refine this setting based on your requirements.
- Select the **ground** object.
- In the **Inspector**, check the **Static** box at the top of the window. This tells Unity that these objects do not move and can be used in baking the **NavMesh**.
- Go to the **Inspector** and locate the **NavMeshSurface** component on your **ground** object.
- Scroll down to the **Bake** section within the **NavMeshSurface** component.
- Click the **Bake** button. A blue overlay will appear in your scene view, indicating the areas that NPCs can navigate.

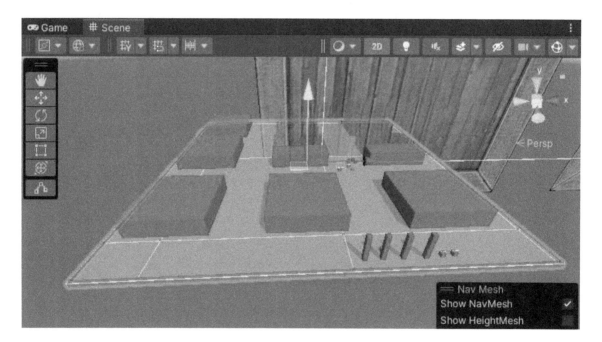

If you are using a version that is older than Unity 2022, then you can do the following instead:

- Select the object called **ground**.
- Open the **Navigation** panel: select **Window | AI | Navigation**.
- This should add a tab called **Navigation** in the **Inspector**, for the object **ground**.

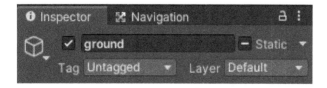

- Click on the **Navigation** tab, this will display the content of the **Navigation** tab, as per the next figure.

- In the default tab **Object**, select check the box for the attribute **Navigation Static**.

- Click on the tab **Bake**, and then on the button called **Bake**.
- You should then notice that the ground turns **blue**, as per the next figure.

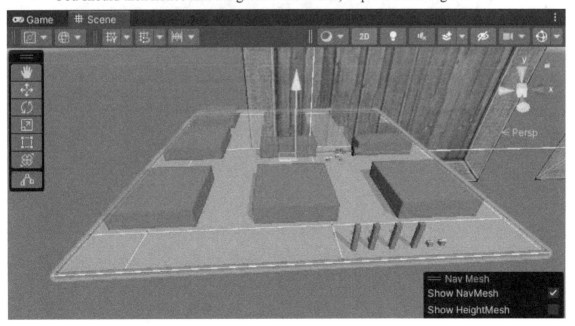

Next, we just need to indicate that the walls should be avoided, so please do the following:

- Select all the walls (i.e., objects called walls) in the **Hierarchy**.
- Click on the **Navigation** tab, then on the **Object** tab, and select the option **Navigation Static** and **Not Walkable**, as per the next figure.

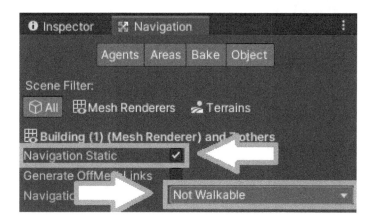

- Again, click on the tab **Bake**, and then on the button labelled **Bake**.
- You should notice that a thin grey area is now drawn around each wall, which shows that they will be avoided for navigation.

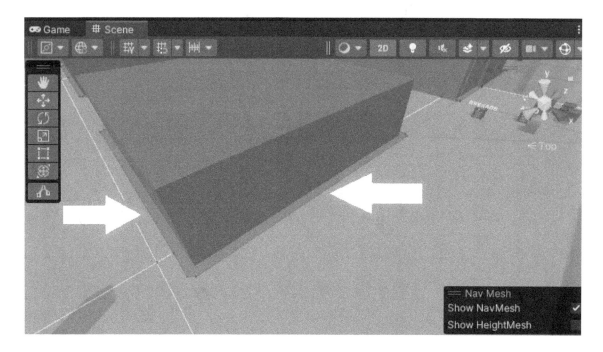

- You can now play the scene and check that the Robots are effectively following the player.

ADDING JUMPING CAPABILITY TO THE PLAYER

Now that we have enabled the robots to follow the player, we will add the ability for them to jump over platforms, to make the game slightly more challenging; so, in this section we will create platforms, and ensure that the **Robot** can jump over them to reach the player.

- We will use a layout similar to the next figure.

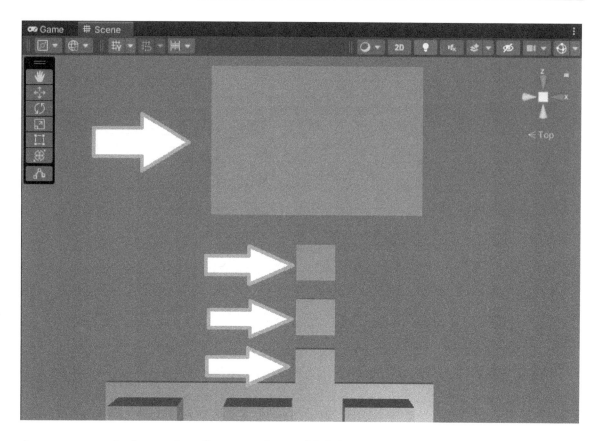

As you can see in the previous figure, we have added three small platforms that the NPC (or the player) will need to jump over to reach the bigger platform located atop of the image.

- Please create a cube, rename it bridge, and change its size to **(10, 1, 10)** and its y coordinate to **0**; duplicate it twice and rename the duplicates **bridge2**, and **bridge3**.
- Place these objects, as per the previous figure.
- Duplicate the object **bridge** and call the duplicate **platform**.
- Change its size to **(64, 1, 43)**.
- Place this object (**platform**) as per the previous figure.

Once this is done, you can try to move your player and jump over the bridges, and you may adjust the distance between them, to make sure that you can effectively move to the platform object by jumping over the bridges.

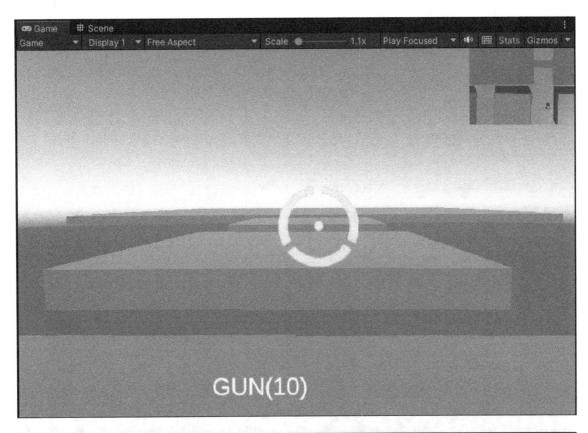

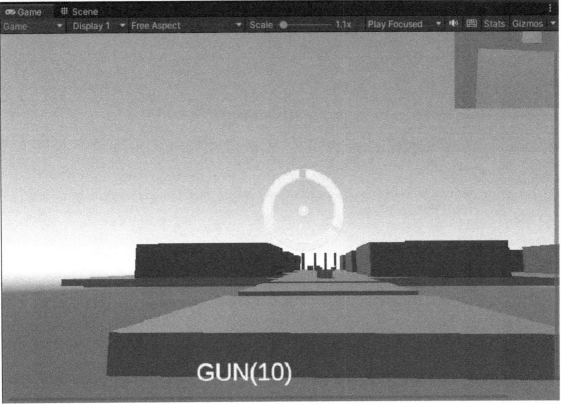

ADDING OFF-MESH LINKS

Once this is done, we need to make it possible for the robot to jump (as you have) through the bridges to reach you; for this purpose, we will use what is often referred to as **Off-Mesh Links**, links between meshes that allow navigation between meshes even if they are not close to each other.

- Using the **Hierarchy** window, select the objects **ground**, **platform**, **bridge**, **bridge2** and **bridge3**.

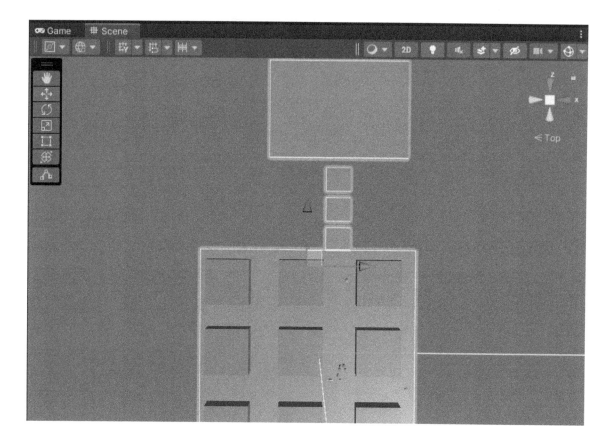

- Once this is done, using the **Navigation** window, in the **Object** tab, select the option "**Generate Off-Mesh Links**".

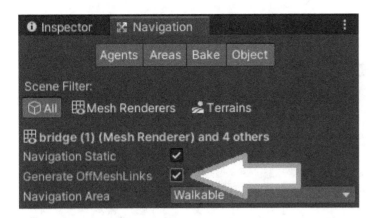

- Click on the **Bake** tab.
- Set the **Jumping Distance** to **8**.
- Click on **Bake**.

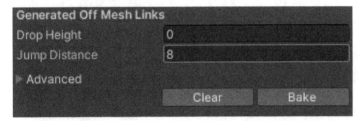

- As soon as you press the **Bake** button, you will notice that links have effectively been created between the bridges and the platforms, as per the next figure.

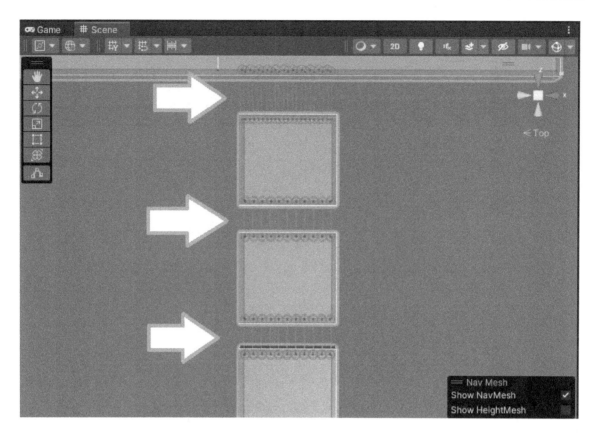

- You can now play your scene, jump over the bridges to attain the other platform and check that the robots are following you and also jumping over the bridges, thanks to these off-mesh links that you have created.

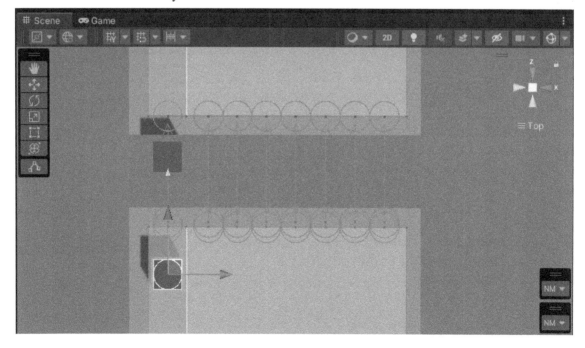

ADDING COSTS AND AREAS TO NAVIGATION

In the previous section, we have managed to create off-mesh links allowing the robots to jump horizontally over gaps to reach the player.

While this is a good addition in terms of challenge, we will push this concept further by adding areas and costs and creating areas that are more difficult to navigate for the robots.

ABOUT COSTS AND AREAS IN UNITY

In Unity's **AI Navigation System**, the concepts of **Areas** and **Costs** play a crucial role in determining how NPCs or agents navigate a scene.

Areas represent types of surfaces in a NavMesh. You can assign different areas (e.g., "Walkable," "Not Walkable," or "Jump Required") to different parts of the terrain. These areas can help define where an agent can or cannot move. Areas are set using the Navigation window or directly in code via NavMeshArea settings. Costs define the difficulty or preference for an agent to traverse a specific area.

Unity allows you to assign a cost value to each area. For example: A low-cost area (e.g., "Walkable" with a cost of 1) encourages agents to prefer it whereas a high-cost area (e.g., "Rough Terrain" with a cost of 5) discourages agents from using it unless necessary. Costs are particularly useful for influencing the pathfinding algorithm, guiding agents to avoid expensive paths unless they are unavoidable. When an agent calculates a path, Unity considers both areas where the agent can move and costs (i.e., how much effort is required to move through specific areas). This enables fine-tuned control of NPC navigation, allowing for more realistic and strategic movement.

For example:

- A road might have a low cost to encourage agents to prefer it.
- A muddy field might have a higher cost to make it a less desirable option.
- A water region could have a prohibitively high cost, essentially making it impassable for most agents unless explicitly allowed.

By combining areas and costs, Unity's navigation system can simulate complex decision-making processes for AI, leading to smarter and more natural behavior.

USING COSTS AND AREAS FOR A SWAMP

In our game we could create a feature whereby NPCs need to navigate a forest to reach a goal, but the forest includes a **swamp** area. This swamp should slow down NPCs or make it a last resort for pathfinding because it's more challenging to traverse. So, in this case, we could do the following:

- Define the Swamp Area: Use Unity's Navigation Window to create a new **Area Type** named "Swamp." Assign this area to the **NavMesh** where the swamp is located in the terrain.

- Set a High Cost for the Swamp Area: Assign a cost of 10 (or higher) to the "Swamp" area in the NavMeshSettings. This makes the swamp much more expensive to traverse compared to normal ground, which might have a cost of 1.
- Observe NPC Behavior:NPCs will now calculate paths that avoid the swamp if alternative routes are available. If there's no other path, they will traverse the swamp but with slowed movement or reluctance.

So, based on this system, players might lure enemies into the swamp to slow them down or use swamp areas strategically for ambushes. Agents will prioritize paths outside the swamp whenever possible due to the high traversal cost. And if an NPC must traverse the swamp (e.g., no other route exists), it will still complete the path but take a longer, more deliberate route, simulating the difficulty of crossing a swampy area.

BUDILDING THE SWAMP

To create the swamp, we will be creating five different platforms, based on the object **platform** as per the next figure.

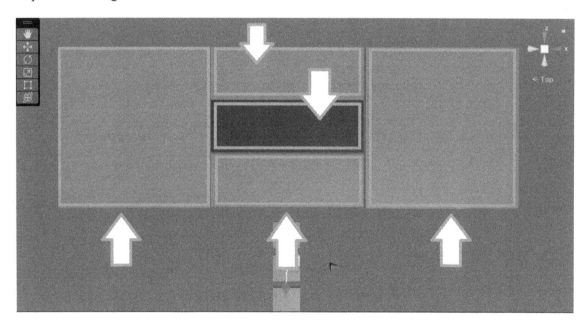

Each of these platforms will have the same costs, except the brown platform, in the middle, that will act as a swamp and therefore have a higher cost, so that NPCs avoid this area as much as possible:

- Please duplicate the object **platform** four times.
- Calle the duplicates **eastSide**, **westSide**, **northSide**, and **southSide**.
- Rename the object **platform** to **swamp**, and change its color to **brown**.
- Resize each of these objects to obtain the layout illustrated in the previous figure.
- Select the objects **eastSide**, **WestSide**, **northSide** and **southSide**, open the **Navigation** panel, and make sure that the navigation area is set to **Walkable** for these objects.

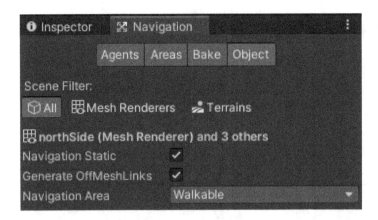

- Select the object called **swamp**, and using the **Navigation** window, select the tab **Areas**, and create a new area called **Swamp** with a cost of **10**, as per the next figure.

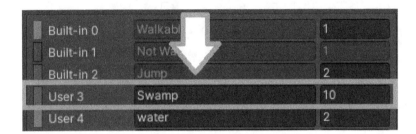

- Then click on the **Object** tab, set the attribute **Navigation Area** to **Swamp**.

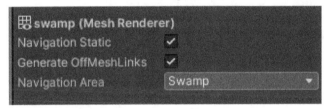

- Click on the **Bake** tab, and then on the button labelled **Bake**.
- You should see that the swamp object has turned purple and that connections (i.e., off-mesh links) have been created on all sides of the swamp.

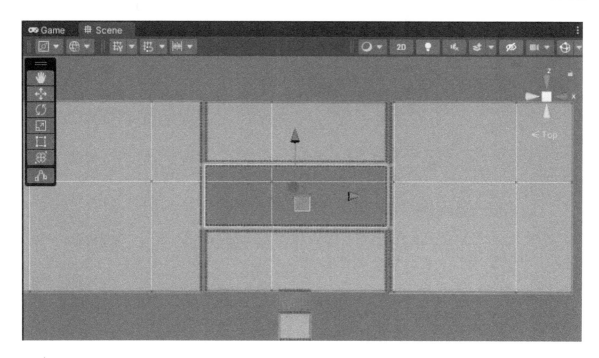

At this stage, everything is set-up. So ,you can play the scene, ensure that the player is on the north side of the swamp, and you should see that the robots, after jumping over the bridges, are avoiding the swamp area in order to reach the player.

ADDING TREES

To add even more obstacles and realism, we could add trees around the swamp and along the way, to make the swamp area more difficult to navigate.

So, let's create a tree:

- Create a new empty object and call it **tree**.
- Add a cylinder as a child of this object.
- Rename the cylinder **trunk** and apply a **brown** color to it.
- Chang the position of the **trunk** to **(0,0,0)** and its **size** to **(0.5, 1, 0.5)**.
- Add a **sphere** object as a child to the **tree** object and rename it **leaves**.
- Apply a green color to the object called **leaves**.
- Change its position to **(0, 1.65, 0)** and its size to **(2, 1.3, 2)**.
- You should now have a tree that looks like the next figure.

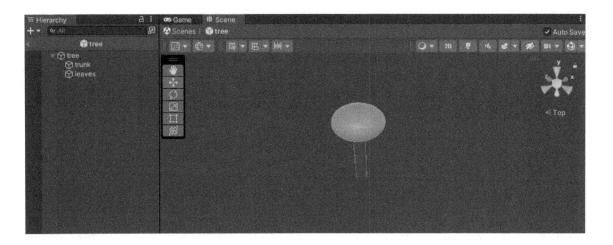

- Once you are happy with the appearance of the tree, you can add an **NavMesh Obstacle** component to it and then drag and drop the tree object to the Project window to create a prefab from it.

The **NavMesh Obstacle** component in Unity is used to define objects that should block or influence the navigation of NPCs using a NavMesh. When added to an object, it marks the area around the object as non-walkable, forcing NavMeshAgents to navigate around it.

- You can now add trees in strategic places, to ensure that they make navigation more challenging for NPCs.

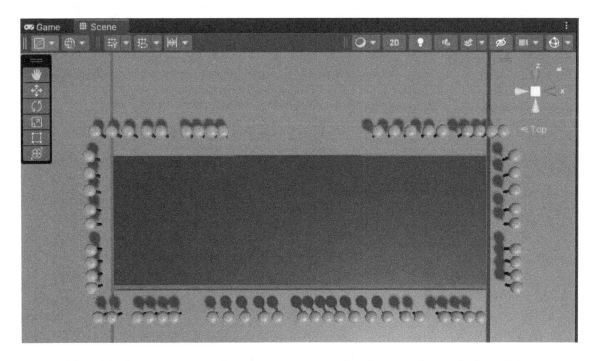

After adding this feature you can play the scene, move the player to the north side of the swamp, and check that the NPCs avoid the swamp and the trees to reach the player.

USING A SIMPLE FINITE STATE MACHINE

CREATING A PATROL STATE

In the previous section, we managed to create NPCs that can navigate the environment and jump over obstacles if needed to reach the player. However, the robots currently exhibit a very basic level of awareness and intelligence.

In this section, we will enhance their behavior by introducing simple actions, such as following a path and tracking the player only when specific events occur—for example, when the player is nearby.

To achieve this, we will modify our **MoveRobot** script and start incorporating a **Finite State Machine (FSM)**, which will allow the robots to make decisions based on their current state.

First, we will create an Animator Controller and the states that will be used for the NPC.

An **Animator Controller** in Unity is a component that manages the animation states and transitions for a game object. It allows you to define how animations are triggered and blend together based on input, parameters, or game logic, enabling dynamic and interactive animations in your project.

Please do the following:

- Create a New **Animator Controller**: In the **Project** window, select **Create | Animator Controller**. Rename it to **RobotAnimatorController**.
- Assign the Animator Controller: Drag and drop the **RobotAnimatorController** onto the **Robot** prefab in the **Hierarchy** (or in the **Project** window).
- Open the **Animator** window: Double-click on the **RobotAnimatorController** object in the **Project** window. This will open the **Animator** window.
- Set Up States and Transitions: Right-click on the canvas in the **Animator** window and select **Create State | Empty**. This will create a new state labelled **New State.**

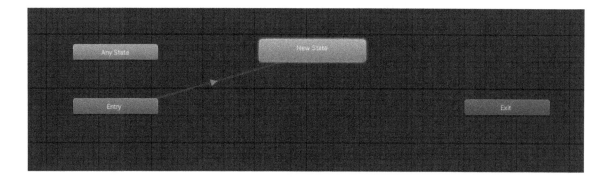

- Select that state (click once on it) and using the **Inspector** window, rename it to **Patrol**.

- You should see that the label of the state has also changed on the canvas.

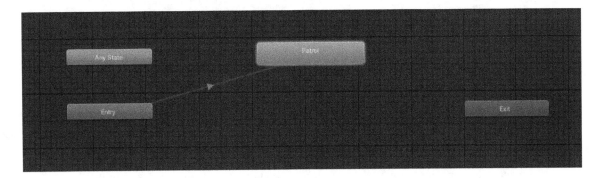

- Using the same steps, create a new state called **Follow_Player**.

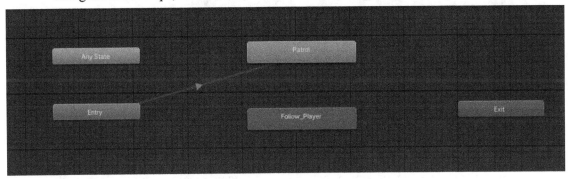

So, at this stage we have two states: **Patrol** and **Follow_Player**.

The idea here is to have the NPC patrolling along a specific path and to start following the player only when it has detected the player, for example when the player is less than 3 meters away from the Robot.

So, we will need to create a transition between the state **Patrol** and the state **Follow_Player**, and this transition will be performed based on a parameter.

- Create a new transition from the state patrol to the state **Follow_Player**: right click on the state called **Patrol**; select **Make Transition** from the contextual menu, and then click on the state called **Follow_Player**; this will create a transition between these two states.

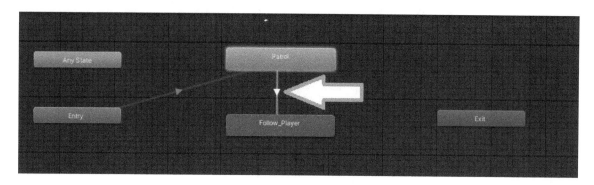

So now that this transition has been created, we just need to specify a condition for it to occur.

Note that you can move states by dragging and moving them and also zoom-in and -put by using the mouse wheel.

- Select (click on) the transition that you have just created (it will turn to blue).
- Click on the + button in the **Parameter** section and select the option **Trigger**.

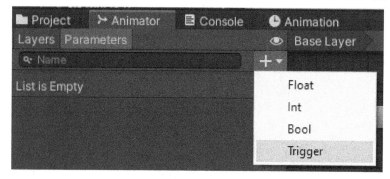

- This will create a new parameter called **New Trigger**: rename it **playerDetected**.

- You can then select the transition that you have created earlier (click on it once) and then, in the **Inspector** window, click on the + button in the section **Conditions**.

- By default, and because we have only one parameter, the condition will be set to **playerDetected**.

So, at this stage, we have an animator controller with two states **Patrol** and **Follow_Player**, for which the transition between the former and the latter will happen if the parameter **playerDetected** is true. So, in the next section, we will modify our code to do the following:

- Move the robot along a pre-defined path.
- Detect when the player is near the player.
- Triger the transition to the state **Follow_Player** where the robot follows the player indefinitely.

LINKING THE **FSM** TO OUR **ROBOT**

Now that animator controller is created, let's control it from the code.

- Please drag and drop the animator controller **RobotAnimatorController** on the **Robot** prefab (if you haven't done that already). You should see that the **Robot** now includes an **Animator** component, as per the next figure.

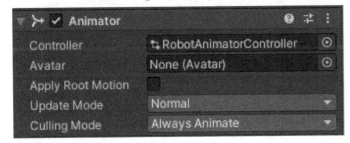

CREATING WAYPOINTS

At this stage, we will create a path for the NPC; this path will be made of waypoints which are basically successive targets that, put together, define the path. So, the idea will be to:

- Create waypoints or empty objects that will be used for navigation.
- The Robots will navigate towards a particular waypoint.
- When close to this waypoint (e.g., less than 1 meter), they will start to move towards the next waypoint.
- After reaching the last waypoint, the NPCs will follow the first waypoint again.

So, let's get started:

- Please create a new cube (**GameObject | 3D Object | Cube**).
- Rename it **WP1** (as in WayPoint1).
- Using the **Inspector** window, deactivate its collider, as illustrated in the next figure.

- Select the object **WP1** in the **Hierarchy**.
- Duplicate this object three times (i.e., **CTRL + D**) and call the duplicates **WP2**, **WP3**, and **WP4**.
- Move these three objects at each corner of the object ground, just above the ground, as per the next figure.

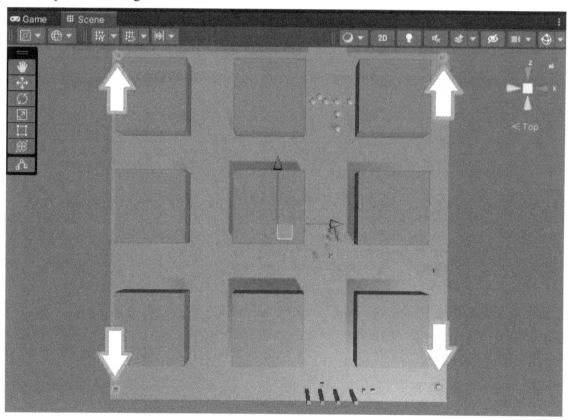

Once the waypoints have been created, we can modify the script **MoveRobot** so that the Robots follow these waypoints successively.

CONTROLLING THE ROBOTS' STATES WITH THE CODE

Let's write the code to control the robots.

- Please open the script **MoveRobot**.
- Add this code at the beginning of the class.

```
public GameObject WP1, WP2, WP3, WP4;
int WPCount;
GameObject[] WayPoints;
Animator anim;
AnimatorStateInfo info;
```

In the previous code, we do the following:

- **Define waypoint objects**: We specify multiple waypoints that act as markers in the game environment. These waypoints are often used to guide the NPC or represent locations the NPC must navigate to.
- **Track waypoint progression**: A variable is used to keep count of the current waypoint or how many waypoints the NPC has passed or interacted with.
- **Store waypoints in a collection**: An array is created to hold all the waypoint objects together. This makes it easier to manage and loop through them systematically, especially for tasks like NPC pathfinding.
- **Set up an Animator**: A reference to the Animator component is included. This allows control over the animations linked to the NPC or player, enabling smooth transitions between animation states.
- **Track animation states**: Another variable is used to monitor the current state of the Animator. This helps in determining which animation is currently active or when a transition between animations occurs.

So, overall, with this code we:
- Prepare and manage waypoints for NPC navigation.
- Track progress through these waypoints.
- Use an Animator to control animations and monitor their states for seamless behavior transitions.

Next, we will initialize these variables:

- Please add the following code to the **Start** function:

```
anim = GetComponent<Animator> ();
target = new GameObject ();
WP1 = GameObject.Find ("WP1");
WP2 = GameObject.Find ("WP2");
WP3 = GameObject.Find ("WP3");
WP4 = GameObject.Find ("WP4");
WayPoints = new GameObject[]{ WP1, WP2, WP3, WP4 };
WPCount = 0;
```

In the previous code, we do the following:

- **Retrieve the Animator component**: The Animator component attached to the GameObject is accessed and stored in a variable. This enables control over animations, allowing us to trigger, stop, or modify animation states programmatically.

- **Initialize a target object**: A new GameObject is created and stored in a variable called target. This can be used later for purposes like setting navigation goals or representing an NPC's point of focus.
- **Locate waypoint objects in the scene**: Several waypoints (WP1, WP2, WP3, WP4) are identified in the scene using their names and assigned to corresponding variables. These waypoints are likely pre-defined objects placed in the game world to direct NPC movement.
- **Store waypoints in an array**: The waypoints retrieved earlier are grouped into an array called **WayPoints**. This collection simplifies navigation logic, making it possible to iterate through or randomly select waypoints.
- **Initialize waypoint counter**: A counter variable is set to 0, likely to track which waypoint the NPC is currently navigating to or how many waypoints it has traversed.

So, overall, with this code we:
- Set up essential components (Animator and waypoints) to enable navigation and animation control.
- Organize waypoints into an array for efficient processing and use in movement logic.
- Establish a starting point for tracking waypoint progression.

Now that we have defined and initialized these variables, we will write the code to move the Robot from waypoint to waypoint.

- Comment this code that is currently within the function **Update**.

```
//navmeshAgent.SetDestination(target.transform.position);
//navmeshAgent.isStopped = false;
```

- Add the following code inside this function (i.e., **Update**):

```
info = anim.GetCurrentAnimatorStateInfo (0);
if (info.IsName("Patrol"))
{
        if(Vector3.Distance(transform.position,target.transform.position) < 1.0)
        {
                WPCount++;
                if (WPCount > 4)  WPCount = 1;
        }
        target = WayPoints [WPCount];
        navmeshAgent.SetDestination(target.transform.position);
        navmeshAgent.isStopped = false;
}
```

In the previous code, we do the following:

- **Retrieve the current state of the NPC's animation**: The Animator is queried to check the current state of the NPC's animation. This information helps determine if the NPC is in a specific state, such as "Patrol."
- **Check if the NPC is in the "Patrol" state**: The code evaluates whether the NPC is currently patrolling. This conditional logic ensures that the subsequent movement logic only executes when the NPC is in the "Patrol" state.

- **Determine proximity to the target waypoint**: The distance between the NPC's current position and the current waypoint's position is calculated. If this distance falls below a certain threshold, it implies the NPC has reached the waypoint.
- **Update to the next waypoint**: If the NPC has reached the current waypoint, the index of the next waypoint is incremented. If the index exceeds the number of available waypoints, it wraps around to the first waypoint, enabling cyclic patrolling.
- **Assign the next waypoint as the new target**: The target for the NPC's movement is updated to the next waypoint. This keeps the NPC moving along the path.
- **Direct the NPC to move towards the next waypoint**: The NPC's navigation system is instructed to move to the position of the updated target waypoint. Movement is resumed if the NPC was previously stopped.

So, overall, with this code we:
- Determine the NPC's current state to ensure it is patrolling.
- Check if the NPC has reached its current waypoint and, if so, update to the next waypoint in the patrol path.
- Continuously cycle through waypoints, creating a looping patrol behavior.
- Use the navigation system to guide the NPC to the updated target.

You can now save your code, check that it is error free and play the scene; as the game begins, you should see that the robots start to follow the waypoints sequentially.

DETECTING THE PLAYER AND CHANGING THE ROBOTS' BEHAVIOUR

Now that the robots are following the waypoints, we can look into transitioning to the **Follow_Player** state, whereby the Robot detects and starts to follow the player; so in this section we will write the code that:

- Detects the player (based on distance).
- Set the **playerDetected** parameter accordingly.
- Ensure that the Robot follows the player after the detection.

So, let's get started:

- Please add this code at the beginning of the class **MoveRobot**:

```
GameObject player;
```

- Add this code to the **Start** function:

```
player = GameObject.Find("Player");
```

- Add this code in the **Update** function in the conditional statement for the state **Patrol**.

```
if(Vector3.Distance(transform.position,player.transform.position) < 3.0)
{
        anim.SetTrigger("playerDetected");
}
```

In the previous logic, we do the following:

- **Calculate the distance between the NPC and the player:** The distance between the NPC's position and the player's position is computed to determine proximity.
- **Check if the player is within a specific range:** A condition verifies if the player is closer than a predefined distance (e.g., 3 meters). This acts as the NPC's detection threshold.
- **Trigger a behavior change through the animator:** If the player is detected within range, a command is sent to the animator to activate a specific behavior (e.g., transitioning from one state, such as "**Patrol**," to another, like "**Follow_Player**").

So, overall, with this logic we evaluate the player's proximity to the NPC, we identify when the player enters the NPC's detection radius, and we then dynamically trigger a behavior change, allowing the NPC to react to the player's presence.

- Add this code in the **Update** function, after the conditional statement for the state **Patrol**.

```
if (info.IsName("Follow_Player"))
{
        target = player;
        navmeshAgent.SetDestination(target.transform.position);
        navmeshAgent.isStopped = false;
}
```

In the previous code, we do the following:

- **Check the current animation state:** The logic verifies if the NPC is in the "**Follow_Player**" state. This ensures that the following behavior only activates when the NPC is meant to track the player.
- **Set the player as the new target:** The target for navigation is updated to the player's current position, allowing the NPC to focus on and move toward the player dynamically.
- **Command the navigation system to move the NPC:** The navigation system (**NavMesh Agent**) is instructed to navigate to the player's position. The agent is explicitly activated to ensure it resumes moving toward the player.

So, overall, with this logic we ensure the NPC follows the player only when in the correct state; we dynamically update the navigation target to the player's current position and we actively control the NPC's movement to maintain engagement with the player.

- You can now save your code, check that it is error-free and play the scene; as the game starts, the robots should move towards the first waypoint; however as soon as the player is within a 3-meter radius, they will start to follow the player indefinitely.
- You can display both the **Animator** and the **Scene** window to see the change.

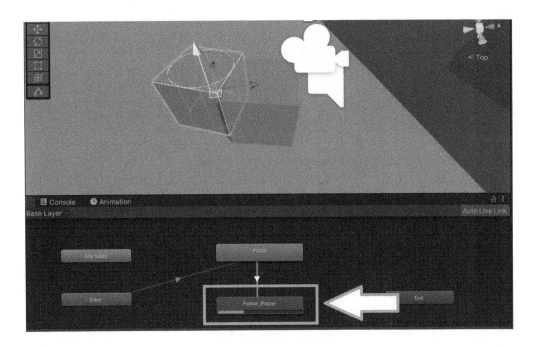

MANAGING HEALTH FOR THE ROBOTS AND THE PLAYER

So, everything seems to work as the NPCs go first patrolling and then follow the player when the latter has been detected. So, in this section, we will just make sure that the player can eliminate these NPCs, by adding health to these NPCs; we will also make sure that the current level restarts if the Robots touch the player.

- Please select both robots (or the **Robot** prefab) and add the component (i.e., script) **ManageNPC** to them; this will ensure that their health can be altered when being shot by the player.
- Apply the tag **target** to both robots.

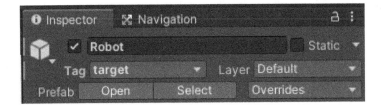

You can now play the scene and ensure that after shooting a Robot three times, that it disappears.

RESTORING SHOOTING ABILITY FOR ROBOTS

Next, we will restore the ability for the Robots to shoot projectiles towards the player; however, we will ensure that this is done only when the robots are chasing the player.

- Add the following code to the class **RobotProjectileThrower**.

```
public bool canShoot = false;
```

- Replace this line in the **Update** function...

```
if (throwTimer >= throwInterval)
```

- by this line...

```
if (throwTimer >= throwInterval && canShoot)
```

- Amend this code in the class **MoveRobot** (new code in bold):

```
if (info.IsName("Follow_Player"))
{
        target = player;
        navmeshAgent.SetDestination(target.transform.position);
        navmeshAgent.isStopped = false;
        GetComponent<RobotProjectileThrower>().canShoot = true;
}
else
{
        GetComponent<RobotProjectileThrower>().canShoot  = false;
}
```

In the previous code, we set the variable **canShoot** to true only when the Robot is following the player.

You can test the scene and you should see that after detecting the player, the robots will start firing at the player, causing the scene to reload automatically.

So, at this stage we have managed to implement damage both for the player and the Robots; however, for the player, being touched by a projectile will cause the scene to restart automatically.

This being said, to make the gameplay smoother, we could, instead, make sure that the player has 100 health points initially, and that its health decreases as it is hit by the projectiles.

ADDING DAMAGE TO THE PLAYER

To manage the player's health, we will start by creating a class that will be attached to the player.

- Please create a new class called **ManagePlayerHealth**.
- Attach this script to the object **Player**.
- Add tis code at the beginning of the class.

```
int health = 100;
int maxHealth = 100;
```

- Add this function:

```
public void DecreaseHealth(int deltaAmount)
{
        health -= deltaAmount;
        if (health <0) health = 0;
        print ("Just Got Hit; health = "+health);
}
```

In the previous code, we do the following:

- **Decrease Health**: The health variable is reduced by the value of deltaAmount, representing the amount of damage received.
- **Clamp Health to Zero**: If the new health value is less than 0, it is reset to 0 to prevent invalid negative health values.
- **Print Feedback**: A message is printed to the console, showing that the object was hit and displaying the updated health value for debugging or gameplay purposes.

Overall, this code ensures that health decreases appropriately when damage is applied, avoids negative health values, and provides feedback about the health state for better gameplay management or debugging.

We can now create a function to increase the player's health; it could be used, for example, when picking up health packs.

- Add this function:

```
public void IncreaseHealth(int deltaAmount)
{
        health += deltaAmount;
        if (health > maxHealth) health = maxHealth;
}
```

In the previous code, we do the following:

- **Increase Health**: The health variable is increased by the value of deltaAmount, representing the amount of healing or health boost received.
- **Clamp Health to Maximum**: If the new health value exceeds the **maxHealth**, it is capped at **maxHealth** to prevent the health from surpassing its defined limit.

Overall, this code ensures that health increases appropriately when healing is applied, avoids exceeding the maximum health value, and maintains consistency within the health system.

Now that these functions have been created, we can modify the code executed when projectiles collide with the player:

- Save your code.
- Open the script **Projectile**.
- Add this code in function **OnCollisionEnter** within the conditional statement

```
//SceneManager.LoadScene(SceneManager.GetActiveScene().name);
collision.gameObject.GetComponent<ManagePlayerHealth>().DecreaseHealth(10);
Destroy(gameObject);
```

In the previous code, upon collision between a projectile and the player, we decrease the player's health by 10, and we then destroy the projectile.

You can now save your code and play the scene; as the player is detected by the robots, and projectiles are thrown towards the player, the player's health will decrease and a corresponding message should appear in the **Console** window, as illustrated in the next figure.

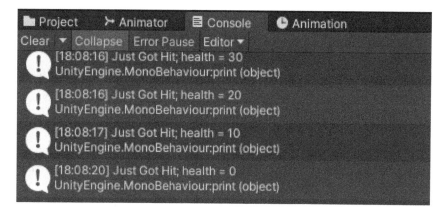

ADDING A SCREENFLASH

While we can now decrease the player's health when s/he is being it would be great to add feedback as to when we have been hit by the Robots. One common way to do this is to add a screen flash; that is, a brief moment when the screen flashes to red. There are many ways to achieve this effect, and one of them is to create a texture or color material and quickly fade its alpha (i.e., transparency) value from opaque to fully transparent. So here, we will achieve this effect using a **UI Image** component.

- Please create a new **UI | Image** object.
- Rename it **screenFlash**.
- Change its **Rect Transform** properties as follows:
  - Type: **Stretch/Stretch**.
  - Left: **0**.
  - Top: **0**.
  - Pos Z: **0**.
  - Right: **1**.
  - Bottom: **1**.

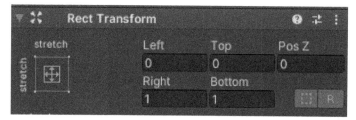

- This will ensure that the image fills the entire screen.

- Please change its **color** to **red** and its **transparency to 100%** (Alpha = 0). The transparency attribute is marked as **A**.

We will now modify the script **ManagePlayerHealth** so that this red screen appears briefly whenever the player is hit.

- Please open the script **ManagePlayerHealth**.
- Add this code at the beginning of the file.

```
using UnityEngine.UI;
using UnityEngine.SceneManagement;
```

- Add the following code at the beginning of the class.

```
public float alpha;
public bool screenFlashBool;
```

- Then add the following code at the end of the method **DecreaseHealth**.

```
ScreenFlash();
if (health == 0) SceneManager.LoadScene(SceneManager.GetActiveScene().name);
```

- Add the following to the **Start** method.

```
alpha = 0;
GameObject.Find("screenFlash").GetComponent<Image>().color = new Color (1,0,0,alpha);
screenFlashBool = false;
```

In the previous code, we set the color of the **screenFlash** object, using the RGB code (i.e., Red = 1, Green = 0, Blue = 0) to red and its alpha value to 0 (i.e., transparent). The RGB values are normalized here; this means that the values will range between 0 and 1;

- Add the following method at the end of the class:

```
private void ScreenFlash ()
{
        screenFlashBool = true;
        alpha = 1.0f;
        print ("Screen Flash");
}
```

- In the previous code, we specify that the screen flash effect should start, and we then set the **alpha** value of the **screenFlash** object to **1** (i.e., it will initially be opaque and progressively become transparent).

- Finally, add the following code to the **Update** method.

```
if (screenFlashBool)
{
        alpha -= Time.deltaTime;
        GameObject.Find("screenFlash").GetComponent<Image>().color = new Color (1,0,0,alpha);
        if (alpha <=0)
        {
                screenFlashBool = false;
                alpha = 0;
        }
}
```

In the previous code we decrease the alpha value of the **screenFlash** object; when this value has reached **0** (i.e., totally transparent) the screen flash effect can be stopped.

- Please save your code and check that the screen flash appears whenever the player has been hit and that when the player's health has reached 0, that the level reloads automatically.

ADDING A HEALTH BAR

In your games, you will often need to keep track of the player's health, and a health bar is a very easy and clear way to do so; the idea is to create a horizontal bar that will be filled and colored depending on the value of the players' health. In the next sections, our health bar will be based on an image that we will scale up and down, and also color, based on the value of the health.

Please do the following:

- In Unity, create a new image (**GameObject | UI | Image**) and rename it **healthBarBg**.
- Set its color to black, and its width and height to **200** and **20**, respectively.

- Duplicate the object **healthBarBg**, rename the duplicate **healthBarFg**, and add this new object as a child of the object **healthBarBg** (i.e., drag and drop atop).
- Select the object **healthBarFg**, set its color to green.

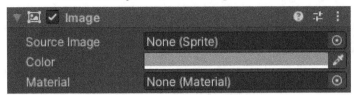

- Set its anchor to **Stretch/Stretch** and its attribute **Min** to **(0,0)**, **Max** to **(1,1)**.

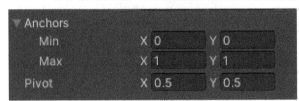

- Set the attributes **left/right/top/ bottom** to 2 as per the next figure.

- Import the file **whiteImg** from the resource folder (i.e., drag and drop to the **Project**
- window)
- Select this image, and using the **Inspector**, set its **Texture Type** attribute to **Sprite (2D and UI)** and press the button labelled **Apply** that is located at the bottom of the **Inspector** window.

- You can now drag and drop this image to the attribute **Source Image** (in the section called **Image**) for the object **healthBarFg**.

- In the **Inspector**, set the attribute **Image Type** to **Filled** and set the **Fill Method** attribute to **Horizontal**.

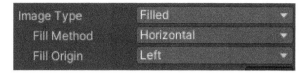

- Lastly, we will also add some text to that health bar so that we can see the actual value of the health, in addition to a scaled and colored health bar. So please add a new **Text** object (**GameObject | UI | Text Mesh Pro**) as a child of the object **healthBarFg**. Set its name to **healthBarText**. You can also set the font size to **15**, the horizontal and vertical alignment of that text object to center/middle.

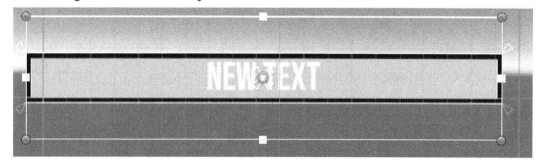

At this stage, the different UI elements are created, and we just need to create the code that will make it reflect the value of the player's health, as it varies.

- Please create a new script, name it **ManageHealthBar** and attach it to the object **healthBarFg**.
- Add this code at the top of the script.

```
using UnityEngine.UI;
using TMPro;
```

In the previous code, we add the name spaces that will be needed to manage the object used for the health bar.

- Add the following code, just before the method **Start**.

```
const float MAX_HEALTH = 100f;
Image healthBar;
TextMeshProUGUI healthText;

[Range(0,100)]
public float health = MAX_HEALTH;
```

- Next, we will initialize the health value for the health bar; so please add the following code to the **Start** function.

```
healthBar = GetComponent<Image>();
healthText= GameObject.Find("healthBarText").GetComponent<TextMeshProUGUI>();
```

In the previous code, link the variable **healthBar** to the object **healthBarText** in the scene.

- Finally, add the following code to the **Update** function:

```
if (health > 50) healthBar.color = Color.green;
else if (health > 30) healthBar.color = Color.yellow;
else healthBar.color = Color.red;

if (health < 0) health = 0;
healthBar.fillAmount = health / MAX_HEALTH;
healthText.text = "" + Mathf.Floor(health);
```

In the previous code, we color the health bar based on the value of the variable health. We then resize the object linked to this script (**healthBarFg**) based on the value of the variable health.

You can now save your code, and play the scene, modify the value of the variable health in the **Inspector**, and see how the **healthbar** is resized and changes color.

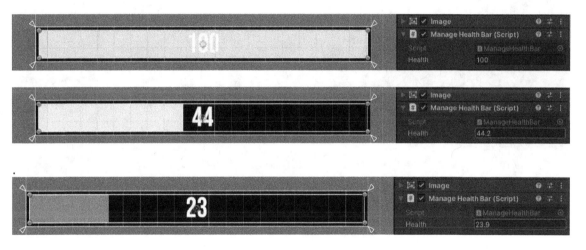

Once you have checked that the health bar is working as a standalone unit, we just need to connect tit to the player's health.

- Move the object **healthBarBg** to the top left corner, or any other location of your choice.
- Open the script **ManageHealthBar**, and add this function:

```
public void SetHealth(int newHealthValue)
{
        health = (float)newHealthValue;
}
```

- Open the script **ManagePlayerHealth**.
- Add this code at the beginning of the class:

```
GameObject healthBar;
```

- Ad this code to the **Start** function.

```
healthBar = GameObject.Find("healthBarFg");
```

- Add this code to the function **DecreaseHealth**.

```
healthBar.GetComponent<ManageHealthBar>().SetHealth(health);
```

- Add the same code to the function **IncreaseHealth**.

You can now play the scene, and check that after being detected by a Robot, every time they hit you with a projectile, that the player's health decreases accordingly.

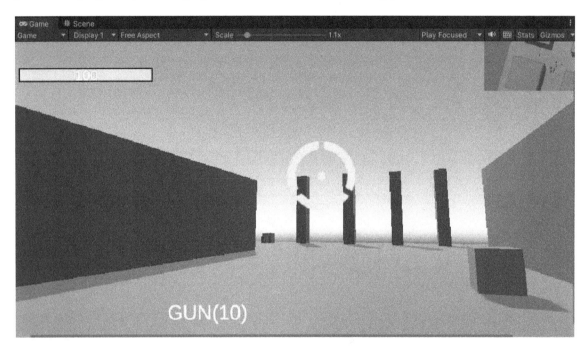

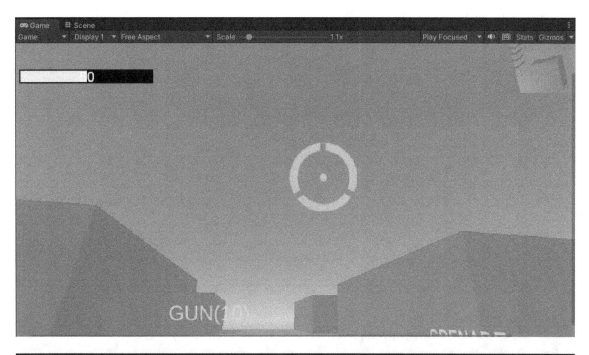

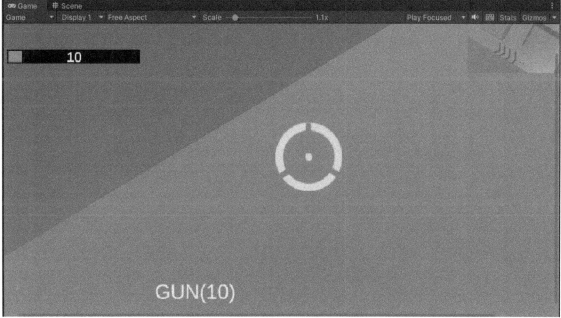

COLLECTING HEALTH PACKS

Now that our level is complete, we just need to add the ability to collect health packs so that the player can top-up its health as it's running low after being hit by robots.

- Duplicate the prefab **ammo_gun** and rename the duplicate **health_pack**.
- Open this prefab.
- Use a different texture (for example the texture **healthPack** from the resource pack).

- Change its tag to **health_pack** and its label to **Health**.

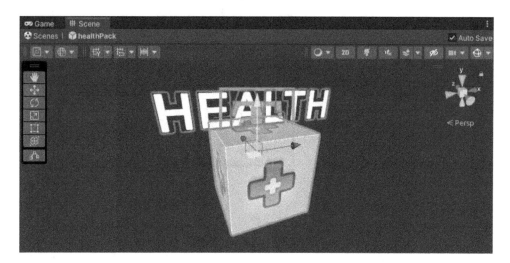

- Close the prefab.
- Open the script **BoxCollector**.
- Replace this code…

```
HashSet<string> ammoTags = new HashSet<string> { "ammo_gun", "ammo_automatic_gun",
"ammo_grenade" };
```

- With this code…

```
HashSet<string> ammoTags = new HashSet<string> { "ammo_gun", "ammo_automatic_gun",
"ammo_grenade","health_pack" };
```

- Open the script **ManageWeapons**.
- Add this code to the function **ManageAmmoCollection**.

```
if (tagOfAmmo =="health_pack")
{
        GetComponent<ManagePlayerHealth>().IncreaseHealth(100);

}
```

- Last but not least, you can add a few health packs to the level.

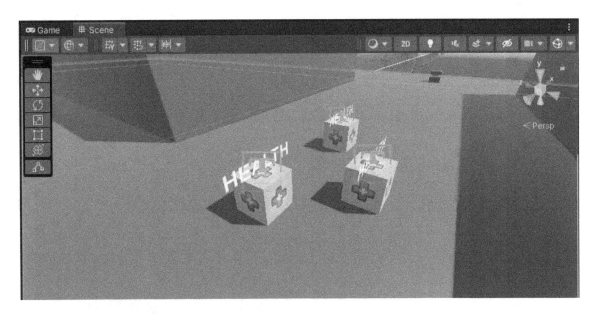

You can now play the scene, and check that after being hit a few times, collecting a health pack replenishes the player's health.

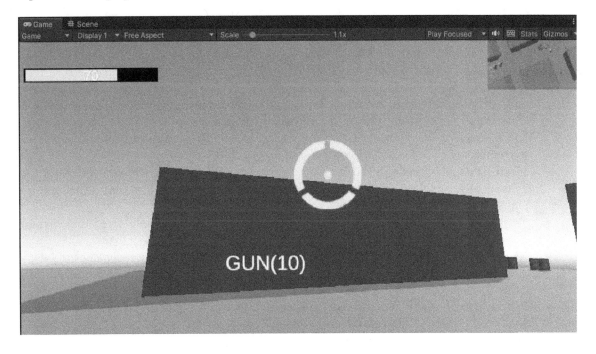

SUMMARY

In this chapter, we delved into creating more intelligent and interactive gameplay mechanics by focusing on both NPC behaviors and player interface elements. Here's what we achieved:

- **Simple NavMesh Navigation:** We set up a NavMesh system to enable NPCs to navigate through the environment and reach designated targets, starting with a box robot.
- **Cost-Based Navigation Areas:** We introduced the concept of navigation costs, allowing NPCs to prioritize paths and avoid specific areas, like a swamp, to optimize their movements.
- **Finite State Machine (FSM):** We implemented a basic FSM to manage NPC behaviors dynamically, enabling them to switch between states like patrolling and following the player based on specific conditions.
- **Waypoint Navigation:** We configured NPC movement using both fixed and random waypoints, adding variety and unpredictability to their navigation.
- **NPC Health and Damage Systems:** We added health and damage mechanics to NPCs, allowing them to take damage and respond accordingly, providing a foundation for combat scenarios.
- **Player Health Bar:** We created a visual health bar for the player, giving real-time feedback on their health status during gameplay.
- **Screen Flash on Player Damage:** We enhanced player feedback by introducing a screen flash effect that triggers when the player is hit, increasing immersion and awareness during encounters.

This chapter significantly enriched the gameplay experience by combining advanced AI behaviors for NPCs with intuitive UI elements for the player. NPCs are now more interactive and adaptable, and players receive real-time visual feedback, enhancing engagement and game depth.

QUIZ: TEST YOUR KNOWLEDGE

Please specify whether the following statements are True or False (the solutions are at the end of the book).

1. NPCs use NavMeshAgent components for pathfinding in Unity.
2. To set up navigation areas, a NavMeshSurface component must be added to every NPC in the scene.
3. Costs in Unity navigation determine the ease or difficulty for NPCs to traverse certain areas.
4. Off-mesh links allow NPCs to navigate across disconnected platforms, such as gaps or obstacles.
5. A NavMeshSurface component must always be baked to make the ground navigable for NPCs.
6. Finite State Machines (FSMs) are used for NPC navigation rather than behavior control.
7. Assigning a higher cost to an area, such as a swamp, will make NPCs prefer to avoid that area.
8. The "Swamp" navigation area in Unity cannot have a different cost than other navigation areas.
9. Adding a NavMesh Obstacle component to an object like a tree will prevent NPCs from passing through it.
10. Unity's Navigation system can only handle flat surfaces for NPC pathfinding.

CHALLENGE

For this challenge, you just need to do the following:

- Add more waypoints for a longer path for robots
- Apply different types of damage depending on the distance between the robot and the player.
- Add different types of health packs: some with 50 health points and other with 100 health points.

6
ADDING AND MANAGING 3D ANIMATIONS

The goal of this chapter is to deepen your understanding of how to create dynamic and engaging NPC behaviors within a game environment. By leveraging Finite State Machines (FSM), advanced navigation techniques, and event-driven triggers, you will learn how to make NPCs more interactive and responsive to the player's actions. These concepts are critical for designing immersive and engaging gameplay that feels realistic and challenging.

In this chapter, you will follow these steps:

- **Configuring NavMesh and NPC Navigation**: Set up NPC pathfinding and movement along predefined waypoints.
- **Implementing Finite State Machines (FSM)**: Introduce state-based logic to control NPC behavior dynamically.
- **Creating State Transitions**: Enable NPCs to switch between states such as patrolling and following the player.
- **Integrating Player Detection**: Add proximity-based triggers to enhance NPC responsiveness.
- **Adding Visual Feedback**: Implement animations and visual cues for state transitions and interactions.

By the end of this chapter, you will have learned how to:

- Build an FSM system to manage NPC behaviors dynamically.
- Configure navigation paths using NavMesh and waypoints.
- Use event-driven triggers for NPC actions, such as detecting the player or returning to patrol.
- Combine animations with state transitions for seamless visual feedback.
- Enhance gameplay with intelligent and interactive NPCs that respond to player input.

This chapter equips you with essential tools for crafting AI-driven gameplay, setting the stage for more complex mechanics in future chapters. Let's get started!

ADDING 3D ANIMATED CHARACTERS FOR NPCS

In this section, we will start to progressively replace the box robot by actual 3D characters; this will provide an improved visual appeal to our game.

This will involve:

- Importing 3D characters
- Applying animations to specific states for the Robots.
- Modifying the code, in places where needed to account for these animations.

IMPORTING 3D CHARACTERS

In this section, we will replace our cubic NPC with an animated character and make some modifications to our script also.

First, let's import the animated character:

- In Unity, create a new folder (if you wish, so that it is easier to find your animations) in the **Project** window (for example **military**).
- In your file system, please locate the folder called **animations** in the resource pack. Then locate the folder called **military** within the folder **animations**.
- Drag and drop the content of this folder (i.e., all files within the folder **military**) into your **Project** window (e.g., to the new folder that you have just created).
- Unity will then import these assets.
- If a window labeled **NormalMap Settings** appears, you can press the option to **Fix Now**, as illustrated on the next figure.

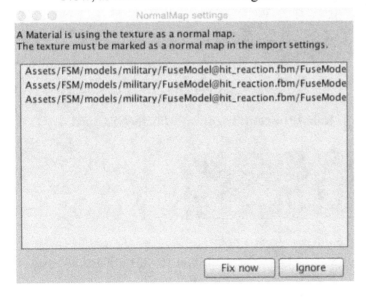

- This should add several prefabs and folders that we will be able to use for the character animation.

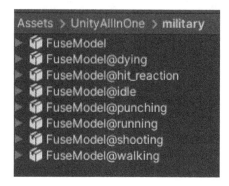

Now we just have to create a new type of robot:

- Drag and drop the object **FuseModel** to the **Scene** view and rename it **NPC**.
- Set its tag to **target**.
- Add an empty object as a child of the **NPC** object and rename the new object **throwPoint**.

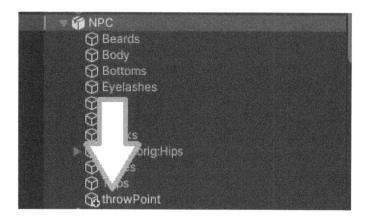

- Change the position of this object (**throwPoint**) to **(0, 0.5, 0.5)**.
- Select the object **NPC**.
- Attach the following scripts to it: **RobotProjectileThrower**, **ManageNPC**, and **MoveRobot**.

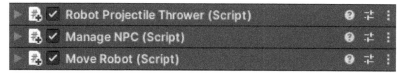

- Add a **NavMeshAgent** component to the object **NPC**.
- Add a **Capsule Collider** to it also, and set its **Center** attribute to **(0, 1, 0)**, and its height to **1.8**.

- It should look as the next figure.

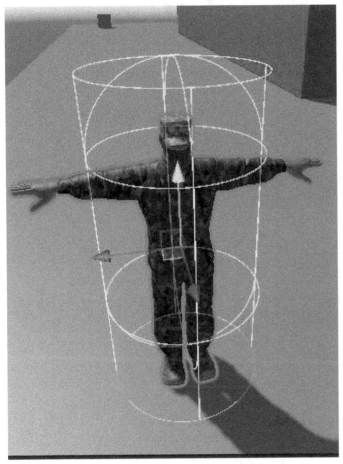

- Finally, drag and drop the **AnimatorController** called **RobotAnimatorController** on the object NPC.

So at this stage, the object NPC should have the component illustrated in the next figure:

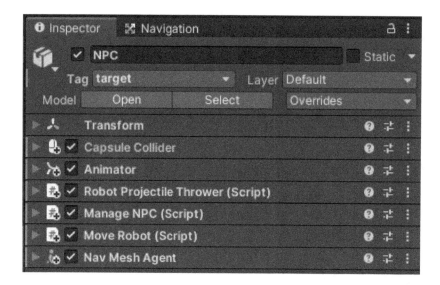

- You can now deactivate the robots in the scene and play the scene. You should see the NPC character moving around the level.

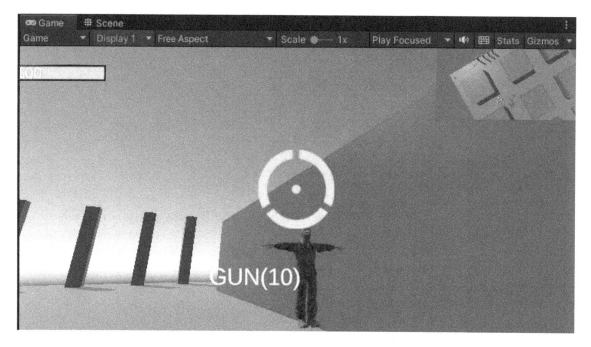

This being said, this character is static and we need to ensure that it moves according to its state (e.g., walk).

- Open the Animator Controller called **RobotAnimatorController**.

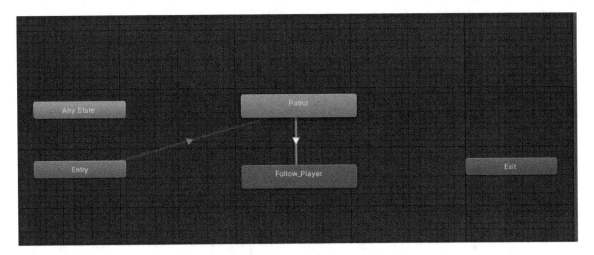

- Click once on the state called **Patrol**.
- In the **Inspector**, locate the attribute called **Motion**.

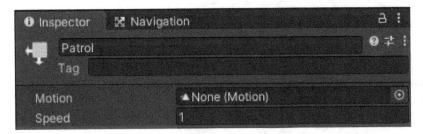

- Click on the cogwheel to the right of the attribute and type the text '**walk**' in the contextual search field.

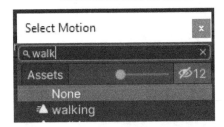

- Select the option **walking** from the results.

- Double click on the state called **Patrol**.
- This will open a new window.

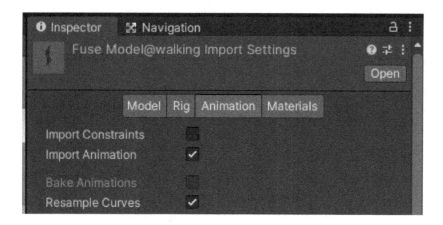

- Select the tab **Animation** and scroll down to the bottom of that window.
- Set the attributes **Loop Time** and **Loop Pose** to **True**, as per the next figure.

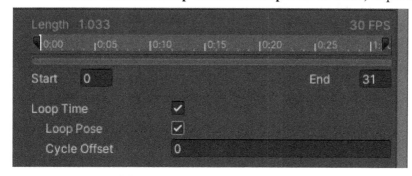

- Then press the button labelled '**Apply**' located at the bottom of that window.

- Repeat these steps for the state called **Follow_Player**.

Finally, so that the NPCs are not constantly looking at the player, even when patrolling, please do the following:

- Open the script called **RobotProjectileThrower**.
- Comment this line in the function **Update**.

```
LookAtPlayer();
```

Once this is done, you can play the scene and check that the NPC is now represented by an animated (i.e., walking) 3D characters.

Next, we will need to add custom animations for when the NPC is hit, when it dies, and when it is shooting.

- Open the Animator Controller used for the NPC.
- Create a new state called **Hit**.
- Create a transition from this state to the state **Follow_Player**.
- Create a transition from the state **AnyState** to the state **Hit**.

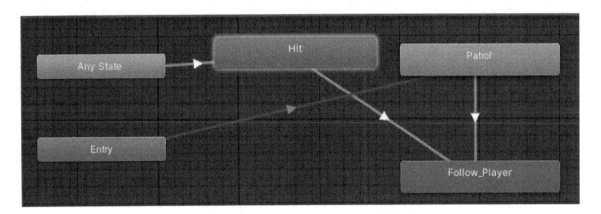

- Create a trigger parameter and rename it **gotHit**.
- Select the first transition (between **Any State** and **Hit**), set the transition to **gotHit**.

- Set the attribute **Can Transition To Self** to **False**.

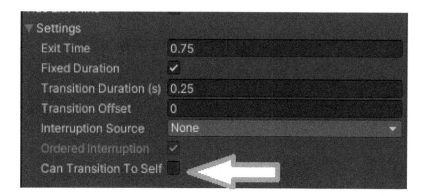

- Add this function to the script **MoveRobot**:

```
public void SetHitReaction()
{
        anim.SetTrigger("gotHit");
        print ("Set Hit reaction");
}
```

- Add this code to the function **GotHit** in the class **ManageNPC**.

```
public void GotHit()
{
        health -=50;
        GetComponent<MoveRobot>().SetHitReaction();
}
```

In the previous code, we ensure that the NPC transitions to the state **Hit** by **setting** the parameter **gotHit** whenever the player is hit.

You can now play the scene and ensure that whenever the NPC is hit, that it briefly transitions to the state **Hit** with a hit reaction animation.

ADDING AN ANIMATION FOR SHOOTING

So, at the moment, our NPC can patrol and follow the player, and is using 3D animations; while the NPC can also shoot at the player, we haven't yet applied a corresponding animation for that state, so in this section we will do the following:

- Define a state called **Shoot**.
- Attach an animation to it.
- Trigger that state from the code, ensuring that the NPC is not moving while shooting.

So, let's make these changes:

- Open the Animator Controller **RobotAnimatorController**.
- Create a state called **Shoot**.

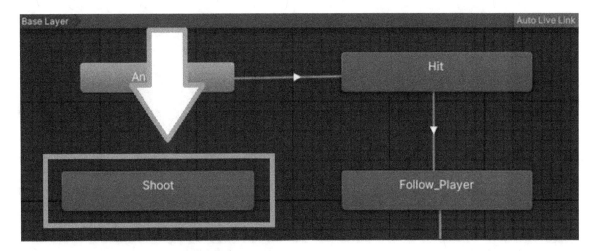

- Associate the animation **shooting** to it.

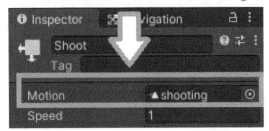

- Create a trigger parameter called **startToShoot**.

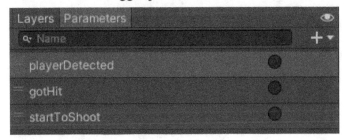

- Create a transition from the state **Any State** to the state **Shoot**.

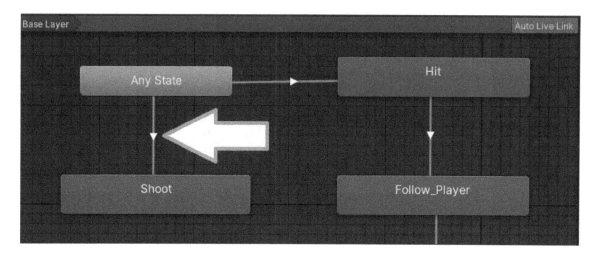

- Select the transition and, using the **Inspector**, set the condition for this transition to **startToShoot**.

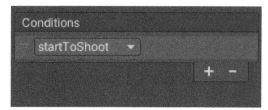

- Create a transition between the states **Shoot** and **Follow_Player**.

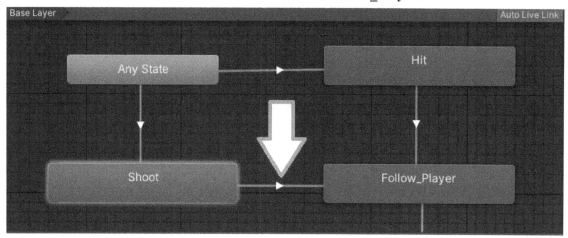

There is no need to set a condition for this transition as we want a transition to the state **Follow_Player** just after the animation has completed.

Now that the Animator Controller has been updated, we just need to modify our code, to trigger the change to the state **Shoot** when the NPC throws projectiles.

- Add this function in the script **MoveRobot**:

```
public void SetStartToShoot()
{
        anim.SetTrigger("startToShoot");

}
```

- Add this code (in bold) to the function **Update** in the script **RobotProjectileThrower**:

```
if (throwTimer >= throwInterval && canShoot)
{
        ThrowProjectile();
        GetComponent<MoveRobot>().SetStartToShoot();
        throwTimer = 0f; // Reset the timer
}
```

In the previous code, we call the function **SetStartToShoot** that will, in turn, set the parameter **startToShoot**, triggering a transition to the state **Shoot**, and the corresponding animation to be played.

- Add this code to the **Update** function:

```
if (info.IsName("Shoot"))
{
        navmeshAgent.isStopped = true;
}
```

This code ensures that the NPC does not walk while shooting.

Once this is done, you can play the scene and check that when the NPCs are shooting, and that the corresponding animation is used.

ADDING AN ANIMATION FOR CLOSE COMBAT ATTACKS

Next, while the shooting mechanism works, and for more realism, it should only be used when the NPC is far away from the player; when close, the NPC should use a close combat technique such as punches, so in this section we will do the following:

- Create a state called **Attack_Close_Range**.
- Check the distance between the NPC and the player
- Trigger a transition to that state when the NPC is within a 1-meter radius from the player.

So, let's get started:

- Open the Animator Controller **RobotAnimatorController**.
- Create a **Boolean** parameter called **isAtCloseRange.**

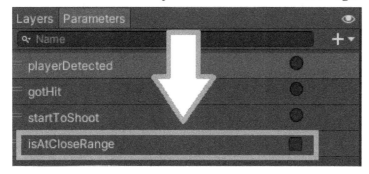

- Create a new state called **Punch**.
- Create a transition from the state **Any State** to the state **Punch**.
- Select that transition.
- For this transition, using the **Inspector**, set the condition to **isAtCloseRange = True**.

- For this same transition, set the attribute **Can Transition To Self** to **false** (from the **Settings** section).

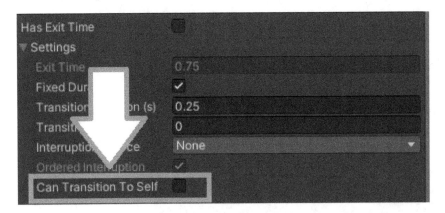

- Create a transition from the state **Punch** to the state **Follow_Player**.

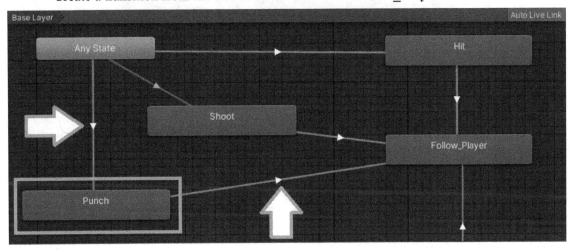

- Add this code to the function **Update** in the script **MoveRobot**:

```
if (Vector3.Distance (player.transform.position, transform.position) <1.5) anim.SetBool("isAtCloseRange",
true);
else anim.SetBool("isAtCloseRange", false);
```

- You can now play the scene and check that when the NPC is very close to you, it starts punching.

While we have managed to create a close-range attack for the NPC, it would be good to add damage to the player, every time the NPC is punching, just as we have done with the projectiles.

For this purpose, we are going to use a **Behaviour Script**, a script attached to a state that can, amongst other things, use function launched only once during the animation linked to that state.

- Click once on the state called **Punch**.
- Click on the button labeled "**Add Behaviour**"

- In the next text field, type '**Punches**'.

- Then select the option '**New Script**'.

- Then press '**Create and Add**'.

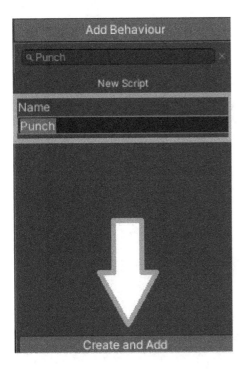

- This will create a script called **Punches**.

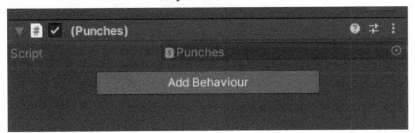

- Open this script.
- You should see that it includes several functions that are commented.
- Uncomment the function **OnStateEnter**.

```
override public void OnStateEnter(Animator animator, AnimatorStateInfo stateInfo, int layerIndex)
{

}
```

This function is called only when we enter the state linked to that script, so effectively, it will be called only once while the state is active.

- Add this code to the function **OnStateEnter**.

```
GameObject.Find("Player").GetComponent<ManagePlayerHealth>().DecreaseHealth(5);
```

In this code we apply a damage of **5** to the player by calling the function **DecreaseHealth** in the script **ManagePlayer** that is attached to the player.

You can now play the scene and check that the player's health decreases as the NPC is punching at close-range; you should also notice a screen flash every time the player is hit, as illustrated in the next figure.

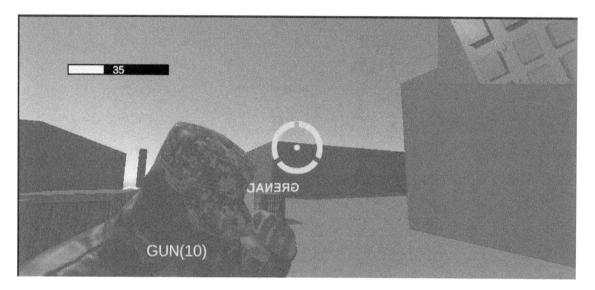

ADDING AN ANIMATION WHEN THE NPC DIES

In this section we will ensure that when the NPC dies, an animation is played, where it falls to the ground before disappearing; for this purpose, we will do the following:

- Create a state called **Die**.
- Trigger an animation to this state when the NPC's health is 0.
- Remove the NPC after the animation is completed.

So, let's start:

- Open the Animator Controller **RobotAnimatorController**.
- Create a state called **Die**.

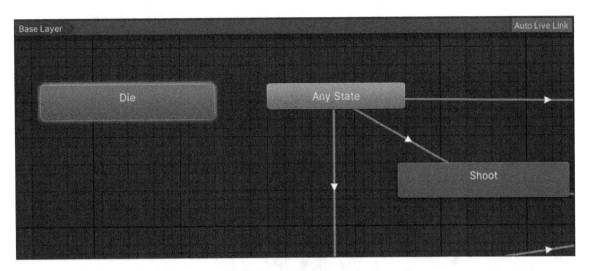

- Link it to the animation called dying.

- Create a **Boolean** parameter called **lowHealth**.
- Create a transition between the state **Any State** and the state **Die**.
- For this transition, using the **Inspector**, set the condition to **lowHealth = True**.

- For this same transition, set the attribute **Settings | Can Transition To Self** to **false**.

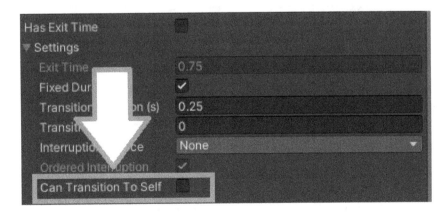

So that other transitions do not fire when we are in the state **Die**, we will need to ensure that the other transitions are triggered only if the parameter **lowHealth** is false.

- Select the transition between the states **Any State** and **Hit**.
- Using the **Inspector**, add the condition **lowHealth = false**.

- Do the same for the transition between the states **Any State** and **Shoot**.

- Do the same for the transition between the states **Any State** and **Punch**.

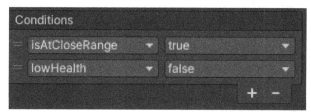

Once this is done, we just need to modify our code so that his transition to the state **Die** is triggered.

- Modify the function **Destroy**, in the script **ManageNPC** as follows (new code in bold):

```
public void Destroy()
{
        GetComponent<MoveRobot>().SetLowHealth();
        Destroy(gameObject, 4);
}
```

- Add this function to the script **MoveRobot**:

```
public void SetLowHealth ()
{
        anim.SetBool("lowHealth", true);

}
```

- Add this code to the **Update** function

```
if (info.IsName("Die") || info.IsName("Hit"))
{
          navmeshAgent.isStopped = true;
}
```

You can now save your code, and play the scene; after being hit several times, the NPC will fall to the ground.

USING A THIRD-PERSON VIEW

While we have been using a First-Person view in the last sections, it would be great to implement a Third-Person view, as it is a feature often found in games; so, in this section, we will do the following:

- Create a character for the player.
- Modify our scripts so that the 3D animated Player Character can move.
- Create and adjust animations for when the player is walking, shooting, or being hit.
- Modify the camera position so that it can follow the player smoothly over time.

CREATING OUR 3RD PERSON PLAYER CHARACTER

Please do the following:

- Deactivate the object called **Player** for now, and rename it **PlayerFP**.
- Drag and drop the object **FuseModel** from the **Project** window to the **Scene** view.

- This will create a new object called **FuseModel** in the **Hierarchy**; rename this new object **Player**.

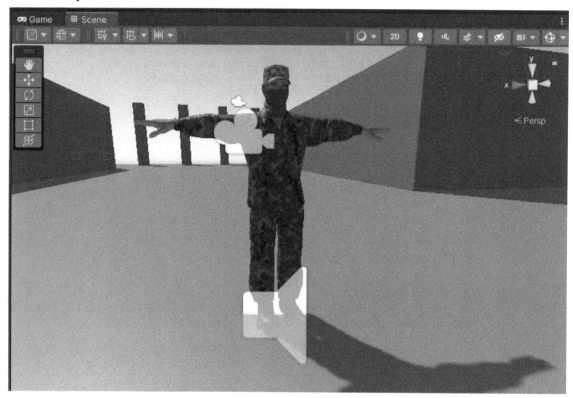

- Once this is done, please add the following script component to this object **Player**: **ManagePlayerHealth**, **ManageWeapons**, **BoxCollector**, **FPS Controller**.

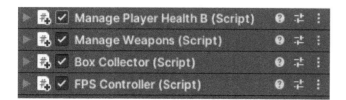

- Open the component **BoxCollector** and drag and drop the objects (from the Hierachy) **box1**, **box2**, **box3**, **box4**, and **transitionImage** to their corresponding slots, as illustrated in the next figure.

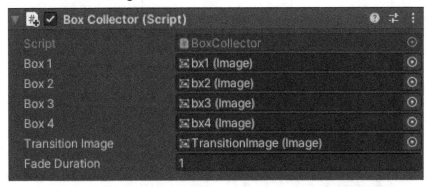

- Open the component **ManageWeapon** and drag and drop the prefab **grenade** to its corresponding slot.

- Add an **Audio Source** component and set its **AudioClip** property with the clip **gun_shot** (from the **Project** window).

- Add a **CharacterController** component to this object and set its attribute as follows: **Center = (0, 0.79, 0); Height = 1.7**.

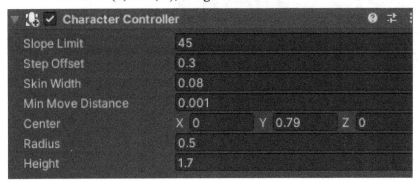

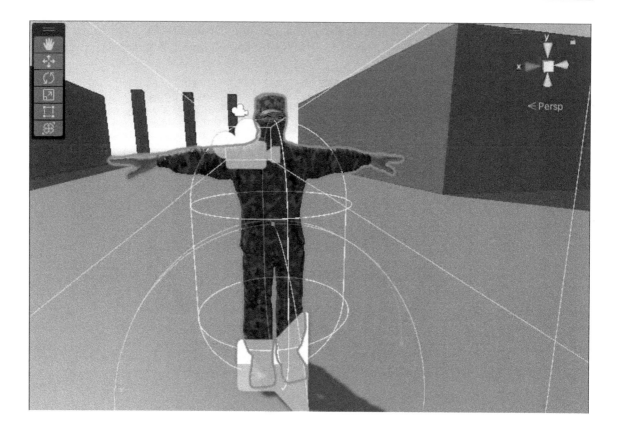

- Last but not least, using the **Hierarchy** window, copy the objects **playerCamera**, **launcher**, and **topView**.
- Right click on the object **Player** and select **Paste as Child** from the contextual menu.

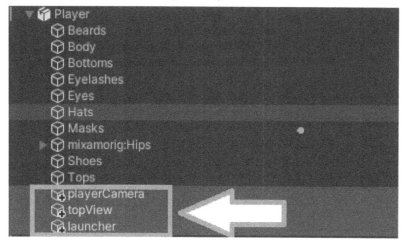

CREATING AND MANAGING A BLEND TREE

Next, we will create an Animator Controller that will manage the different animations for our player character.

- Create a new **AnimatorController** and rename it **PlayerAnimatorController**.
- Drag and drop it on the object **Player**, this will create an **Animator Component**.

Next, we will create states for the player; for this purpose we will create a **Blend tree**, a type of state that manages to blend 3D animations for a smooth transition between them; in our case, we will blend between the states **Idle** and **Walk**:

- Open the **AnimatorController PlayerAnimatorController**.
- Right click on the canvas and select the option **Create State | From New Blend Tree**.

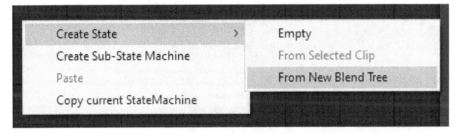

- This will create a state called **Blend Tree**.

- Double click on that state, a new window should appear, as per the next figure.

- In the **Parameters** section, create a new **float** parameter called **speed** by pressing the + button.

- Select the **blend tree**, and, using the **Inspector**, change the attribute **Parameter** to **speed**.

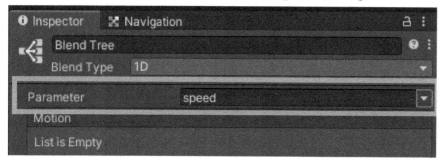

- In the **Inspector**, click on the + button located under the label **Motion**.

- Then select the option '**Add Motion Field**' from the contextual menu.

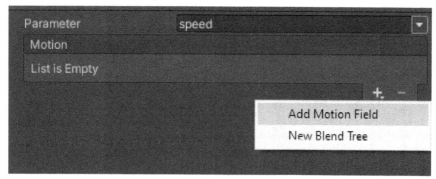

- This will create a new **Motion** field

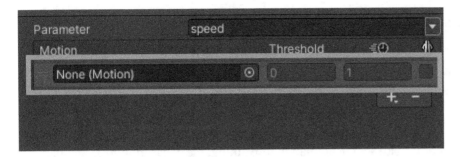

- Repeat the last steps to create three additional **Motion** fields (i.e., click on the + button)

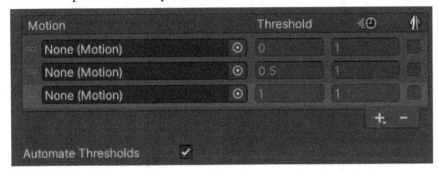

So far, we have created three **Motion** fields, these will refer to three distinct states between which we will apply blending.

In our case, we will need to use and blend animations for when the player is moving forward, back, and also when it is idle. So let's set up these fields.

- Untick the box for the option "**Automate Thresolds**".

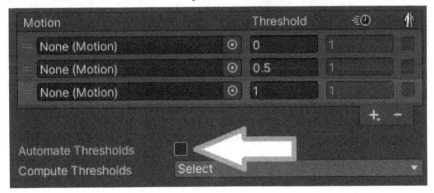

- Click on the cogwheel for the first **Motion** and select the animation **walking** from the contextual menu.

- Set the threshold to **-1** and the speed to **-1**.

- For the second **Motion** field: set the animation to **idle**, the **Threshold** to **0**, and the **speed** to **-1**.
- For the third **Motion** field: set the animation to **walking**, the T**hreshold** to **1**, and the **speed** to **1**.

- You should also see that the **Blend Tree** has been modified accordingly:

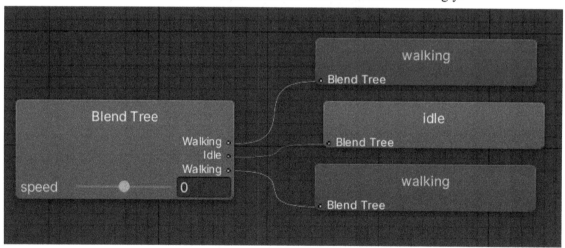

So, our blend tree is now set up and we just need to configure the code to interact with it.

- Click on the button labelled **Base Layer** (top-right corner of the **Animator** window), to return to the **Base Layer**.

- This will display the entire **Animator Controller**.

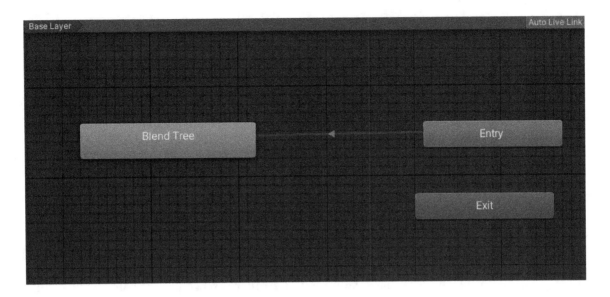

CONTROLLING THE BLEND TREE

Now that the **Blend Tree** has been created, it is time to control it from the code to make it possible to animate the player character:

- Open the script **FPSController** and add this code at beginning of the class.

```
Animator anim;
public float speed = 3.0F;
public float rotateSpeed = 3.0F;
```

In the previous code, we define three variables that will be used to animate, move and rotate the character.

- Add this code to the **Start** function:

```
GameObject.Find ("crossHair").SetActive(false);
anim = GetComponent<Animator>();
```

In the previous code, we deactivate the crosshair, since this is only meant to be used for the **First-Person Controller**. We also link our variable **anim** to the Animator component for the **Player** object, so that we can animate the player character.

Next, we are going to create a function that will control the player character; it is needed because the movement in the Third-Person view is quite different from the one in the First-Person mode as we won't be using **MouseLook** and the character's rotation will be handled with the arrow keys.

- Create a new function called **MovePlayer3rdP** and add this code to it:

```
private void MovePlayer3rdP()
{
        CharacterController controller = GetComponent<CharacterController>();
        transform.Rotate(0, Input.GetAxis("Horizontal") * rotateSpeed, 0);
        Vector3 forward = transform.TransformDirection(Vector3.forward);
        float curSpeed = speed * Input.GetAxis("Vertical");
        controller.SimpleMove(forward * curSpeed);
        print("Setting speed: " + speed);
        anim.SetFloat("speed", curSpeed);
}
```

In the previous code:

- We capture whether the player is pressing the arrows on the keyboard.
- The up and down arrow will determine the moving speed.
- The left and right arrows will serve to rotate the player around the y axis.
- The parameter **speed** from the **Animator Controller** is set so that the animation blending can occur. A negative value will move the character back, a null value will trigger the **idle** mode, and a positive value will move the character forward.
- Modify this code in the **Update** function as follows:

```
//MovePlayer();
//RotateCamera();
MovePlayer3rdP();
```

In this version of the player (Third-Person view) we use a different function to move the player (i.e., **MovePlayer**) and we no longer need the function **RotateCamera** as **MouseLook** is not used in the **Third-Person** view.

Next, we will create a function that will make it possible for the player to jump:

- Add this function

```
private void Jump()
{
        isGrounded = controller.isGrounded;
        if (isGrounded && velocity.y < 0)
        {
                velocity.y = -2f;
        }
        if (Input.GetButtonDown("Jump") && isGrounded)
        {
                velocity.y = Mathf.Sqrt(jumpHeight * -2f * gravity);
        }
        velocity.y += gravity * Time.deltaTime;
        controller.Move(velocity * Time.deltaTime);
}
```

In the previous code, we do the following:

- **Check if the player is on the ground**: Use a condition to determine whether the player is grounded, ensuring that actions like jumping are only allowed when the player is in contact with a surface.
- **Reset downward velocity**: When the player is grounded and has a downward velocity, the velocity is reset to a small value to keep the player grounded and prevent issues like sinking through the ground.
- **Trigger a jump**: Check if the jump button is pressed while the player is grounded. If so, calculate the upward velocity using a physics formula based on the jump height and gravity.
- **Apply gravity**: Continuously increase the downward velocity to simulate the effect of gravity pulling the player downward over time.
- **Move the character**: Use the character controller to move the player, applying the velocity updates for both jumping and gravity.

Overall, this code ensures that the player can jump when grounded, simulates realistic gravity, and applies smooth vertical movement during jumping and falling.

- Add this code to the Update function:

```
Jump();
```

Next, we will create a script that will serve to control and manage the camera attached to the player, so that it can follow the player.

- Create a new script called **MovePlayerCamera**.
- Attach this script to the object **playerCamera**.
- Add this code at the beginning of the class:

```
GameObject player;
```

- Add this code in the **Start** function:

```
player = GameObject.Find("Player");
```

- Add this function:

```
void MoveMode1()
{
        transform.LookAt(player.transform.position);
}
```

- Add this code to the **Update** function.

```
void Update()
{
        MoveMode1();
}
```

In the previous code, we make sure that the camera attached to the player is always looking at the player.

- Finally set the position of the object **playerCamera** to **(0, 3, -2)**.

You can now play your scene, and you should see that you can move the player character around while the camera is following your movement, as per the next figure.

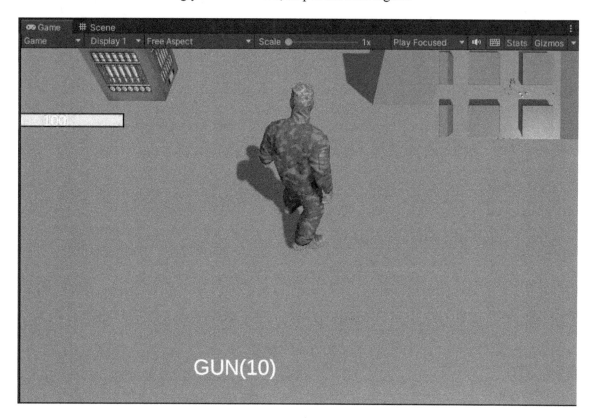

ADDIN CAMERA EFFECTS

While this works and while you can see the scene properly, from a **Third-Person** view, we will change the camera mode so that it follows the player more smoothly. For this purpose, we will use position interpolation, so that the camera can smoothly, and over time, move from its current position to being very close to the player, as a camera would do in most movies of cartoons; this creates a smoother and more realistic effect.

> The idea of position interpolation is to set a path (linear or not) between two points and to move an object along this path at regular intervals.

- Please open the script **MovePlayerCamera**.
- Add this code at the beginning of the class.

```
float speed = 0.5f;
```

- Add this code to the **Start** function:

```
gameObject.transform.parent = null;
```

In the previous code, we detach the camera from the player, since it will be moving around the scene to follow the player.

- Add this function:

```
void MoveMode2()
{

        float interpolation = speed * Time.deltaTime;
        Vector3 position = this.transform.position;
        Vector3 behindPlayer = player.transform.position - 3 * player.transform.forward + 3 *
Vector3.up;
        position.x = Mathf.Lerp(this.transform.position.x, behindPlayer.x, interpolation);
        position.z = Mathf.Lerp(this.transform.position.z, behindPlayer.z, interpolation);
        position.y = Mathf.Lerp(this.transform.position.y, behindPlayer.y, interpolation);
        this.transform.position = position;
        transform.LookAt(player.transform.position);

}
```

In the previous code:

- We determine at which speed the camera will move along its path.
- We define the starting and ending position (i.e., just behind the player) for the path followed by the camera.
- We then define the position of the camera, overtime, on the path defined earlier. The function **Mathf.Lerp** is used to perform the interpolation.
- We then ensure that the camera is always looking at the player.

Finally, we just need to call this new function every frame.

- Add this code to the **Update** function:

```
void Update()
{
        MoveMode1();
        //MoveMode2();
}
```

You can now save your code and play the scene, and you should see that the camera follows the player from a distance, always placed behind the player.

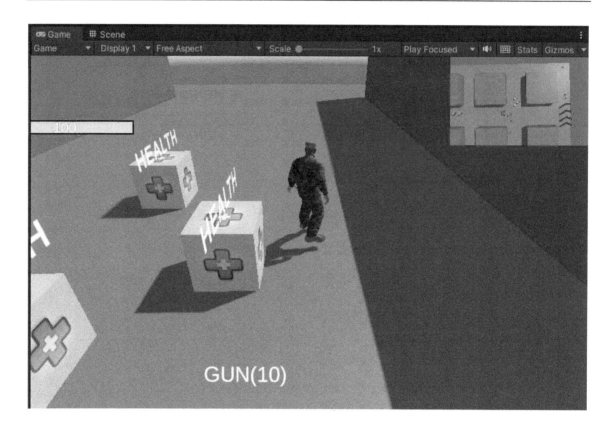

ADDING MORE ANIMATIONS FOR THE PLAYER CHARACTER

So, at this stage you can move around the scene using a third-person view with a camera that follows smoothly the character; this being said, we will also need to include and use animations for this character for when it is shooting and when it is being hit by an NPC.

First, we will update the corresponding **Animator Controller** to include states to be used when the player is shooting and when it is being hit by an NPC.

- Please open the Animator Controller **PlayerAnimatorController**.
- Create two new parameters: a trigger parameter called **gotHit**, and a trigger parameter called **startToShoot**.

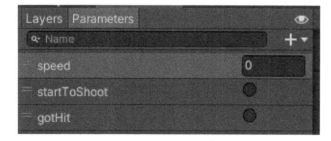

- Create two new states: **Hit** and **Fire**.

First, we will set up the transition for the state **Hit**.

- Create a transition between the states **AnyState** and **Hit**.
- Select that transition, and using the **Inspector**, set the condition for the transition to **gotHit** and the attribute **Settings | Can Transition To Self** to **False**.
- Create a transition between the states **Hit** and **Blend Tree**.

Next, we will set up the transition for the state **Fire**.

- Create a transition between the states **AnyState** and **Fire**.
- Select that transition, , and using the **Inspector**, set the condition for the transition to **startToSHoot** and the attribute **Settings | Can Transition To Self** to **False**.
- Create a transition between the states **Shoot** and **Blend Tree**.

So after setting up these two states, your **Animator Controller** will look like the following figure.

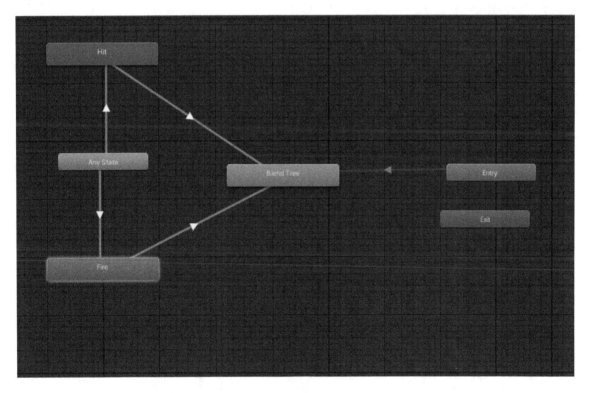

Now that we have set up the **Animator Controller**, its time to modify our code so that these transitions can be triggered when the player is hit and when it is firing the gun.

- Please add these two functions to the script **FPSController**:

```
public void SetGotGit()
{
        anim.SetTrigger("gotHit");
}
public void SetShoot()
{
        anim.SetTrigger("startToShoot");
}
```

In the previous code, we create two public functions (i.e., accessible from outside the class) that we will call whenever the player character is hit or shooting, so that the corresponding animations can be played; this will be done in the next code snippets:

- Please add this line to the function **DecreaseHealth** in the script **ManagePlayerHealth**.

```
GetComponent<FPSController>().SetGotGit();
```

- Add this code to the function **Update** in the class **ManageWeapons** (new code in bold):

```
if (Input.GetKey(KeyCode.F))
{
        GetComponent<FPSController>().SetShoot();
```

- You can now save your code and check that when you fire the gun, a shooting animation is played, as per the next figure.

You can also check that every time the player character is hit by the Non-Player Character, that the corresponding animation is played, as per the next figure.

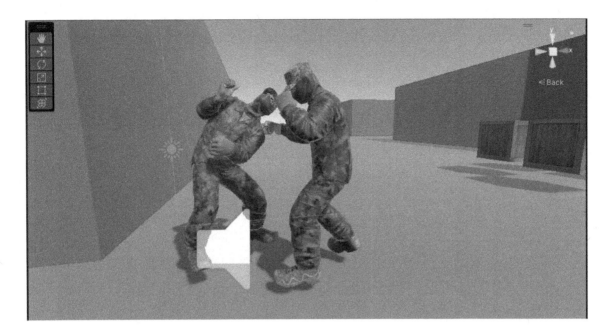

SUMMARY

So, well done! You have successfully mastered 3D character animations in this chapter. Throughout the last sections, you progressively implemented additional features that made your game more engaging and efficient. These included 3D animated characters, a third-person view, blend trees, a smooth camera-follow effect, and additional animations to enhance realism. You've covered a lot in this chapter, and your game now looks much more polished and realistic, thanks to the incorporation of 3D animations and camera effects.

QUIZ: TEST YOUR KNOWLEDGE

Please specify whether the following statements are True or False (the solutions are at the end of the book).

1. NavMesh navigation is used to create basic pathfinding for NPCs in a game.
2. A finite state machine (FSM) allows NPCs to transition between different behaviors based on their state.
3. Waypoints can only be fixed and cannot include random points for NPC navigation.
4. Assigning costs to areas in a navigation mesh enables NPCs to prefer or avoid specific paths.
5. Health bars in games only display the health of players, not NPCs.
6. Adding a screen flash effect enhances player feedback when damage is taken.
7. Random waypoints are used to create predictable NPC movement patterns.
8. Damage systems in games can be used for both players and NPCs to track health changes.
9. NavMesh areas with higher costs are typically preferred over lower-cost areas.
10. A health system for NPCs is often combined with visual cues like health bars to enhance gameplay.

CHALLENGE

For this challenge, you just need to do the following:

- Add more NPCs.
- Increase the initial speed of the player.
- Create random navigation for the NPCs, whereby they follow random waypoints.

7

ADAPTIVE GAMEPLAY

In the previous chapter, we explored techniques to enhance game dynamics through responsive systems, focusing on elements such as interactive NPC behaviors, health systems, and environmental interactions. These foundational mechanics added depth to the game, allowing players to experience a more engaging and immersive world.

This chapter, **Adaptive Gameplay**, builds on those mechanics to introduce intelligent systems that adjust the game environment and challenges based on player performance and progression. This approach ensures that the game provides the right balance of difficulty and enjoyment, keeping players engaged and motivated.

In this chapter, we will ensure that the player is challenged at the right level by the addition of a game level choice at the start, and by making sure that the game environment accounts for this; so, this will involve:

- Creating a splash screen where the player can choose the difficulty level.
- Saving the difficulty level and using it to amend the gameplay accordingly.
- Modifying game elements such as NPC speed, fire power, or intelligence based on the difficulty level.
- Adding helpers that will follow the player and also attack specific targets when ordered to so by the player

Together, these changes and additions will make your game more appealing, and responsive to the user's experience levels, as it is often found in video games.

SPAWNING ENEMIES

In this section, we will implement a mechanism through which enemies are added to the scene at regular intervals; this will increase the challenge and motivate the player to complete the level quickly before it becomes over crowed; for this purpose, we will just use an empty object with a script that instantiates NPCs at regular intervals; so let's get started:

- Please create a prefab from one of the NPCs in the scenes by dragging and dropping it to the **Project** window.
- If you see the following message, select the option '**Original Prefab**'.

Create Prefab or Variant?

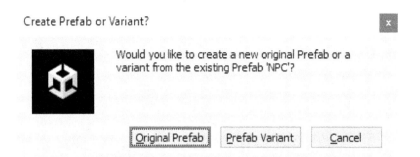

Would you like to create a new original Prefab or a variant from the existing Prefab 'NPC'?

| Original Prefab | Prefab Variant | Cancel |

- Create an empty new cube, deactivate its box collider and rename it **spwanNPCs**.
- Create a new script called **SpawnNPCs** and attach it to the object **spwanNPCs**.
- Open the script **SpawnNPCs** and add this code at the beginning of the class:

```
public GameObject NPC;
float timer;
GameObject newNPC;
spwanfrequency = 5;
```

- Then add this code in the **Update** function:

```
timer += Time.deltaTime;
if (timer > spawFrequency)
{
        newNPC = Instantiate(NPC, gameObject.transform.position, Quaternion.identity);
        newNPC.name = "NPC Clone";
        timer = 0;
}
```

In the previous code:

- We increase the value of the variable **timer** as time progresses.
- We check whether it's time to spawn a new NPC.
- If that's the case, we instantiate an NPC at the same position as the object attached to this script (i.e., the object **spawnNPC**).
- We also set the name of the new NPC and reset the **timer** variable to 0.

We can now add a reference to the **player** object:

- Add this code to the **Start** function in the script **RobotProjectileThrower**:

```
player = GameObject.Find("Player").transform;
```

You can now save your code, play the scene and check that new NPCs are spawn every five seconds, and that they follow the waypoints that we have created earlier.

ADDING RANDOM STARTING POINTS

Now that we have managed to instantiate NPCs at regular intervals, we will make sure that they start at random positions, to keep the player guessing; for this purpose, we will create four different spawning points, and select one at random to instantiate new NPCs.

- Please create four new cubes, set their tag to **spawningPoint**, deactivate their colliders, and place them far apart, for example in the four corners of the scene you have created.
- Open the script **SpawnNPCs**.
- Add this code at the beginning of the class:

```
GameObject [] spawningPoints;
```

- Add this code to the function **Start**.

```
spawningPoints = GameObject.FindGameObjectsWithTag("spawningPoint");
```

In the previous code, we initialize the array **spawningPoints** by including all the objects with the tag **spawningPoint**.

- Add this function

```
GameObject SelectSpawningPoint()
{
        return spawningPoints[Random.Range(0, spawningPoints.Length)];

}
```

In the previous function, we return one of the spawning points randomly, using the function **Random.Range**.

- Finaly, modify the **Udpate** function as follows:

```
//newNPC = Instantiate(NPC, gameObject.transform.position, Quaternion.identity);
newNPC = Instantiate(NPC, SelectSpawningPoint().transform.position, Quaternion.identity);
print("NPC Created at "+newNPC.transform.position);
```

In the previous code, we instantiate a new NPC using the position of the random spawning point returned by the function **SelectSpawningPoint**.

You can now save your code, play the scene and check that he NPCs are instantiated at different positions, by verifying the printouts in the **Console** window.

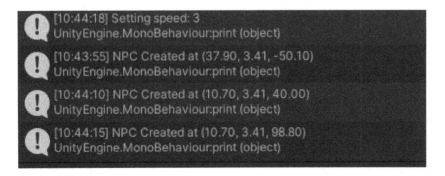

STARTING THE LEVEL IN RANDOM POSITIONS

Similarly to the previous section, we will make the game slightly different every time we start by placing the player in a different location every time the game restarts; this will challenge the players, as they can't guess where they will start the game and they will need to readjust their strategy accordingly.

- Please create two cubes, rename them **spawningPoint**, set them with the tag **spawningPoint**, and deactivate their components **Mesh Rendrer** and **Collider**.
- Place these boxes in strategic areas, for example, one near the second platform and one near the main platform.
- Open the script **FPSController**.
- Add this code at the beginning of the class

```
GameObject [] startingPoints;
```

- Create this new function:

```
GameObject SelectStartingPoint()
{
        return startingPoints [Random.Range(0, startingPoints.Length)];
}
```

- Add these lines to the function **Start**.

```
startingPoints = GameObject.FindGameObjectsWithTag("startingPoint");
transform.position = SelectStartingPoint().transform.position;
```

In the previous code we select a random starting point determined (or returned) by the function **SelectStartingPoint**, and we move the player to its location.

You can now save your code and play the scene; you should see that every time to restart the scene, your player character will be in a different location.

ADDING HEALTH PACKS AND AMMUNITIONS WHEN THE PLAYER NEEDS IT

In this section, we will add a feature through which health packs will be added to the level at regular intervals; the idea here is to help the player by detecting when there is only a few health packs left and to then instantiate additional ones; so, the process will be as follows:

- Create random spawning points for health packs.
- Scan the number of health packs available in the level at regular intervals.
- When there is no health pack, instantiate a new health pack at a random location.

Let's start to create the object that will spawn health packs:

- Create an empty object called **spawnHealthPacks**.
- Create a script called **SpawnHealthPacks** and attach it to that object.
- Open the script.
- Add this code at the beginning of the class:

```
float timer, spawnFrequency = 5;
GameObject [] HPSpawningPoints;
public GameObject healthPack;
int nbSpawningPoints, randomLocationNumber;
```

- Add this code to the **Start** function.

```
HPSpawningPoints = GameObject.FindGameObjectsWithTag("HPSpawningPoint");
```

In the previous code, we identify and save all the objects with the tag **health_pack** into the array **HPSpawningPoints**.

- Add this function:

```
void SpawnPacks()
{
        Vector3 spawnLocation;
        nbSpawningPoints = GameObject.FindGameObjectsWithTag("HPSpawningPoint").Length;
        randomLocationNumber = Random.Range(0,nbSpawningPoints);
        spawnLocation = HPSpawningPoints[randomLocationNumber].transform.position;
        Instantiate(healthPack, spawnLocation, Quaternion.identity);
        print("Just Added 1 Health Pack");
}
```

In the previous code, we instantiate a health pack at a random position using one of the spawning points defined earlier.

- Add this code to the function **Update**:

```
void Update()
{
        timer += Time.deltaTime;
        //if (timer >= SPAWN_TRIGGER_TIME * PlayerPrefs.GetInt("difficultyLevel"))
        if (timer > spawnFrequency)
        {
                print("Checking Health Packs");
                if (GameObject.FindGameObjectsWithTag("health_pack").Length < 1)
                {
                        SpawnPacks();

                }
                timer = 0;
        }
}
```

In the previous code, we create a timer for which the value will increase overtime; once it has reached the threshold **spawnFrequency**, we check whether there are health packs in the scene; if that's not the case, we instantiate a new health pack.

- You can now save your code.
- Make sure that the script is attached to the object **spawnHealthPacks**.
- Create an object called **HPSpawnPoint** and set its tag to 'HPSpawningPoint'.

- Duplicate this object and place these duplicates in different locations.
- Select the object **HPSpawnPoint**, and use the **Inspector** to drag and drop the prefab **health_pack** to the placeholder **health pack**, as per the next figure.

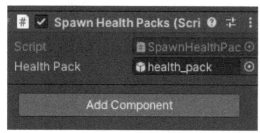

You can now play the scene, check that the message '**Checking Health Packs**' is displayed regularly in the **Console** window. You can also remove (or deactivate) all the health packs in the scene, wait for 5 seconds, and check that a new heal pack has been created, along with the message '**Just Added 1 Health Pack**' in the **Console** window.

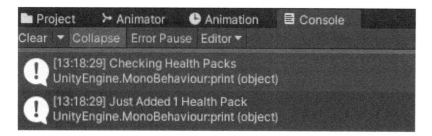

ADDING DIFFICULTY LEVELS

In the previous section, we have managed to improve the game play by adding randomized events, such as the addition of health packs in different locations, or a random starting point for the player; while these can really improve the game play, it would also be great to make sure that the player can choose, from the start, a difficulty level, and then modify the gameplay accordingly.

So, in this section, we will do the following:

- Create a splash screen where the player can choose the level of difficulty (i.e., easy, medium or advanced).
- Save this choice.
- Adjust the game play so that several aspects of the game reflect this preference (e.g., the speed of the NPCs, the frequency for the health packs spawning, or the damage inflicted by the NPC).

By managing to implement this feature, we will be able to offer an experience that is adapted to the player's level of proficiency, ensuring that the challenge is appropriate and that it keeps the player motivated.

First, we will create a splash screen:

- Save your current scene.

- Create a new scene.
- Save it as called **splashScreen** (i.e., select **File | Save Scene As**).
- Open that scene.
- Create a new empty object called **manageButtons**.
- Create a new script called **ManageButtons** and attach it to the object **manageButtons**.
- Open the script.
- Add this code at the beginning of the script:

```
using UnityEngine.SceneManagement;
```

- Add this function:

```
public void LoadScene (int level)
{
        PlayerPrefs.SetInt("difficultyLevel", level);
        SceneManager.LoadScene("level1");
}
```

In the previous code:

- We define a public function that will be accessible from outside the class.
- It takes one parameter that will be used to set the difficulty level.
- When called, this function sets the difficulty level, and it also loads the first level.

PlayerPrefs is a simple data storage system in Unity used to save and retrieve small amounts of data, such as player preferences, settings, or game progress. It stores data as key-value pairs and is ideal for saving information like volume settings, high scores, or user preferences.

Once this is done, we just need to create the three buttons that will make it possible to choose the difficulty level.

- Create a new button (**GameObject | UI | Button Text-Mesh Pro**)
- Rename this button **btEasy.**
- Set its text to '**Easy**': select the child object of the object **btEasy** called **Text (TMP)** and then change the attribute **TextMeshPro | Text Input** to "**Easy**".

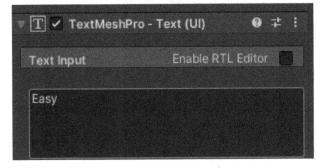

- Select the button (i.e., the object **btEasy**).

- In the **Inspector**, scroll to the bottom and click on the + button (below the label **List is Empty**).

- This will create a new empty placeholder.

- Drag and drop the empty object **manageButtons** to the empty field, as per the next figure.

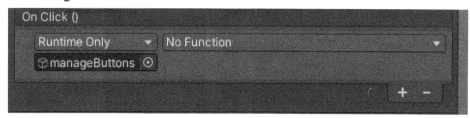

- From the drop-down menu labelled '**No Function**', select, **ManageButtons | LoadScene**.

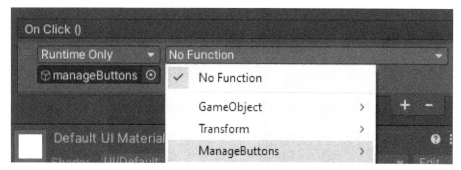

- Type the number **1** in the field to the right.

- Switch to the 2D mode to see the button in the Scene View.

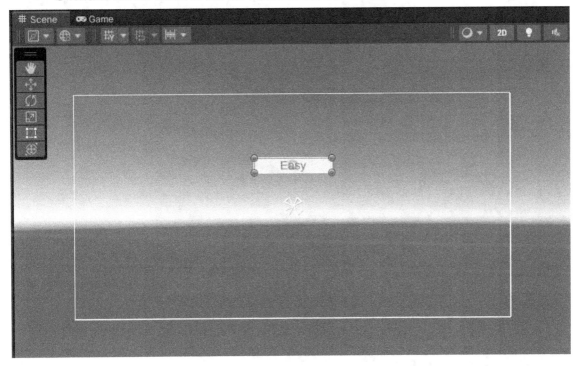

So altogether, we have specified that if the player presses this button, we call (and pass the value 1 to) the function called **Loadscene** from the script **Managebuttons**, to specify that we are selecting the **Easy** level.

Once this is done, you can create two additional buttons (e.g., by duplicating the button **btEasy**) named **btMedium** and **btAdvanced**, with labels called '**Medium**' and '**Advanced**' and associated with the values **2**, and **3** respectively.

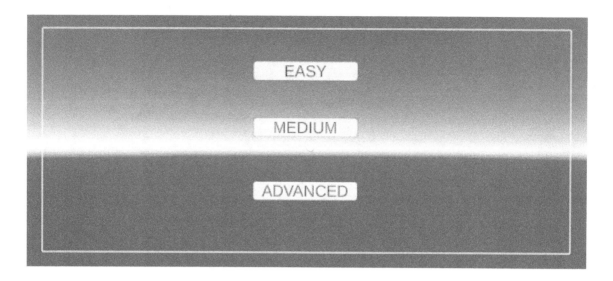

- Make sure that for the **Medium** button, you pass **2** to the function **ManageButtons**, as per the next figure.

- Also make sure that for the **Advanced** button, you pass **3** to the function **ManageButtons**, as per the next figure.

Once this is done, we just need to make sure that the scene to be loaded (i.e., **level1**) is included in the **Build Settings**, and we also need to check that the player preferences have been saved properly after pressing one of the buttons.

First, let's configure the **Build Settings**:

- Open the **Build Settings** window: Select **File | Build Settings**.
- Drag and drop the main scene (the one we have been working on in the previous chapters) from the **Project** folder to the **Build Settings** window.
- Make sure that **level1** and **level2** are both present and selected (i.e., ticked) in that window.

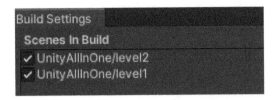

- You can now close the **Build Settings**.

Last but not least, we will add some code in **level1** to print the current difficulty level and therefore check that it was saved properly.

- Open the script **ManageNPC**.
- Add this code to the **Start** function:

```
print ("Current Level is: " + PlayerPrefs.GetInt("difficultyLevel"));
```

- Save the code, and check that it is error-free.
- Open the **splashScreen** scene and play that scene; after selecting the **Beginner** level, the main scene should open and you should see a message in the **Console** window that confirms your choice, as per the next figure.

Now that we know that the difficulty level is saved properly, we will amend some of the scripts in our game so that the difficulty level applies to several areas including:

- The starting health amount for the NPCs.
- The NPCs speed.
- The fire power of the NPCs (i.e., the damage they can apply).
- The detection radius for each NPC.
- The spawning frequency for the health packs.

Let's start with the NPCs health and resistance:

- Open the script **ManageNPC**:
- Add this code at the beginning of the class:

```
int difficultyLevel;
```

- Add this code at the beginning of the **Start** function:

```
difficultyLevel = PlayerPrefs.GetInt("difficultyLevel");
health = 100 * difficultyLevel;
```

In the previous code we increase the health of the NPC proportionally to the difficulty level; so, the more advanced the level and the more difficult the NPC will be to eliminate (i.e., greater health).

- In the same script, modify the function **GotHit** as follows:

```
public void GotHit()
{
        health -= (50 - difficultyLevel *10);
        GetComponent<MoveRobot>().SetHitReaction();
}
```

In the previous code, we make sure that the more advanced the difficulty level and the less damage the NPCs take when they are hit.

Next, we will modify the speed of each NPC based on the difficulty level:

- Open the script **MoveRobot**:
- Write this code at the end of the function **Start**.

```
navmeshAgent.speed *= PlayerPrefs.GetInt("difficultyLevel");
```

In the previous code, we make sure that the speed of the NPCs will increase with game difficulty.

Next let's look into the fire power of the NPCs (i.e., the damage they can apply):

- Open the script **Projectile**.
- Add this code at the beginning of the class:

```
int difficultyLevel;
```

- Add this code in the **Start** function:

```
difficultyLevel = PlayerPrefs.GetInt("difficultyLevel");
```

- In the function **OnCollisionEnter** change this line...

```
collision.gameObject.GetComponent<ManagePlayerHealth>().DecreaseHealth(10);
```

- with this line...

```
collision.gameObject.GetComponent<ManagePlayerHealth>().DecreaseHealth(10 * difficultyLevel);
```

- Open the script **Punches**:
- Change this line...

```
GameObject.Find("Player").GetComponent<ManagePlayerHealth>().DecreaseHealth(5);
```

- with this line...

```
GameObject.Find("Player").GetComponent<ManagePlayerHealth>().DecreaseHealth(5 *
PlayerPrefs.GetInt("difficultyLevel"));
```

Next, we will modify the detection radius for the NPCs:

- Open the script **MoveRobot**.
- Change this code in the **Update** function...

```
if(Vector3.Distance(transform.position,player.transform.position) < 1.5)
```

- with this code...

```
if(Vector3.Distance(transform.position,player.transform.position) < 1.5 *
PlayerPrefs.GetInt("difficultyLevel"))
```

In the previous code, advanced NPCs can detect the player from a greater distance.

The last aspect of the game that needs to be modified is the spawning frequency for both the NPCs and the health packs. As the difficulty level increases, we want the NPCs to be spawn more frequently and health packs to be checked and spawn less frequently.

- Open the script **SpawnNPCs**.
- Add this line at the end of the **Start** function.

```
spawnFrequency /= PlayerPrefs.GetInt("difficultyLevel");
```

- Open the script **SpawnHealthPacks**.
- Add this code at the end of the **Start** function:

```
spawnFrequency *= PlayerPrefs.GetInt("difficultyLevel");
```

You can now save your scripts, check that they are error-free and play the scene. As you do, please check the following:

- Play the **splashScreen** scene several times, choosing a different option every time; for example, start at a **Beginner** level and then move up to an **Advanced** level.
- Observe how the NPCs' speed and detection accuracy increases as you select higher levels of difficulty.
- Also check that they are more difficult to eliminate.

ADDING HELPERS

So, so far, we have managed to include different levels of difficulty for the player, and to make sure that the challenge is adjusted accordingly; in this section, we will create helpers; these are often found in video games, and they are NPCs that assist, follow and support the player throughout the game.

We will create three helpers, who will initially follow the player, and then follow orders to either attack an NPC controlled by the game AI or withdraw from the battle. This will add another layer of complexity to the game and the ability for the player to handle many enemy NPCs thanks to its own army.

In this new scene, we will create NPCs that follow a particular character that we will refer to as **the leader**; in this particular case, the leader will be the player, so the NPCs will follow the player, and stop walking whenever they are close to the player. For this purpose, we will complete the following tasks:

- Create friendly NPCs (i.e., helpers).
- Create a finite state machine for these NPCs.
- Coordinate the movement of the NPCs as a group.

So, let's get started:

- Open the scene **level1**.
- From the folder called **military**, that you have imported in Unity in the previous chapters, select the prefab called **FuseModel** and drag and drop it to the scene; this will create a new object called **FuseModel**; rename this object **teamMember**.

- Place it above the **ground**.
- Select the object **teamMember** and add a **NavMesh Agent** component to it (i.e., select **Component | Navigation | NavMeshAgent**). This will be necessary so that the NPCs can navigate the scene.

Next, we will create an **Animator Controller** that will be used for the helper NPCs.

- From the **Project** menu, select **Create | Animator Controller**. This will create an asset called **New Animator Controller**; please rename this asset **teamMember**.
- Open this **Animator Controller** by double-clicking on it.
- Create a new state called **Idle** and associate the animation **idle** with this state.
- Then create another state called **moveTowardsLeader**,and associate the animation **walking** to this state.
- Create a new **Boolean** parameter called **closeToLeader**. This parameter will be used to determine when the NPC is close to its leader.
- Create a transition from the state **Idle** to the state **MoveTowardsLeader** and use the condition **closeToLeader=false** as a condition for the transition. So, the NPC will walk towards the leader until it is close enough.
- Create a transition from the state **MoveTowardsLeader** to the state **idle** and use the condition **closeToLeader=true** as a condition for the transition, as illustrated in the next figure.

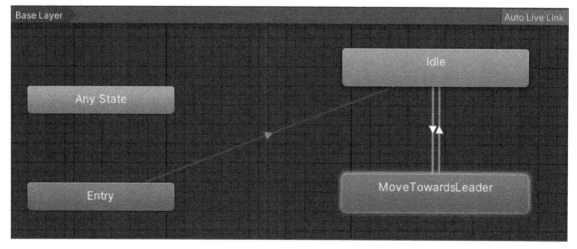

- You can now drag and drop the **Animator Controller** called **teamMember** to the object called **teamMember**. This will create a new **Animator** component for the object **teamMember, as** illustrated in the next figure.

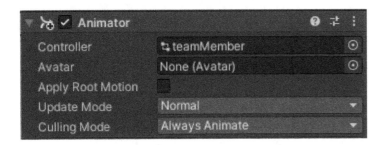

Now that we have set up the **Animator Controller**, we will create a script that will be employed to trigger transitions between the two states that we have defined earlier.

- Please create a new C# script and rename it **TeamMember**.
- Drag and drop this script on the object called **teamMember**.
- Open the script.
- Add this code at the beginning of the script:

```
using UnityEngine.AI;
```

- Add the following code at the beginning of the class.

```
GameObject leader;
Animator anim;
AnimatorStateInfo info;
float distanceToLeader;
```

- Modify the **Start** method as follows (new code in bold)

```
void Start ()
{
        anim = gameObject.GetComponent<Animator>();
        leader = GameObject.Find ("Player");
}
```

In the previous code, we create a reference to the **Animator Controller** linked to the NPC and we also define the object that will act as a leader for this NPC. In this particular case, the player will be the leader; so, in other words, this type of NPC will be following the player.

- Please add the following code to the **Update** function (new code in bold).

```
void Update ()
{
        info = anim.GetCurrentAnimatorStateInfo(0);
        distanceToLeader = Vector3.Distance (leader.transform.position,
gameObject.transform.position);
        if (distanceToLeader < 5.0f)
                anim.SetBool ("closeToLeader", true);
        else anim.SetBool ("closeToLeader", false);
```

In the previous code:

- We update the variable called **info** so that we can detect the current (or active) state.
- We calculate the distance between the NPC and the leader (i.e., the **player**).
- If this distance is greater than **5 meters**, then we set the Boolean parameter **closeToLeader** (from the Animator Controller) to **true**; otherwise, this parameter is set to **false**.

We can now add the code that will be executed when we are in the states called **Idle** or **MoveTowardsPlayer**.

- Please add the following code just after the code that you have added in the **Update** function.

```
if (info.IsName ("Idle"))
{
        GetComponent<UnityEngine.AI.NavMeshAgent> ().isStopped = true;
}
if (info.IsName ("MoveTowardsLeader"))
{
        GetComponent<NavMeshAgent> ().SetDestination (leader.transform.position);
        GetComponent< NavMeshAgent> ().isStopped = false;
}
```

In the previous code:

- If we are in the state called **Idle**, we ensure that the navigation is not active for the NPC; in other words, it will be stopped.
- If we are in the state called **MoveTowardsLeader**, we set the destination (or the target) to be the leader (i.e., the player); we also ensure that the navigation resumes.

You can now save this script and drag and drop it to the object called **teamMember** (if not done yet). So, at this stage, we have implemented most of the features that will make it possible for the friendly NPCs to follow the player.

If you have not already done so, please bake the scene, so that navigation can be performed correctly.

Finally, when this is done, we can create a prefab from our friendly **NPC** and create duplicates to create a team of helper NPCs that share the same features.

- Please create a prefab from the object called **teamMember** and rename this prefab **teamMember**.

- If you see the following message appearing as you drag and drop your object to the **Project** window, select the option **Original Prefab**.

- Drag the prefab **teamMember** twice to the scene; this will create three additional objects called **teamMember(1)**, **teamMember(2)**, and **teamMember(3)**.

Lastly, to make sure that the friendly NPCs can be identified easily, we will add a small green disc just above their heads:

- Please open the **teamMember** prefab.
- Right-click on the object **teamMember** and select: **3D Object | Cylinder**. This should create a new cylinder as a child of the object **teamMember**.
- Change its color to **green** (after creating a new material or reusing an existing one).
- Change its scale to **(0.3, 0.01, 0.3)**.
- Move it slightly above the NPC's head, for example at the position **(0, 1.83, 0)**.
- After these modifications, your prefab should look like the following figure:

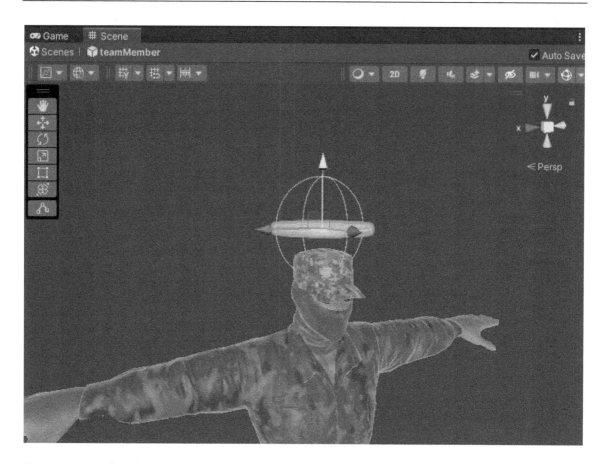

You can now play the scene; you should see that the NPCs follow the player and stop once they are about five meters away from the player.

ATTACKING SEVERAL TARGETS AS A GROUP

In this section, we will start to coordinate group attacks as follows: The leader will order the team members to launch an attack, and every team member will be attacking one target.

So, let's go ahead!

- Please open the **Animator Controller** called **teamMember** (i.e., from the **Project** window).
- Create a sub-state machine called **Attack-one-to-one** (i.e., right-click on the canvas and select **Create Sub-State Machine**).

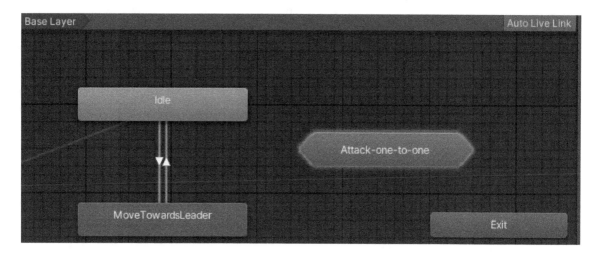

- Double-click on this sub-state machine (i.e., **Attack-one-to-one**) to open it.
- Create two states within: a state called **GoToTarget**, and then a state called **AttackTarget**.
- Associate the animation **walking** to the state **GoToTarget** and the animation called **punching** to the state called **AttackTarget**.
- You will need to edit the **punching** animation to set the attribute **Loop Pose** and **Loop Time** to true, so that it loops indefinitely, as we have done earlier for the walking animation.
- Create a **Boolean** parameter called **closeToTarget**.
- Create a transition from the state **GoToTarget** to the state **AttackTarget** using the condition **closeToTarget=true**.
- Create a transition from the state **AttackTarget** to the state **GoToTarget** using the condition **closeToTarget=false**.
- Once this is done, your **Animator Controller** should look like the next figure.

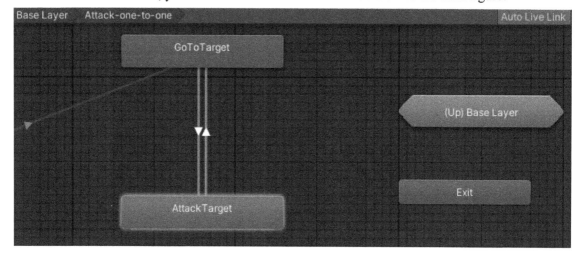

- Create a new **Trigger** parameter called **attackOneToOne**.
- We will be using this parameter to create a transition between the **Idle** state and the sub-state machine **Attack-one-to-one**.
- In the **Animator** window, click on the tab called **Base Layer**.

- Create a transition from the state **Idle** to the sub-state machine: right-click on the state **Idle** and select the option **Make Transition** from the contextual menu.
- Then click on the sub-state machine called **Attack-one-to-one** and select the option: **States | GoToTarget**, as illustrated in the next figure. This means that the transition is made from the state **Idle** to the state **GoToTarget** that is within the sub-state machine called **Attack-one-to-one**.

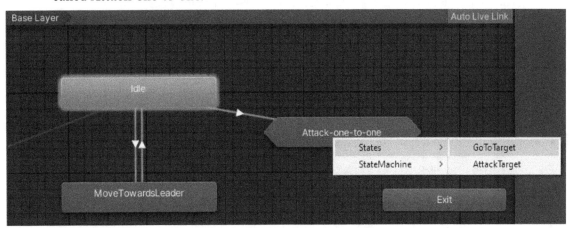

- As you open (i.e., double click on) the sub-state machine, you should see that the new transition appears from a state called **(Up) Base Layer** as illustrated in the next figure.

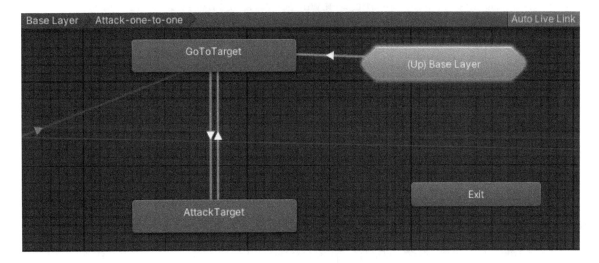

- Select the transition that you have just created and set the condition to **attackOneToOne**.

Now that our sub-state machine has been configured, we can start to modify the script for the NPC to specify what should be done in the different states that we have defined in the sub-states.

- Please open the script **TeamMember**.
- Add this code at the beginning of the class.

```
GameObject target;
float distanceToTarget;
```

In the previous code:

- We define two variables: **target** and **distanceToTarget**.
- The first variable will define the target that the NPC has to attack.
- The second variable will be used to determine whether the NPC is close enough to the target to start attacking; it will also be used to set the corresponding parameter in the **Animator Controller**.

Now that these variables have been defined, we can define a few methods that will be used to control the friendly NPCs.

- Please, add the following method to the script **TeamMember**.

```
public void Attack (GameObject t)
{
        target = t;
        anim.SetTrigger ("attackOneToOne");
}
```

In the previous code:

- We define a method called **Attack**.
- Note that this method is **public**; so it will be accessible from outside the class.
- This method will be accessed by the leader, when sending an order (to attack a target) to the NPC. The target will be defined by the leader (not the NPC), so that a group attack can be coordinated easily.
- When the method is called, the target is defined and the trigger parameter **attackOneToOne** is also set.

We can now define the actions to be performed in the states present in the sub-state machine.

- Please add the following code in the **Update** method within the script **TeamMember**:

```
if (info.IsName ("GoToTarget"))
{
        GetComponent<NavMeshAgent> ().SetDestination (target.transform.position);
        GetComponent<NavMeshAgent> ().isStopped = false;
        distanceToTarget = Vector3.Distance (target.transform.position, gameObject.transform.position);

        if (distanceToTarget < 2.0f) {
                anim.SetBool ("closeToTarget", true);
                GetComponent< NavMeshAgent> ().isStopped = true;
        }
        else anim.SetBool ("closeToTarget", false);
}
```

In the previous code:

- We check that we are in the state called **GoToTarget**.
- The destination is set for the NPC.
- The NPC moves towards the target until it is close enough.

Now, let's define the actions for the state **AttackTarget**.

- Please add the following code to the **Update** method:

```
if (info.IsName ("AttackTarget"))
{
        GetComponent<NavMeshAgent> ().isStopped = true;
        distanceToTarget = Vector3.Distance (target.transform.position, gameObject.transform.position);
        if (distanceToTarget > 2.0f)
        {
                anim.SetBool ("closeToTarget", false);
                GetComponent< NavMeshAgent> ().isStopped = false;
        }
}
```

In the previous code, the NPC will stop moving forward as soon as it is in the state called **AttackTarget**. However, if the distance between the helper and the enemy NPC is greater than **3**, then we make sure that the helper follows the enemy NPC.

You can now save your script. Now that we have defined how the NPCs should behave when receiving orders to attack, we just need to create a communication channel between the leader and the NPCs, so that the latter can receive orders from the former; this will consist in:

- Identifying all team members.
- Detecting when orders need to be sent to the team members.
- Allowing the player to send orders to these members.

First, let's create a script that will be used to establish communication between the leader and the other team members.

- Please create a new C# script called **Leader**.
- Drag and drop this script on the object called **Player**.
- Open the script.
- Add this code at the beginning of the class.

```
GameObject [] teamMembers;
GameObject[] allTargets;
int nbTeamMembers, nbTargets, nbBattles;
```

In the previous code, we define several variables.

- **teamMembers** will include all the team members in the scene.
- **Alltargets** will include all the enemy NPCs in the scene (they all have a tag called target).
- **nbTeamMembers** will be the total number of helpers in the scene.
- **nbTargets** will be the total number of targets (enemy NPCs) in the scene.

- **nbBattles** will be used to define how we pair-up friendly NPCs and their targets.

We can now add the code to identify the team members and send them orders.

- Please add this function:

```
void Attack()
{
        teamMembers = GameObject.FindGameObjectsWithTag("teamMember");
        allTargets = GameObject.FindGameObjectsWithTag("target");
        print("Battle Mode: Found " + nbTargets + " targets and " + nbTeamMembers + "members");
        nbTeamMembers = teamMembers.Length;
        nbTargets = allTargets.Length;
        nbBattles = nbTeamMembers;
}
```

In the previous code: we look for all the NPCs that are part of the team, based on their tag, and add them to the array called **teamMembers**; we also store the number of NPCs in this team. We do the same for the targets, storing them in the array called **alltargets**, and storing their number in the variable **nbTargets**.

Now that we have identified the NPCs that are part of the team, and the targets, we can add the code to send them orders.

- Please add this code to the function **Attack**:

```
if (nbTeamMembers > nbTargets) nbBattles = nbTargets;


for (int i = 0; i < nbBattles; i++)
{
        teamMembers[i].GetComponent<TeamMemberB>().Attack(allTargets [i]);
}
```

In the previous code:

- We check whether we have more friendly NPCs than targets.
- We then select the corresponding NPCs and ask each of them to attack a target, by accessing one of their public methods called **Attack**.

We could customize this script to account for the fact that there could be more targets than NPCs or vice-versa; however, for the time being, we will assume (and set-up our environment accordingly) that there is one target for each NPC.

The only thing that we need to do now, is to trigger attacks; in our case, this will be done when the player presses the **P** key on the keyboard.

- Please add the following code to the **Update** function in the script called **Leader** (new code in bold):

```
void Update ()
{
        if (Input.GetKeyDown (KeyCode.P))
        {
                Attack ();
        }
}
```

- Please deactivate the static targets that we created in the previous chapters (cubes with a **target** tag).

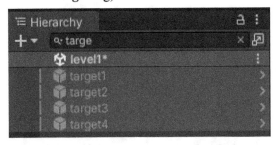

- Save your script and play the scene (after checking that you have added the script called **Leader** to the object called **player**). The NPC will start to gather around the player. As you press the **P** key, the NPCs will start to go towards and attack enemy NPCs.

You may notice that while the helpers start to hit an enemy NPC, the latter keeps walking, which is not a realistic behavior; instead, we would expect the NPC to stop and fight back.

So, we need to modify the behavior of the enemy NPCs to implement just this:

- Open the AnimatorController **RobotAnimatorController**.
- Add a Trigger variable called **gotHitByHelper**.
- Add a Boolean parameter called **closeToHelper**.

- Add a Trigger variable called **startPatrol**.

- Create a sub-state machine called **Chase_Helper**.

- Double click on it to open it.
- Create two states within the sub-state machine: **Follow_Helper** and **Attack_Helper**.
- Associate the animation **walking** to the state **Follow_Helper**, and the animation **punching** to the state **Attack_Helper**.
- Create transitions between these states.

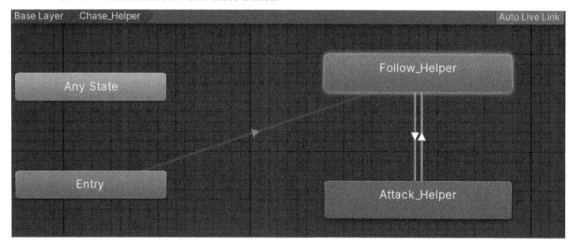

- Set the condition for the transition from the states **Follow_Helper** to **Attack_Player** to **closeToHelper = true**.
- Set the condition for the transition from the states **Attack_Player** to **Follow_Helper** to **closeToHelper = false**.

- Create a transition from the state **Any State** to **Follow_Helpers** and set the condition to **gotHitByHelper**.
- Also ensure that for this transition, the attribute **Settings | Can Transition >To Self** is set to **False** (i.e., unchecked)
- Click on the button for the **Base Layer** (in the top-left corner of the **Animator** window).

Now that we have amended the **Animator Controller**, we will modify the code for both the helpers and the enemy NPCs to apply damage and set the NPCs to hit back.

- Open the script **MoveRobot**.
- Add this code at the beginning of the class.

```
GameObject helperTarget;
float distanceToHelperTarget;
```

- Add this code to the **Update** function:

```
if (info.IsName("Follow_Helper"))
{
        if (helperTarget != null )
        {
                target = helperTarget;
                navmeshAgent.SetDestination(target.transform.position);
                navmeshAgent.isStopped = false;
                if (distanceToHelperTarget < 3) anim.SetBool("closeToHelper", true);
                else anim.SetBool("closeToHelper", false);
        }
        else anim.SetTrigger("startPatrol");

}
```

In the previous code, we make sure that he we are following an existing target (i.e., that it has not been destroyed yet); in that case we move the NPC towards the helper and set it to attack the helper when the distance between them is less than **3** meters. If the target (i.e., the helper that had attacked the NPC first) has been destroyed then the NPC will resume the patrol.

- Add this code just after the previous code:

```
if (info.IsName("Attack_Helper"))
{
        if (helperTarget !=null )
        {

        }
        else anim.SetTrigger("startPatrol");
}
```

In the previous code, we check that we are in the state called **Attack_Helper**; we also check that the helper has not been destroyed yet; otherwise, the NPC resumes the patrol.

- Include the following code within the conditional statements that you have just added:

```
if (distanceToHelperTarget > 2) anim.SetBool("closeToHelper", false);
else anim.SetBool("closeToHelper", true);
if (info.normalizedTime % 1.0 >= .98)
{
        helperTarget.GetComponent<TeamMember>().DecreaseHealth(10 *
PlayerPrefs.GetInt("difficultyLevel"));
}
```

In the previous code we check whether the NPC is close to the helper that attacked it in the first place; if they are no longer close, we set the NPC to follow the helper by setting the attribute **closeToHelper** to false; Finally, as the animationslinked to that state moves on, we call the function **DecreaseHealth**, from the script **TeamMember** as we have reached 98% of the animation.

- Add this function to the script MoveRobot:

```
public void SetGotHitByHelper(GameObject g)
{
        anim.SetTrigger("gotHitByHelper");
        helperTarget = g;
}
```

In the previous code, the function **SetGotHitByHelper** takes a GameObject as a parameter, and sets the target from the NPC accordingly; it also sets the trigger parameter **gotHGitByHelper** to **true**, so that the NPC can start chasing and attacking the helper that attacked it in the first place.

Now that we have set up the NPC, let's look at the helpers so that these can apply damage to the NPCs:

- Open the Animator Controller **teamMember**.
- Add a new **Trigger** Parameter called **retreat**.
- Create a transition from the state **Any State** to the state **MoveTowardsLeader** and set the transition to **retreat**.

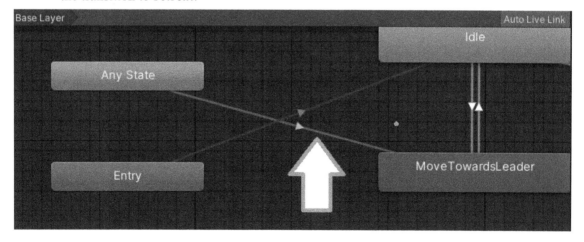

- Open the script **TeamMember**.

- Add this code at the beginning of the class.

```
int health = 100;
```

- Add this function:

```
public void DecreaseHealth (int amount)
{
        health -= amount;
        if (health <1) Destroy();
}
```

- Add this function:

```
void Destroy ()
{
        anim.SetTrigger ("lowHealth");
        Destroy (gameObject, 4);
}
```

- In the **Update** function, amend the code related to the state **GoToTarget** as follows (new code in bold):

```
if (info.IsName ("GoToTarget"))
{
        if (target!=null)
        {
                GetComponent<NavMeshAgent> ().SetDestination (target.transform.position);
                GetComponent<NavMeshAgent> ().isStopped = false;
                distanceToTarget = Vector3.Distance (target.transform.position,
gameObject.transform.position);
                if (distanceToTarget < 2.0f) {
                        anim.SetBool ("closeToTarget", true);
                        GetComponent< NavMeshAgent> ().isStopped = true;
                }
                else anim.SetBool ("closeToTarget", false);
        }
        else anim.SetTrigger("retreat");
}
```

- In the **Update** function, amend the code related to the state **AttackTarget** as follows (new code in bold):

```
if (info.IsName ("AttackTarget"))
{
        if (target!=null)
        {
                GetComponent<NavMeshAgent> ().isStopped = true;
                distanceToTarget = Vector3.Distance (target.transform.position,
gameObject.transform.position);
                target.GetComponent<ManageNPC>().GotHitByHelper(gameObject);

                if (distanceToTarget > 2.0f) {
                        anim.SetBool ("closeToTarget", false);
                        GetComponent< NavMeshAgent> ().isStopped = false;
                }
        }
        else anim.SetTrigger("retreat");
}
```

In both code snippets we ensure that the target has not been destroyed yet; if that's the case, the helper will follow its leader.

Add this code to the script ManageNPC:

```
public void GotHitByHelper(GameObject g)
{
        GotHit();
        GetComponent<MoveRobot>().SetGotHitByHelper(g);
}
```

You can now save both scripts, ensure that the script **Leader** is attached to the object **Player**, that each team member has the tag **teamMember** and test the scene. Press the **P** key so that the NPCs attack their respective targets; then press the **O** key; all NPCs should now retreat and follow the leader again.

POLISHING OUR LEVEL

While the game works, we will, in this section, polish it up by enhancing by doing the following:

- Enhancing the Splash-screen.
- Giving several lives to the player (and an opportunity to restart the level up to 3 times).
- An End screen that gives the opportunity to restart the game.
- Improved graphics for the game.

ENHANCING THE SPASH-SCREEN

Let's improve the spasl-screen:

- Open the scene **splashScreen**.
- Move the buttons at the bottom of the screen, as per the next figure.

- Add a new text element (**GameObject | UI | TextMeshPro-Text**), rename it **gameTitleText**, and set its text to **"Robot Escape"**.

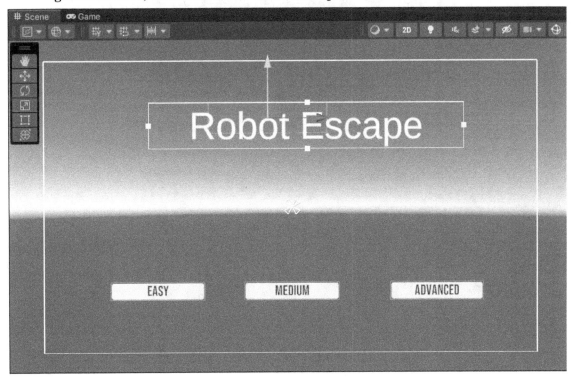

- Import the font **BebasNeue-Regular** from the resource pack: drag and drop this file to the **Project** folder.
- Select the object **gameTitleText**, and using the **Inspector**, click on the cogwheel to the right of the label **TextMeshPro | Main Settings | Font Asset**.

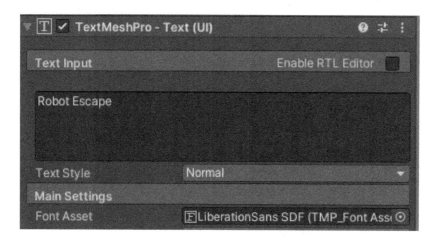

- Select the option **BebasNeue-Regular**.

- You should see that the font for the game title has now changed.

- Create a new text element, rename it **gameInstructions** set its text to "**Collect 4 Boxes and avoid Getting Killed.**", apply a font of your choice, and place it just below the title.

- Import the image **splashImage** from the resource pack.
- Select it in Unity and, using the **Inspector**, set its type to **Sprite (2D and UI)**.

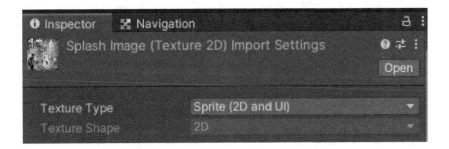

- Then press Apply (at the bottom of the Inspector window).
- Create a new Panel (**GameObject | UI | Panel**).
- Drag and drop this image to the attribute **Image | Source Image** for the object **Panel**.

- Click on the attribute **Color** just below the attribute **Source Image**.

- Set the color to white.

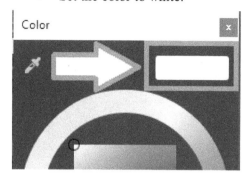

- Set the **transparency** (Alpha value) to **255**.

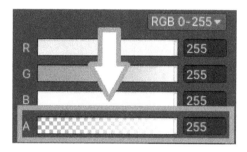

You should now see that the background of the splash-screen has changed.

CREATING THE END SCREEN

In this section we will create an end screen that will display either game over or congratulations based on whether the player has managed to collect the boxes or has used all of its lives.

- Duplicate the scene **splashScreen** and rename the duplicate **endScreen**.
- Open the scene **endScreen**.
- Rename the object **gameInstructions** to **endMessage**.
- Delete the buttons **btEasy** and **btAdvanced**.
- Change the name of the button **btMedium** to **btRestart**, and change its label to **Restart**.
- Change the text of the object **gameInstructions** to **Message**.

MODIFYING THE SCRIPTS

Once this is done, we will just need to modify some of our script to do the following:

- Set the number of lives to **3**.
- Decrease the number of lives of the player, and restart the current level every time the **health** has reached **0**.
- Detect when the players have collected four boxes or used all their lives, and load the scene **endScene** to display either "**Congratulations**" or "**Game Over**".

Let's start making these modifications:
- Open the script **ManageButtons**.

- Add this code at the beginning of the script.

```
using TMPro;
```

- Add this function:

```
public void RestartGame()
{
        SceneManager.LoadScene("splashScreenTechCheck");
}
```

- Select the object **btRestart**, using the **Inspector**, scroll down to the section 'OnClick' and set the function from **LoadScene** to **RestartGame**.
- Add the scene **splashScreen** to the **Build settings**, and play the scene; after pressing the **Restart** button, the splash-screen will be displayed.

Next, we will manage the message displayed:

- Add this line to the script **ManageButtons**.

```
string message="";
```

- Add this code to the Start function:

```
PlayerPrefs.SetString("endMessage", "GAME OVER");
if (SceneManager.GetActiveScene().name == "endScreen")
{
        message = PlayerPrefs.GetString("endMessage");
        GameObject.Find("endMessage").GetComponent<TextMeshProUGUI>().text = message;
}
```

- You can save your code and play the scene, and you should see the message "**Game Over**".

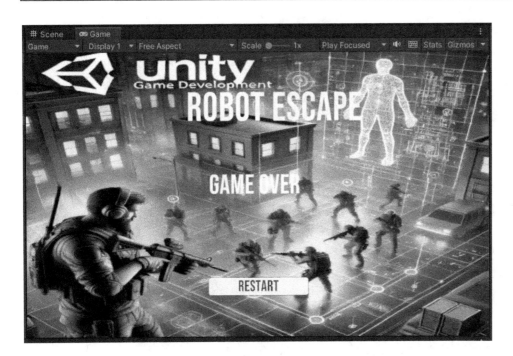

Next, we just need to detect when the player has either collected 4 boxes or ran out of lives:

- Add this code to the function **LoadScene** in the script **ManageButtons**:

```
PlayerPrefs.SetInt("nbLives", 3);
```

Open the script BoxCollector
Modify the function LoadScene as follows.

```
void LoadNewScene()
{
        Debug.Log("Load New Scene");
        //SceneManager.LoadScene("level2");
        //StartCoroutine(LoadSceneWithTransition("level2"));
        PlayerPrefs.SetString("endMessage", "CONGRATULATIONS!");
        SceneManager.LoadScene("endScreen");
}
```

In the previous code, we ensure that, after collecting 4 boxes, that we display the end screen with the corresponding message.

Next, we will look after the number of lives:

- Open the script **ManageButtons**.
- Add this code at the beginning of the function **LoadScene**.

```
PlayerPrefs.SetInt("nbLives", 3);
```

- Open the scene **level1** (the main scene).
- Import the image called **heart** from the resource pack.
- Set its **Type** attribute to **Sprite (2D and UI)**.
- Create a new Raw Image, and rename it heart.

- Set its **width** and **height** to **50**.
- Apply the **heart** image to its attribute **Texture**.

- In the **Scene** view, move this image near the health bar.

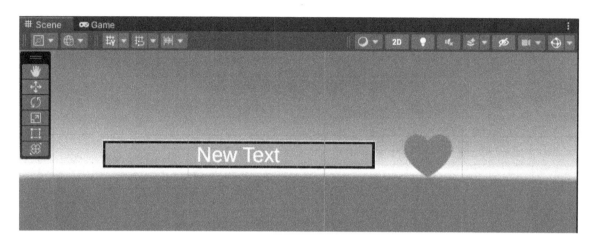

- Add a new text object as a child of the object **heart** and call this new object **heartText**.

- Set its text to **0**, change its font size and move it so that it fits within the heart.

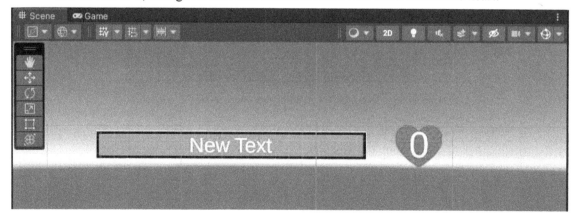

Now that we have set the UI for the number of lives, we will modify our code to display the actual number of lives:

- Open the script **ManagePlayerHealth**.
- Add this code at the beginning of the script:

```
using TMPro;
```

Add this code at the beginning of the class:

```
int nbLives;
GameObject heartText;
```

Add this function

```
void UpdateNbLives()
{
        heartText.GetComponent<TextMeshProUGUI>().text = ""+nbLives;
}
```

Add this code to the Start function:

```
nbLives = PlayerPrefs.GetInt("nbLives");
heartText = GameObject.Find("heartText");
UpdateNbLives();
```

- You can now save your code and play the scene, and check that three lives are displayed in the user interface, as per the next figure.

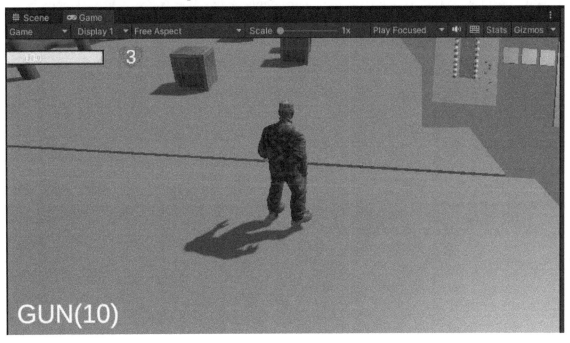

Next, we just need to decrease the number of lives every time the health reaches 0, and to then open the end screen when the player has no lives left.

Open the script ManagePlayerHealth.

Comment this line in the function Decreasehealth.

```
if (health == 0) SceneManager.LoadScene(SceneManager.GetActiveScene().name);
```

- Add this code instead:

```
if (health == 0)
{
        nbLives = PlayerPrefs.GetInt("nbLives");
        nbLives--;
        PlayerPrefs.SetInt("nbLives", nbLives);
        if (nbLives >=0 )
        {
                SceneManager.LoadScene(SceneManager.GetActiveScene().name);
        }
        else
        {
                PlayerPrefs.SetString("endMessage", "GAME OVER!");
                SceneManager.LoadScene("endScreen");
        }
}
```

In the previous code, when health is 0, we check the number of lives remaining for the player; when the player has no lives left, the end screen is loaded with the corresponding message.

Finally, open the script **ManageButtons**, and comment this line (since it was essentially for testing purposes).

```
PlayerPrefs.SetString("endMessage", "GAME OVER");
```

You can now save your script, ensure that the scenes **splashScreen** and **endScreen** are part of the Build Settings.

Play the game and check that your see the end screen with a different message ("**Congratulations**" or "**Game Over**") depending on whether you collect four boxes or lose all your lives.

Summary

In this chapter, you've added impactful new mechanics and features to enhance your game, pushing both the gameplay experience and your development skills to the next level. These improvements not only make your game more interactive and engaging but also demonstrate your growing expertise as a developer.

What You've Achieved:

- **Enhanced Camera Effects:** You've implemented dynamic camera movements and transitions, creating a more immersive and cinematic gameplay experience. These effects allow the player to feel more connected to the game world.
- **Player Abilities Expansion:** Introducing new abilities for the player, such as crouching, sprinting, or interacting with the environment, you've made the gameplay more versatile and engaging. These mechanics encourage exploration and add depth to the player's interaction with the world.
- **Improved NPC Interactions:** By refining how NPCs behave and interact with the player, you've made the world feel more alive and responsive. These additions create meaningful challenges and add personality to the game.
- **Polished Visuals and Feedback:** You've enhanced the game's visuals and feedback systems, ensuring that every action—whether a player-triggered event or NPC behavior—feels satisfying and clear.

Game Improvements:

- Your game now offers a more engaging experience with fluid camera effects that immerse the player in the action.
- The addition of player abilities increases gameplay variety, making exploration and problem-solving more rewarding.
- NPC interactions now feel smarter and more reactive, providing dynamic challenges and narrative potential.
- Polished visual and feedback enhancements elevate the professional feel of your game.

By completing this chapter, you've not only added meaningful improvements to your game but also gained skills that are fundamental for creating advanced, immersive gameplay experiences. Each new feature is a stepping stone toward making your game a polished and memorable creation. Keep up the fantastic work—you're mastering the art of game development!

Quiz: Test Your Knowledge

Please specify whether the following statements are True or False (the solutions are at the end of the book).

1. A spawning mechanism can be used to dynamically add enemies or objects in a game scene at regular intervals.
2. Using random starting points for the player or NPCs ensures predictable gameplay.
3. Health packs should always spawn in fixed locations to maintain balance in the game.

4. Difficulty levels in games can influence NPC behavior, including speed, health, and damage output.
5. Adjusting game mechanics based on difficulty settings can enhance player engagement and immersion.
6. A splash screen can allow players to select their desired difficulty level at the start of the game.
7. Spawning points are essential for randomizing the placement of objects or NPCs in a scene.
8. Helper NPCs are designed to assist the player and can follow specific commands such as attacking or retreating.
9. Adding animation states to NPCs is unnecessary for creating complex behaviors.
10. NPCs can have distinct roles, such as helpers or attackers, depending on their assigned tasks.

CHALLENGE

For this challenge, you just need to do the following:

- Add more helpers.
- Create a box that, once collected by the player, adds three more helpers.
- Create an end screen that offers the player to replay or to quit the game.

8
FREQUENTLY ASKED QUESTIONS

What is the purpose of using a NavMesh in Unity?
NavMesh helps define navigable areas in the game, allowing NPCs to move intelligently within the environment by following paths and avoiding obstacles.

How do I add NavMesh areas with specific costs?
You can define specific areas in the NavMesh and assign cost values to them. For instance, a swamp can have a higher cost, discouraging NPCs from crossing it unless necessary.

What is a Finite State Machine (FSM), and how is it used in the book?
The FSM is implemented to control NPC behavior dynamically. For example, an NPC can switch between patrolling and chasing the player based on proximity or events.

How do waypoints enhance NPC movement?
Waypoints provide predefined locations for NPCs to navigate through, which can be set as random or fixed points, adding diversity to their movement patterns.

How do I add a health system for both players and NPCs?
You can define a health variable in a script and update it based on damage taken. This can be visualized with health bars and tied to animations or effects for damage feedback.

What steps are needed to create a health bar for the player?
Use Unity's UI system to create a health bar, then link it to the player's health variable in a script so the bar dynamically updates as health changes.

What are the benefits of adding a screen flash when the player takes damage?
The screen flash provides immediate visual feedback to the player, enhancing immersion and making the game more engaging.

What is the role of animation in NPC behavior, as covered in the book?
Animations help NPCs visually represent their actions, such as patrolling or attacking. Unity's Animator Controller and transitions are used to switch between these states.

How can you use NavMesh to make NPCs avoid dangerous areas?
By defining specific areas with high costs in the NavMesh, NPCs can be programmed to avoid those areas unless absolutely necessary.

How do you create transitions between animation states?
Transitions are created in Unity's Animator window by linking states with parameters. For example, a transition from "Patrol" to "Chase" can be triggered when the player is detected.

What are the key steps to import 3D animated characters for NPCs?
The book covers importing 3D character models, applying animations, and using the Animator Controller to manage their states.

How do you set up random waypoint navigation for NPCs?
Create an array of waypoint objects, and use a random number generator to select one as the next destination for the NPC.

What techniques are discussed for enhancing NPC awareness?
The book explores using triggers, raycasting, and finite state machines to give NPCs awareness of their surroundings and dynamic reactions to the player.

How can you implement a damage system for NPCs?
Create a health variable for NPCs, deduct values when hit, and destroy the NPC when health reaches zero, optionally with a visual effect.

What is the significance of switching between first-person and third-person views?
Switching views allows players to experience the game from different perspectives, adding variety and accessibility to gameplay.

What tools are recommended for creating visually appealing environments?
Unity's terrain editor, lighting tools, and particle systems are used to enhance the aesthetic appeal of the game environment.

How do you set up triggers to detect the player's presence?
Triggers are added using colliders marked as triggers. Scripts then respond to events like the player entering the area.

What is the role of costs in navigation for NPCs?
Costs define the difficulty of traversing certain areas, helping NPCs make intelligent decisions about the best path to take.

How do you implement camera effects for enhanced gameplay?
Camera effects such as depth of field, motion blur, or dynamic transitions between perspectives can be added using Unity's post-processing tools.

How does the book help you create dynamic interactions between NPCs and the player?

The book teaches techniques like state transitions, pathfinding, and event-driven behavior to ensure NPCs interact dynamically and meaningfully with the player

9
SOLUTIONS TO QUIZZES

CHAPTER 1

1. **False**: The shortcut for the Console window is not CTRL + 1. It varies depending on system configurations and Unity version.
2. **False**: Unity does not have a default shortcut for opening the Project window using CTRL + 2.
3. **False**: Unity does not use CTRL + 4 as a default shortcut for opening the Hierarchy window.
4. **False**: The Console window is used to display messages, warnings, and errors related to your project, not scene objects.
5. **False**: The Project window is used to manage assets in your project, while errors and messages appear in the Console window.
6. **False**: Assets in the Project window are accessible across all scenes within the same project.
7. **False**: Deactivating an object only disables it in the scene; it is not deleted from the project.
8. **False**: Child objects are created by dragging one object onto another in the Hierarchy window, not through a "Create Child" menu option.
9. **True**: Unity's coordinate system follows a right-hand convention where the positive Z-axis typically points forward.
10. **False**: Unity provides offline documentation that can be downloaded and accessed without an internet connection.

CHAPTER 2

1. **False**: The value of a variable can change unless it is declared as a constant.
2. **False**: Methods do not always return information; some methods perform actions without returning a value.
3. **True**: A method may not return information, especially if it is declared with a void return type.
4. **False**: If a method is void, it does not return any value, including integers.
5. **True**: An array can store multiple variables of the same data type at the same time.
6. **True**: A class usually includes a constructor, which is a special method used to initialize objects of that class.
7. **True**: A for loop is commonly used to iterate through all the elements of an array.

8. **True**: A public method is accessible from any other class or location within the project.
9. **True**: A private variable is accessible only within the class where it is declared.
10. **False**: A protected variable is accessible to the class itself and its derived (child) classes, not just members of the class.

CHAPTER 3

1. **True**: The ground object in the game environment was created using a cube resized to form a flat surface.
2. **False**: The walls were not created as spheres; they were typically created as cubes or other appropriate shapes for walls.
3. **True**: The First-Person Controller allows players to navigate using keyboard inputs for movement and mouse inputs for camera control.
4. **True**: Jumping mechanics in the FPS controller are implemented using Unity's built-in CharacterController component.
5. **True**: The collectible items were created as spheres and tagged as "collectible" for collision detection.
6. **True**: The player's progress in collecting items is visually represented using dynamically activating UI images.
7. **True**: The transition effect between scenes includes a fade-to-black animation followed by a fade-from-black animation.
8. **True**: The robot throwing projectiles uses physics-based rigid body mechanics to launch objects toward the player.
9. **False**: The mini-map's position can vary, but it is not necessarily displayed in the bottom-left corner unless specifically designed to be there.
10. **True**: Prefabs enable developers to create reusable and scalable game objects, such as collectible boxes and robot enemies.

CHAPTER 4

1. **True**: The script ManageWeapons uses raycasting to detect objects in the player's line of sight.
2. **False**: Debug.DrawRay is used for visualization purposes only and does not detect collisions.
3. **True**: The crosshair helps players aim by aligning with the center of the screen.
4. **True**: The Physics.Raycast method requires a ray and outputs collision data when the ray intersects with an object.
5. **False**: Ammo collection includes checks to ensure the player's ammo does not exceed the maximum limit.
6. **True**: The weapon management system uses arrays to store properties such as ammo count, reload times, and weapon availability.
7. **True**: The grenade launcher propels grenades using Unity's AddForce method applied to a Rigidbody component.
8. **True**: The Physics.OverlapSphere function identifies all objects within a defined radius and applies damage to them.

9. **False**: The particle system for explosions is configured to play once and does not loop continuously.
10. **False**: The ManageNPC script reduces health incrementally, and targets are destroyed only when their health reaches zero.

CHAPTER 5

1. **True**: NPCs use NavMeshAgent components for pathfinding in Unity.
2. **False**: A NavMeshSurface component is added to the ground or navigable surfaces, not to NPCs.
3. **True**: Costs in Unity navigation determine the ease or difficulty for NPCs to traverse certain areas.
4. **True**: Off-mesh links allow NPCs to navigate across disconnected platforms, such as gaps or obstacles.
5. **True**: A NavMeshSurface component must always be baked to make the ground navigable for NPCs.
6. **False**: Finite State Machines (FSMs) are used for NPC behavior control, not just navigation.
7. **True**: Assigning a higher cost to an area, such as a swamp, will make NPCs prefer to avoid that area.
8. **False**: The "Swamp" navigation area in Unity can have a different cost than other navigation areas, allowing for dynamic pathfinding.
9. **True**: Adding a NavMeshObstacle component to an object like a tree will prevent NPCs from passing through it.
10. **False**: Unity's Navigation system can handle uneven or sloped surfaces for NPC pathfinding, not just flat surfaces

CHAPTER 6

1. **True**: NavMesh navigation is used to create basic pathfinding for NPCs in a game.
2. **True**: A finite state machine (FSM) allows NPCs to transition between different behaviors based on their state.
3. **False**: Waypoints can include both fixed and random points for NPC navigation.
4. **True**: Assigning costs to areas in a navigation mesh enables NPCs to prefer or avoid specific paths.
5. **False**: Health bars in games can display the health of both players and NPCs.
6. **True**: Adding a screen flash effect enhances player feedback when damage is taken.
7. **False**: Random waypoints are used to create unpredictable NPC movement patterns, not predictable ones.
8. **True**: Damage systems in games can be used for both players and NPCs to track health changes.
9. **False**: NavMesh areas with higher costs are typically avoided in favor of lower-cost areas.
10. **True**: A health system for NPCs is often combined with visual cues like health bars to enhance gameplay.

CHAPTER 7

1. **True**: A spawning mechanism can be used to dynamically add enemies or objects in a game scene at regular intervals.
2. **False**: Using random starting points for the player or NPCs ensures unpredictable, not predictable, gameplay.
3. **False**: Health packs can spawn in both fixed and random locations depending on the desired game balance.
4. **True**: Difficulty levels in games can influence NPC behavior, including speed, health, and damage output.
5. **True**: Adjusting game mechanics based on difficulty settings can enhance player engagement and immersion.
6. **True**: A splash screen can allow players to select their desired difficulty level at the start of the game.
7. **True**: Spawning points are essential for randomizing the placement of objects or NPCs in a scene.
8. **True**: Helper NPCs are designed to assist the player and can follow specific commands such as attacking or retreating.
9. **False**: Adding animation states to NPCs is necessary for creating complex behaviors and improving realism.
10. **True**: NPCs can have distinct roles, such as helpers or attackers, depending on their assigned tasks.

10
THANK YOU

YOUR REVIEW MATTERS!

If you've enjoyed this book and found the techniques helpful, I would greatly appreciate it if you could take a moment to leave a review. Your feedback is incredibly valuable—not only does it help me understand what worked well and what can be improved, but it also plays a significant role in helping more people discover the book.

Reviews are crucial for authors like me, as they provide visibility and credibility. They make it possible for me to continue creating more books on game development and sharing knowledge with a wider audience. If this book has inspired or taught you something new, your review can inspire others to pick it up and start their own journey.

Thank you for your support, and for being part of this adventure in procedural generation!

For more books on Game Programming, please check the official site (**http://www.learntocreategames.com/books/**) or subscribe to the mailing list to receive weekly news and freebies related to game programming (http://www.learntocreategames.com/subscr